Alastair
Sawday's

Special Places to Stay

A responsible business: we are committed to being a green and socially responsible business. Here are a few things we already do: our pool cars run on recycled cooking oil and low-emission LPG; our award-winning eco-offices are equipped with solar-heated water, wood-pellet heating, and rainwater-fed loos and showers and we were the world's first carbon-neutral publishing company. Find out more at www.sawdays.co.uk

Paper and print: we have sought the lowest possible ecological 'footprint' from the production of this book. Whenever possible, we will use paper that is either recycled (with a high proportion of post-consumer waste) or FSC-certified, and give preference to local companies in order to foster our local economy and reduce our carbon footprint. Our printer is ISO 14001-registered.

Alastair Sawday's

Special Places to Stay

British Hotels & Inns

4   Contents

We are a small company, born in 1994 and growing slowly but surely every year – in 2007 we sold our millionth book. We have always published beautiful and immensely useful guide books, and we now also have a very successful website.

There are about 35 of us in the Company, producing the website, about 20 guide books and a growing series of environmental books under the Fragile Earth imprint. We think a lot about how we do it, how we behave, what our 'culture' is, and we are trying to be a little more than 'just a publishing company'.

Environmental & ethical policies

We have always had strong environmental policies. Our books are printed by a British company that is ISO14001 accredited, on recycled and/or FSC-certified paper, and we have been offsetting our carbon emissions since 2001. We now do so through an Indian NGO, which means that our money goes a long way. However, we are under no illusions about carbon-offsetting: it is part of a strong package of green measures including running company cars on gas or recycled cooking oil; composting or recycling waste; encouraging cycling and car-sharing; only buying organic or local food; not accepting web links with companies we consider unethical; and banking with the ethical Triodos Bank.

In 2005 we won a Business Commitment to the Environment Award and in 2006 a Queen's Award for Enterprise in the Sustainable Development category. All this has boosted our resolve to promote our green policies.

Eco offices

In January 2006 we moved into our new eco offices. With super-insulation, under-floor heating, a wood-pellet boiler, solar panels and a rainwater tank, we have a working environment kind to ourselves and to the environment. Lighting is low-energy, dark corners are lit by sun-pipes, materials are natural and one building is of green oak. Carpet tiles are from Herdwick sheep in the Lake District. The building is a delight to work in.

Ethics

We think that our role as a company is not much different from our role as the individuals within it: to play our part in the community, to reduce our ecological footprint, to be a benign influence, to foster good human relationships and to make a positive difference to the world around us.

Another phrase for the simple intentions above is Corporate Responsibility. It is a much-used buzz-phrase, but many of those adopting it as a policy are getting serious. A world-wide report by the think-tank Tomorrow's Company has revealed quite how convinced the world's major companies are that if they do not take on full responsibility for their impact, social and environmental, they will not survive.

The books – and a dilemma

So, we have created popular books and a handsome website that do good work. They promote authenticity, individuality and good local and organic food – a far cry from corporate culture. Rural economies, pubs, small farms, villages and hamlets all benefit. However, people use fossil fuel to get there. Should we aim to get our readers to offset their own carbon emissions, and the B&B and hotel owners too?

We are gradually introducing green ideas into the books: the Fine Breakfast Scheme that highlights British and Irish B&B owners who use local and organic food; celebrating those who make an extra environmental effort; gently encouraging the use of public transport, cycling and walking. We now give green and 'social' awards to pubs in our pub guide.

In 2006 we published the very successful *Green Places to Stay*, focusing on responsible travel and eco-properties around the globe. Bit by bit we will do more, and welcome ideas from all quarters. Our aim is to be a pioneering green publisher, and to be known as one. We hope one day to offer energy audits to our owners, to provide real help to those who want to 'go green'. And we will continue to champion the small-scale. We will also continue to oppose policies that encourage the growth of air traffic – however contradictory that might seem.

Our Fragile Earth series

The 'hard' side of our environmental publishing is the Fragile Earth series: *The Little Earth Book*, *The Little Food Book* and *The Little Money Book*. They consist of bite-sized essays, polemical, hard-hitting and well researched. They are a 'must have' for anyone who seeks clarity about some of the key issues of our time. We have also published *One Planet Living* with WWF.

A flagship project is the *The Big Earth Book*; it is packed with information and a stimulating and provocative read. It is being promoted, with remarkable generosity, by Yeo Valley Organic.

Lastly – what is special?

The notion of 'special' is at the heart of what we do, and highly subjective. We discuss this in the introduction to every book. We take huge pleasure in finding people and places that do their own thing – brilliantly; places that are unusual and follow no trends; places of peace and beauty; people who are kind and interesting – and genuine.

We seem to have touched a nerve with hundreds of thousands of readers; they obviously long for the independence that our books provide, for the warm human contact of Special Places, and to be able to avoid the banality and ugliness of so many other places.

A night in a Special Place can be a transforming experience.

Alastair Sawday

Yet again the fearless Tom Bell has stridden across the hotel landscape with his unqualified determination to create the best book on the subject. Should anyone ever again accuse us of being less than independent, I will point to Tom's readiness to exclude hotels that don't come up to his exacting standards. He has dropped some that are splendid in many ways but are now owned by faceless corporations. He is quick to spot a lack of warmth, and has developed an eagle eye and gastronome's stomach in the dining room. How he has kept his figure I dare not ask. But he has done a wonderful job, supported by Maria Serrano and the office team generally, and can now be genuinely referred to as an inspired expert. He has inspected, written and organised. This book is his.

Alastair Sawday

Series Editor
Alastair Sawday
Editor
Tom Bell
Editorial Director
Annie Shillito
Writing
Tom Bell
Inspections
Tom Bell
Accounts
Bridget Bishop,
Rebecca Bebbington, Christine Buxton,
Sandra Hasell, Amy Lancastle,
Sally Ranahan
Editorial
Sue Bourner,
Kate Ball, Jo Boissevain, Nicola Crosse,
Melanie Harrison, Jackie King,
Wendy Ogden, Florence Oldfield,
Maria Serrano, Kate Shepherd,
Becci Stevens, Danielle Williams
Production
Julia Richardson,
Tom Germain, Rebecca Thomas,
Emma Wilson
Sales & Marketing & PR
Rob Richardson,
Thomas Caldwell, Sarah Bolton
Web & IT
Russell Wilkinson,
Chris Banks, Isabelle Deakin,
Joe Green, Brian Kimberling
Previous Editor
Nicola Crosse

If hotels are a window into a nation's soul, then what do ours reveal about us? There has recently been a surge in the number of restaurants providing bedrooms, a grand idea for those eating and drinking exceedingly well – which suggests that we are doing more of both. The food, too, has changed subtly. The once-fashionable Mediterranean dishes are yielding to rustic British, such as rhubarb crumble and autumnal game.

Our way of decorating our hotels, too, is changing. Gone are the floral fabrics and wallpapers, the pine and plain colours, leaving us to enjoy a rather delightful mix of minimalism and luxury. Beds are so comfortable that one's own bed seems primitive. Bed linen is of organic cotton and 'toiletries' are of the finest natural quality. All this points to a new interest in eco-friendliness, and an awareness of the need to be seen pointing in that direction. This new interest is very real, especially when it comes to food. It is more and more common to find hotels with their own kitchen gardens, where food-miles become food-metres. This goes well with the trend towards more English cooking – that rhubarb crumble has little distance to travel. Other green measures are also gaining ground: solar panels, discounts for those arriving without a car, encouragement to guests to go hiking, bicycles for them to borrow. The trend is clear, and encourages owners to be extra imaginative.

My own feelings about the counter-trend towards the chillingly chic and very expensive are clear. I mind if the mood is exclusive and indulgent. Where there is imagination and panache galore, then it is stimulating. But I am not moved by any structure that makes people feel apart from and above others – somehow elite. I prefer to be treated as a normal member of the human species. And I prefer not to be part of a culture of over-consumption for consumption's sake.

Let us hope, too, that the small family hotel might one day make a come-back. We love them in France and miss them here. To some extent they are being replaced by restaurants with rooms – a fine idea, especially if you are determined to eat and drink to your very heart's content and not be able to drive home. Very small (even tiny) 'hotels' are also returning, partly because big ones are becoming unaffordable. We have one or two unusual and fascinating examples in this new edition. I think we are keeping up with the times.

Alastair Sawday

Photo: Tom Germain

Over the last three decades soaring property prices have had a profound effect on the world of British hotels. Take the grand old country house, formerly run by a cast of characters such as the eccentric bachelor who inherited the property from his great aunt and thought he'd try his hand at 'entertaining'. These houses once dotted the landscape of Britain. They were bastions of British individualism, hotels that gave the impression of not being hotels at all, where guests could be swept away on flights of fancy before heading back to life in the city.

Thirty years on and the old bachelor has understandably had enough. He has done very nicely and now wishes to retire to the Côte d'Azur. Who can blame him? But his house, now worth a fortune, is beyond the reach of mere hoteliers, so he sells to a company. Consultants are brought in, structures are put in place and the hotel is 'rationalised'. Soon it loses what made it special – the effortless grandeur, the quirky service and the personality of an ever-present owner.

A few of these wonders survive intact. Some are passed down from one generation to another, others are bought by benevolent philanthropists, who refurbish magnificently. Over the last couple of years this guide has striven quietly to bring together those that remain in private hands. Their prices may be high, and a new professionalism may see the owner supported by a general manager, but they remain quintessentially British and deliver the equivalent of a royal flush: impeccable service, delicious food and glorious interiors. They sing the song of days long gone, of afternoon tea served from polished silver, of croquet played on the lawn in summer, of strawberries grown in the kitchen garden, of rivers to fish.

Small is now beautiful...an army of creative souls is working on smaller canvasses

These days, hoteliers wanting to buy their own place must settle for something smaller. In the 90s this brought the rise of the restaurant with rooms. The current trend is for chic inns. Inns are relatively inexpensive to buy and perhaps more popular for their lack of formality. Freshly adorned, they are setting a standard that is tough for others to match; their combination of good prices and plenty of style is proving to be a winning formula.

Photo left: Old Bank Hotel entry 162
Photo right: Miller's at Glencot House, entry 173

With such attention lavished on them, inns are changing dramatically. Some become dining pubs, others turn contemporary, many refurbish in warm traditional style, the brave remain blissfully unreformed, a few splash out on suites with sumptuous furnishings. Inns today represent the biggest growth area in the world of small hotels, and their cooking has begun to attract Michelin stars. Most are quirky and intimate, with hands-on owners doing their own thing – the torch of British individualism still shines brightly, it has just moved house. The vast majority offer great value for money. They draw in locals for food, old boys for ale, travellers for rest. This mix of life adds a vibrancy that some country hotels find hard to match. They remain the de facto community centres of many villages.

Property prices also push hoteliers into more remote areas, where they can buy more for their money. New areas get

discovered, others rediscovered. Take North Wales. It has flourished in the last few years, and an area in which it was once hard to find a decent bed now teems with a whole raft of magical places to stay. If you make the effort and drive the extra hour, you lose the crowds and find you have coast and hills to yourself. There is much to be said for heading to the end of the rainbow.

Despite soaring property prices – or perhaps because of them – small is now beautiful in the world of British hotels. With an army of creative souls working on smaller canvases, we now find an almost endless choice of places to escape to. Standards have shot through the roof in the last ten years. Food, and the passion behind it, has advanced incomparably. When it comes to interior design, you are likely to find the same styles on the Isle of Wight as in Notting Hill Gate. As for fancy bathrooms, they are now pretty much de rigeur. What is certain is that a patchwork quilt of small palaces now covers the land. From Sandwich to Durness, from Royal Dornoch to St Ives, these diminutive boltholes have become the new temples of leisure, places to which we retreat whenever the chance arises, leaving the slog of our daily world far behind. We parachute in for a couple of nights of bliss, sleep cocooned in Egyptian cotton, pour soothing oils into a claw-foot bath, gaze out on glorious country. In short, small British hotels have never been more popular.

Tom Bell

Photo: The Westleton Crown, entry 182

We are fiercely subjective. Those who are familiar with our Special Places series know that we look for comfort, originality, authenticity, and reject the insincere, the anonymous and the banal.

We hope you enjoy these places. They all have something special to offer, whether it be fine views and great antiques, a fire in your bedroom (or bathroom!), food that is fresh as the day or a dazzling garden. The owners often go beyond the call of duty and strive to provide the best that they can.

Inspections

We visit every place in the guide to get a feel for how both house and owner tick. We don't take a clipboard and we don't have a list of what is acceptable and what is not. Instead, we chat for an hour or so with the owner or manager and look round. It's all very informal, but it gives us an excellent idea of who would enjoy staying there. If the visit happens to be the last of the day, we sometimes stay the night. Once in the book, properties are re-inspected every three years so that we can keep things fresh and accurate.

Feedback

We cannot be everywhere at once and things can be mercurial in the world of hotels and inns. So do tell us if your stay has been a joy or not, if the atmosphere was great or stuffy, whether the owners or staff were cheery or bored. The accuracy of the book depends on what you, and our inspectors, tell us. Please use the form on our website at www.sawdays.co.uk, or later in this book. However, please do not tell us if your starter was cold, or the bedside light was broken. Tell the owner, immediately, and get them to do something about it.

Most owners, or staff, are more than happy to correct problems and will bend over backwards to help. Far better than bottling it up and then writing to us a week later! A lot of the new entries in each edition are recommended by our readers, so do keep telling us about new places you've discovered too.

Subscriptions

Owners pay to appear in this guide. Their fee goes towards the high costs of inspecting, of producing an all-colour book and of maintaining our website. We only include places that we like and find special for one reason or another, so it is not possible to buy your way onto these pages. Nor is it possible for the owner to write their own description. We will say if the bedrooms are small, or if a main road is near. We do our best to avoid misleading people.

Disclaimer

We make no claims to pure objectivity in choosing these places. They are here simply because we like them. We try our utmost to get our facts right but we apologise unreservedly if any errors have sneaked in.

We do not check such things as fire alarms, swimming pool security or any other regulation with which owners of properties receiving paying guests should comply. This is the responsibility of the owners.

Finding the right place for you

In these pages you will find swish hotels, cosy inns, restaurants with rooms and other places that defy obvious labels. Hotels can vary from huge, humming and slick to those with only a few rooms that are run by owners at their own pace. In some you may not get room service or have your bags carried in and out. In smaller hotels there may be a fixed menu for dinner with very little choice, so if you have dishes that leave you cold, it's important to say so when you book your meal. If you decide to stay at an inn, remember that they can be noisy, especially at weekends. If these things are important to you, then do check when you book: a simple question or two can avoid regrettable misunderstandings.

All these places are special in one way or another. All have been visited and then written about honestly so that you can take what you like and leave the rest. Those of you who swear by Sawday's books trust our write-ups precisely because we don't have a blanket standard; we include places simply because we like them. But we all have different priorities, so read and choose carefully.

Maps

Each property is flagged with its entry number on the maps at the front. Please don't use these maps as anything other than a general guide or a good starting point for planning your trip. Use a decent road map for real navigation. Most places will send you detailed instructions once you have booked your stay.

We visit every place in the guide to get a feel for how both house and owner tick

Symbols

Below each entry in the book you will see some little black symbols. These are based on information owners give us. At the very back of the book is a short table explaining what each symbol means, but below is a fuller explanation of some of them. Use the symbols as a guide, not as a statement of fact – owners occasionally bend their own rules, so it's worth asking if you may take your child or dog even if they don't have the symbol.

Photo left: The Bath Priory Hotel, entry 5
Photo right: The Punch Bowl Inn, entry 51

least one bedroom and bathroom is accessible without using stairs. The symbol is designed to satisfy those who walk slowly, with difficulty, or with the aid of a stick. A wheelchair may be able to navigate some areas, but these places don't claim to be fully wheelchair friendly. If you use a chair for longer distances, but are not too bad over shorter distances, you'll probably be OK; again, please ring and ask. There may be a step or two, a bath or a shower with a tray in a cubicle, a good distance between the car park and your room, slippery flagstones or a tight turn.

Children – Our ♟ symbol shows places which are happy to accept children of all ages. This does not mean that they will necessarily have cots, high chairs, etc. Having said that, there are several places in this book that are ideal for families with young children. Many have huge swathes of lawn for running and tumbling, a swimming pool for fun and lots of games and other things to do. Plenty of other children around means you won't be quite so embarrassed when your child has the loudest tantrum of its life in the dining room, and a newly found friend for your little dear can sometimes leave you time to read at least the first page of your novel. If you want to get out and about in the evenings, check when you book whether there are any babysitting services. Even very small places can sometimes organise this for you.

Wheelchair access – Some hotels are keen to accept wheelchair users into their hotels and have made provision for them. However, this does not mean that wheelchair users will always be met with a perfect landscape. You may encounter ramps, a shallow step, gravelled paths, alternative routes into some rooms, a bathroom (rather than a wet room), perhaps even a lift. In short, there may be the odd hindrance and we urge you to call and make sure you will get what you need.

Limited mobility – The limited mobility symbol shows those places where at

Pets – Our  symbol shows places that are generally happy to accept pets. It means they can sleep in the bedroom with you, but not on the bed. It's really important to get this one right before you arrive, as many places make you keep dogs in the car. Check carefully: Spot's emotional wellbeing may depend on it.

> Those of you who swear by Sawday's books trust our write-ups precisely because we don't have a blanket standard

Owners' pets – Owners who have pets of their own are given a cat symbol ( ). If you are allergic to or simply don't like animals, beware. Sometimes there are geese, swans, peacocks, ducks, horses.

Smoking – It is now illegal to smoke in public places in Britain. If a hotel permits it you may be able to smoke in bedrooms. Bars, restaurants and sitting rooms have become smoke-free. Smokers must now make do with the garden. Ireland has already proved that you can run a pub or restaurant without a single whiff of smoke and people still come. People now telephone to ask if they really are smoke-free and then come for that reason.

Photo: Eshott Hall, entry 154

Quick reference indices

At the back of the book you'll find a number of quick-reference indices showing those places that offer a particular service, perhaps a room for under £70 a night, or that don't charge a single supplement. They are worth flicking through if you are looking for something specific, like somewhere to get married or to hold an event.

Green entries

For the third time we have chosen, very subjectively, five places which are making a particular effort to be eco-friendly and have given them a double-page spread and extra photos to illustrate what they're up to.

This does not mean there are no other places in the guide taking green initiatives – there are many – but we have highlighted just a few examples. The places that had green pages in previous editions now have a green leaf symbol.

When to go

If I can pass on a single tip to eager travellers, it is this: if you travel out of season, you will avoid the crowds and often pay less for it. Staff will not be rushed, sofas will not be taken, the table by the window will be yours. Often you will be upgraded to better rooms. If you have the chance to travel in April and May or September and October the weather can be good, too. I cannot emphasise enough how wonderful Britain can be at these times. These are the months in which we like to inspect so as not to encroach upon hotels in busy periods. We wouldn't have it any other way.

Rooms

Bedrooms are described as double, twin, single, family or suite. A double may contain a bed which is anything from 135cm wide to 180cm wide. A twin will contain two single beds (usually 90cm wide). Some suites will have separate sitting rooms, but the trend at the moment is for one big room, not two small ones. Family rooms can vary in size and number of beds they hold, so do ask.

All bedrooms have their own bathrooms unless we say that they don't. If you have your own bathroom but you have to leave the room to get to it we describe it as 'separate'. There are very few places in the book that have shared bathrooms and they are usually reserved for members of the same party. Again, we state this clearly.

Meals

Breakfast is included in the room price unless otherwise stated. If only a continental breakfast is offered, we let you know. Often you will feast on local sausage and bacon, eggs from resident hens, homemade breads and jams. In some you may have organic yogurts and beautifully presented fruit compotes. If you want the best porridge and kippers, head north.

A few places serve lunch, most do Sunday lunch (often very well-priced), the vast majority offer dinner. In some places you can content yourself with bar meals, in others you can feast on five courses. Most offer a three-course, fixed-price menu, for £25-£35 without wine. In many restaurants you can also eat à la carte. Very occasionally you eat communally – if you loathe making small talk with strangers avoid these places. Some large hotels (and some posh private houses) will bring dinner to your room if you prefer, or let you eat in the garden by candlelight. Always ask for what you want and sometimes, magically, it happens.

Prices

We quote the lowest price for two people in low season to the highest price in high season. All prices include a full breakfast unless stated. Only a few places have designated single rooms; if no single rooms are listed, the price we quote refers to single occupancy of a double room. In many places prices rise even higher

when local events bring people flooding to the area, a point worth remembering when heading to Edinburgh for the festival, Cheltenham for the racing or Glyndebourne for the opera.

The half-board price quoted is per person per night and includes dinner, usually three courses. Mostly you're offered a table d'hôte menu. Occasionally you eat à la carte and find some dishes carry a small supplement. There are often great deals to be had, mostly mid-week in low season.

Weekends

Most small hotels do not accept one-night bookings at weekends. Small country hotels are rarely full during the week and the weekend trade keeps them going. If you ring in March for a Saturday night in July, you won't get it. If you ring at the last moment and they have a room, you will. Some places insist on three-night stays on bank holiday weekends.

Always ask for what you want and sometimes, magically, it happens

Booking and cancellation

Most places ask for a deposit at the time of booking, either by cheque or credit or debit card. If you cancel – depending on how much notice you give – you can lose all or part of this deposit unless your room is re-let.

Photo: The Inn at Whitewell, entry 126

It is reasonable for hotels to take a deposit to secure a booking; they have learnt that if they don't, the commitment of the guest wanes and they may fail to turn up.

Some cancellation policies are more stringent than others. It is also worth noting that some owners will take this deposit directly from your credit or debit card without contacting you to discuss it. So ask the hotel to explain their cancellation policy clearly before booking so you understand exactly where you stand; it may well avoid a nasty surprise.

Arrivals and departures

Housekeeping is usually done by 2pm, and your room will usually be available by mid-afternoon. Normally you will have to wave goodbye to it between 10am and 11am. Sometimes one can pay to linger. Some inns are closed between 3pm and 6pm, so do try and agree an arrival time in advance, or you may find nobody there.

Parking

Parking can be tricky or expensive in towns; call owners for advice when booking.

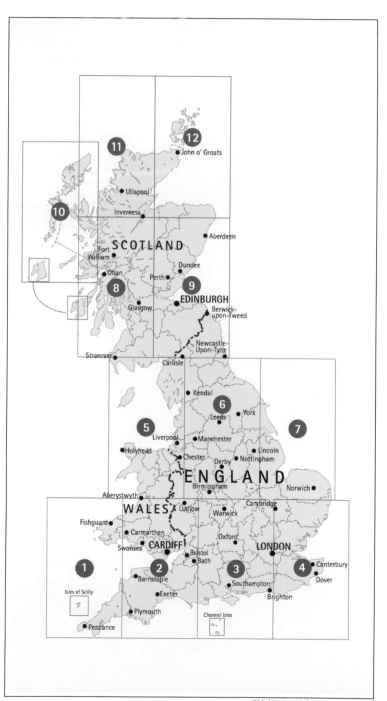

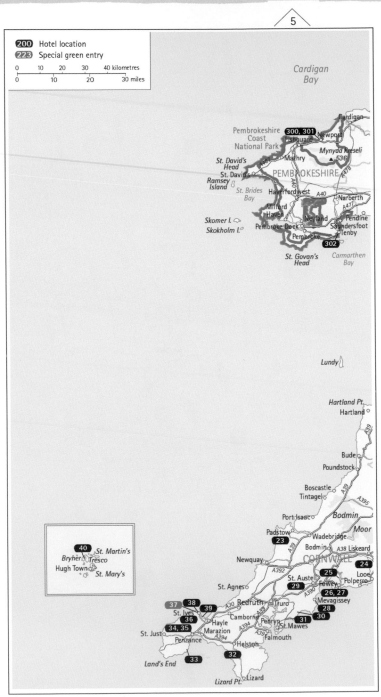

5

200 Hotel location
223 Special green entry

0   10   20   30   40 kilometres
0   10   20   30 miles

Cardigan Bay

Pembrokeshire Coast National Park **300, 301** Fishguard Newport Cardigan

Mynydd Preseli ▲ 536

Mathry

St. David's Head
St. David's
Ramsey Island
St. Brides Bay
Haverfordwest
PEMBROKESHIRE
Narberth
A477
Skomer I.
Skokholm I.
Milford Haven
Neyland
Pendine
Saundersfoot
Tenby
Pembroke Dock
Pembroke
302
St. Govan's Head
Carmarthen Bay

Lundy

Hartland Pt.
Hartland
A39

Bude
Poundstock

Boscastle
Tintagel
A395
Port Isaac
Bodmin Moor
Padstow
Wadebridge
23
Bodmin A38 Liskeard
Newquay
CORNWALL
A392
24
St. Austell
25
Looe
29
Fowey
Polperro
St. Agnes
26, 27
Redruth
Truro
Mevagissey
37 **38**
St. Ives
28
39
30
36
Camborne
Penryn
St. Mawes
34, 35
Hayle
31
St. Just
Marazion
Penzance
A394
Falmouth
A394
Helston
32
Land's End
33
Lizard Pt. Lizard

40 St. Martin's
Bryher *Tresco*
Hugh Town
St. Mary's

©Maidenhead Cartographic, 2007

Map 2   23

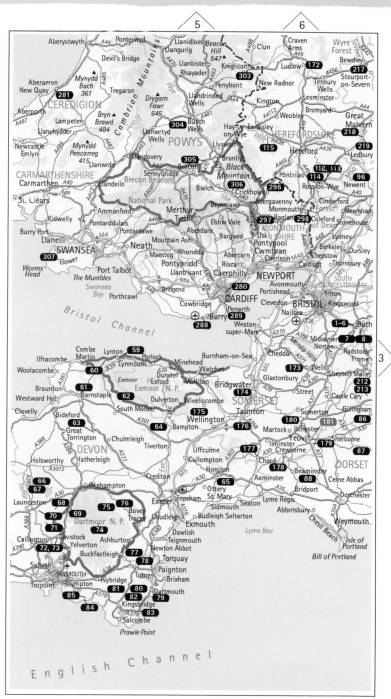

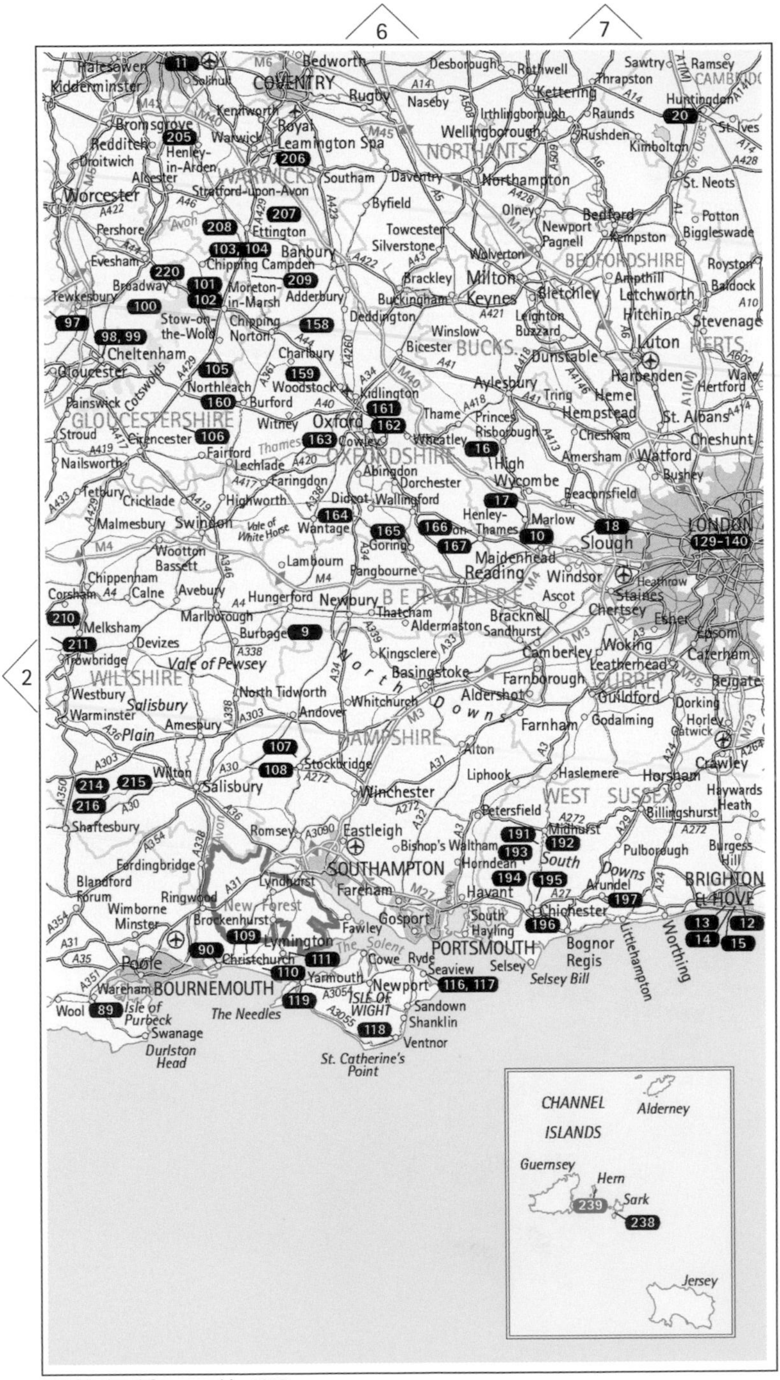
6
7
2
Halesowen
Kidderminster
Solihull
Bedworth
COVENTRY
Rugby
Desborough
Rothwell
Sawtry
Ramsey
Thrapston
Kettering
Huntingdon
St. Ives
Kenilworth
Warwick
Royal Leamington Spa
Naseby
Irthlingborough
Raunds
Wellingborough
Rushden
Kimbolton
Bromsgrove
Redditch
Droitwich
Henley-in-Arden
Alcester
WARWICKS
NORTHANTS
Southam
Daventry
Northampton
St. Neots
Worcester
Stratford-upon-Avon
Byfield
Olney
Bedford
Potton
Biggleswade
Pershore
Ettington
Towcester
Silverstone
Newport Pagnell
Kempston
Evesham
Chipping Campden
Banbury
Wolverton
BEDFORDSHIRE
Royston
Broadway
Moreton-in-Marsh
Adderbury
Brackley
Milton Keynes
Bletchley
Ampthill
Letchworth
Baldock
Tewkesbury
Stow-on-the-Wold
Chipping Norton
Buckingham
Deddington
Leighton Buzzard
Hitchin
Stevenage
Cheltenham
Charlbury
Winslow
Bicester
BUCKS.
Luton
HERTS.
Dunstable
Gloucester
Cotswolds
Northleach
Woodstock
Kidlington
Aylesbury
Harpenden
Ware
Hertford
Painswick
Burford
Tring
Hemel Hempstead
GLOUCESTERSHIRE
Witney
Oxford
Thame
Princes Risborough
St. Albans
Stroud
Cirencester
Cowley
Wheatley
Chesham
Cheshunt
Nailsworth
Fairford
Lechlade
OXFORDSHIRE
High Wycombe
Amersham
Watford
Faringdon
Abingdon
Dorchester
Bushey
Tetbury
Cricklade
Highworth
Didcot
Wallingford
Beaconsfield
Malmesbury
Swindon
Vale of White Horse
Wantage
Goring
Henley-on-Thames
Marlow
LONDON
Wootton Bassett
Lambourn
Pangbourne
Maidenhead
Slough
Chippenham
Reading
Windsor
Heathrow
Corsham
Calne
Avebury
Hungerford
Newbury
BERKSHIRE
Ascot
Staines
Melksham
Marlborough
Thatcham
Aldermaston
Bracknell
Sandhurst
Chertsey
Esher
Devizes
Burbage
Epsom
Trowbridge
Kingsclere
Camberley
Woking
Caterham
Vale of Pewsey
North Downs
Basingstoke
Leatherhead
WILTSHIRE
Farnborough
SURREY
Reigate
Westbury
North Tidworth
Whitchurch
Aldershot
Guildford
Dorking
Warminster
Salisbury Plain
Andover
Farnham
Godalming
Horley
Gatwick
Amesbury
HAMPSHIRE
Alton
Crawley
Stockbridge
Liphook
Haslemere
Horsham
Wilton
Salisbury
Winchester
WEST SUSSEX
Haywards Heath
Petersfield
Billingshurst
Shaftesbury
Romsey
Eastleigh
Bishop's Waltham
Midhurst
Pulborough
Burgess Hill
Fordingbridge
SOUTHAMPTON
Horndean
South Downs
Blandford Forum
Lyndhurst
Fareham
Havant
Arundel
BRIGHTON & HOVE
Ringwood
New Forest
Wimborne Minster
Brockenhurst
Fawley
Gosport
Chichester
South Hayling
Lymington
The Solent
PORTSMOUTH
Bognor Regis
Littlehampton
Worthing
Poole
Christchurch
Cowes
Ryde
Seaview
Selsey
Selsey Bill
BOURNEMOUTH
Yarmouth
Newport
Wareham
ISLE OF WIGHT
Sandown
Shanklin
Wool
Isle of Purbeck
The Needles
Swanage
Ventnor
Durlston Head
St. Catherine's Point
CHANNEL ISLANDS
Alderney
Guernsey
Herm
Sark
Jersey

Map 4

25

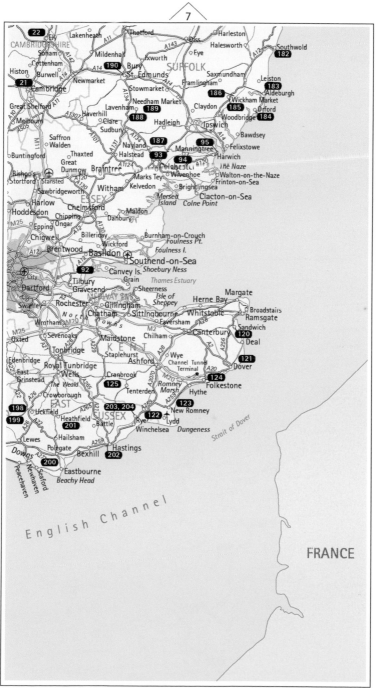

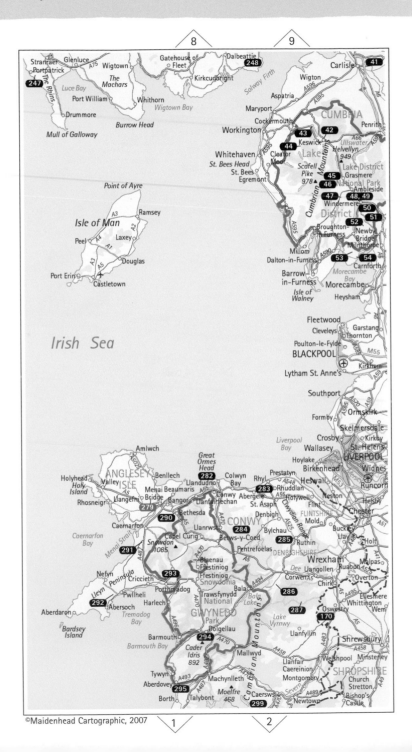

Map 6

27

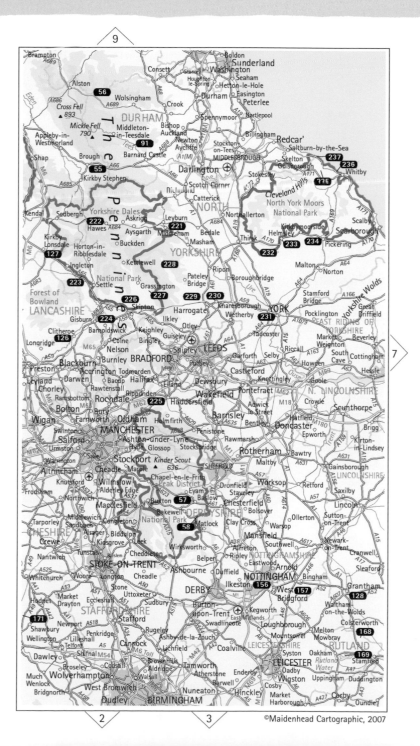

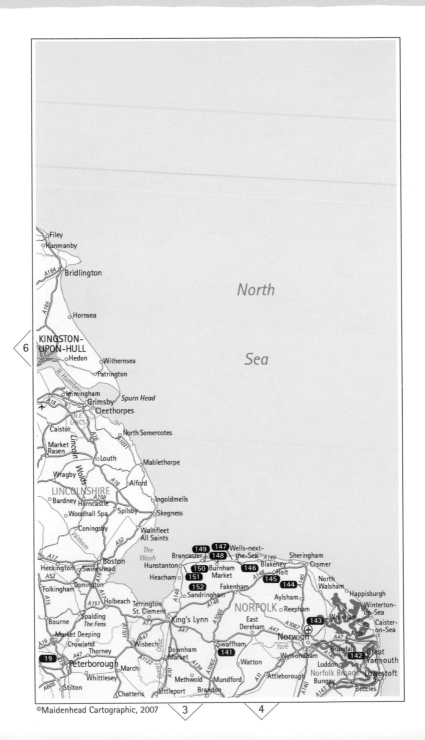

North

Sea

Filey
Hunmanby
A164 Bridlington
A165
Hornsea
6 KINGSTON-
UPON-HULL
Hedon   Withernsea
R. Humber   Patrington
A18 Immingham   Spurn Head
Grimsby
N.E. Cleethorpes
LINCS.
Caistor
North Somercotes
Market
Rasen   Louth   Mablethorpe
Wragby   Alford
LINCOLNSHIRE
A158   Ingoldmells
Bardney Horncastle   Spilsby   Skegness
Woodhall Spa
Coningsby   Wainfleet
Witham   All Saints   149 147 Wells-next-
A17   The   Brancaster 148 the-Sea   A149 Sheringham
A52   Wash   Hunstanton   A148 Holt   Cromer
Heckington Swineshead   150 Burnham   146 Blakeney
A52   Donington   Heacham   Market   145   North
Folkingham   151   Fakenham   A148   144   Walsham Happisburgh
A15   152   Aylsham   Winterton-
Holbeach Terrington   Sandringham   NORFOLK Reepham   on-Sea
Bourne   St. Clement   A148   East   143   Caister-
Spalding   King's Lynn   Dereham   A1067 Wroxham on-Sea
The Fens   A47   A47
Market Deeping   A47   Swaffham   Norwich   A47
Crowland   Wisbech   Ouse   Downham   141   Brundall
19   Thorney   A1122   Market   A134   Watton   Wymondham   142 Great
Peterborough   March   A10   A1065   A11   Loddon Yarmouth
Stilton   Methwold Mundford Attleborough   Norfolk Broads Lowestoft
A805   Whittlesey   Littleport Brandon   Bungay   A143 Beccles
Chatteris

Map 8
29

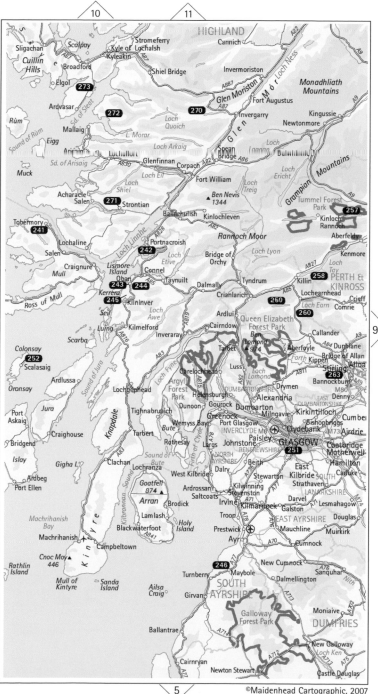

HIGHLAND
Sligachan   Scalpay   Stromeferry
Cuillin   Kyle of Lochalsh   Cannich
Hills   Broadford   Kyleakin
Elgol   273   Shiel Bridge   Invermoriston
Ardvasar   Sd. of Sleat   272   270   Monadhliath
Rùm   Glen Moriston   Mountains
Mallaig   Loch   A887   Fort Augustus
Quoich   Invergarry   Kingussie
Eigg   L. Morar   Newtonmore
Muck   Sound of Rùm   Loch Arkaig   Spean   Loch
Arisaig   Lochailort   Bridge   Laggan   Dalwhinnie
Sd. of Arisaig   Glenfinnan   Corpach   A86
Loch Eil   Loch
Acharacle   Shiel   271   Fort William   Treig   Loch
Salen   Strontian   Ben Nevis   Ericht   Grampian
1344   Mountains
Ballachulish   A9
Tobermory   Kinlochleven   Tummel Forest
241   Rannoch Moor   Park   257
Lochaline   Portnacroish   Kinloch
Salen   242   Aberfeldy   Rannoch
Craignure   Lismore   Loch   Bridge of   Loch Lyon   Kenmore
Mull   Island   Etive   Orchy   Loch
Oban   243   Connel   A827   Tay   PERTH &
Ross of Mull   Kerrera   244   Taynuilt   Dalmally   Tyndrum   Killin   258   KINROSS
Scil   245   Kilninver   Crianlarich   Lochearnhead   Crieff
Loch   A85   260   Loch Earn   Comrie
Luing   Awe   Ardlui   260
Colonsay   Scarba   Kilmelford   Cairndow   Queen Elizabeth   Callander
252   Inveraray   Forest Park   Ben
Scalasaig   Lomond   Aberfoyle   Dunblane
Oronsay   974   A84   Bridge of Allan
Tarbet   Forth   Kippen   Stirling   Alloa
Port   Jura   Garelochhead   Luss   263   Bannockburn
Askaig   Loch   Lomond   Denny   M80
Craighouse   Argyll   Helensburgh   Drymen   EAST
Bridgend   Knapdale   Forest   Dunoon   Gourock   Alexandria   DUMBARTONSHIRE
Islay   Park   Lochgilphead   Greenock   Milngavie   Kirkintilloch   Cumber
Ardbeg   Tighnabruaich   Port Glasgow   Bishopbriggs   Airdrie
Port Ellen   Gigha I.   Tarbert   Bute   Wemyss Bay   Dumbarton   Clydebank   M73
Rothesay   Largs   Paisley   GLASGOW   Coatbridge
Clachan   Sound   Johnstone   251   Motherwell
Machrihanish   of   West Kilbride   RENFREWSHIRE   Hamilton
Bay   Bute   Dalry   NORTH   Beith   East   SOUTH   Carluke
AYRSHIRE   Stewarton   Kilbride   LANARKSHIRE
Machrihanish   Goatfell   Ardrossan   Kilwinning   Strathaven   Lesmahagow
874   Saltcoats   Stevenston   Darvel
Cnoc Moy   Arran   Irvine   Galston   Douglas
446   Brodick   Troon   Kilmarnock   EAST AYRSHIRE
Mull of   Lamlash   Prestwick   Mauchline   Muirkirk
Kintyre   Blackwaterfoot   Holy   Ayr   A70
Sanda   Island   Cumnock
Rathlin   Island   Mauchline   New Cumnock   Sanquhar
Island   246   Maybole   Nith
Turnberry   Dalmellington
Ailsa   SOUTH   DUMFRIES
Craig   AYRSHIRE   Moniaive
Girvan   Galloway
Forest Park   New Galloway
Ballantrae   Loch Ken   A75
Cairnryan   Castle Douglas
Newton Stewart

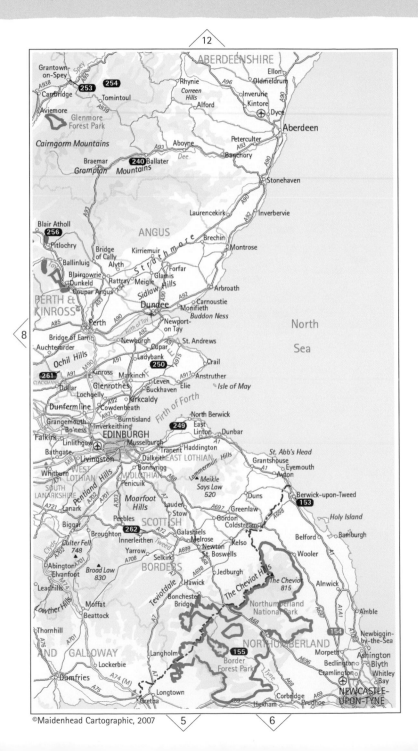

Map 10

31

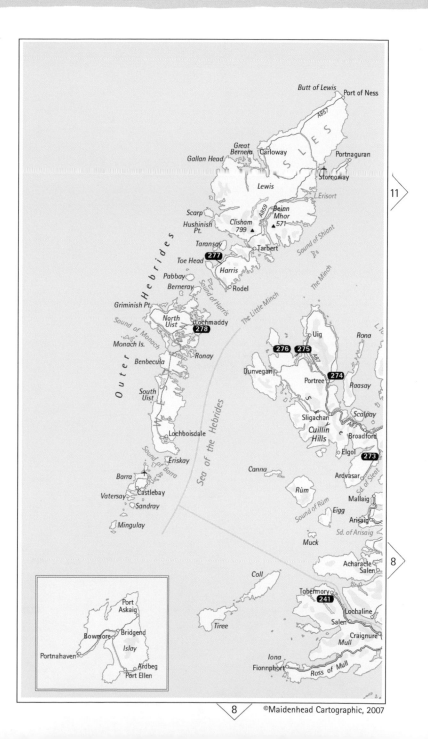

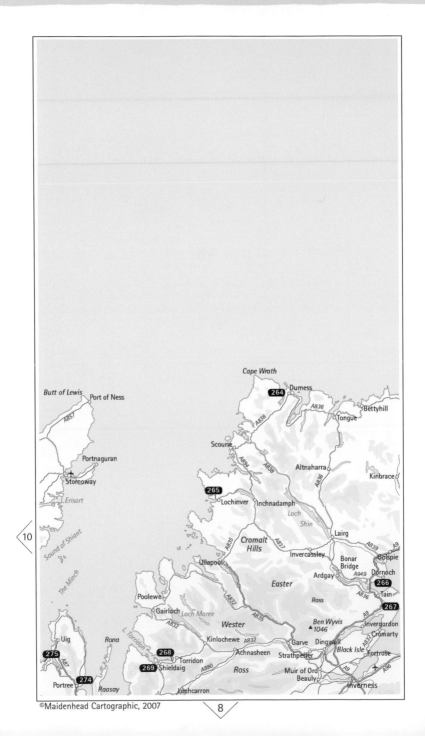

Map 12   33

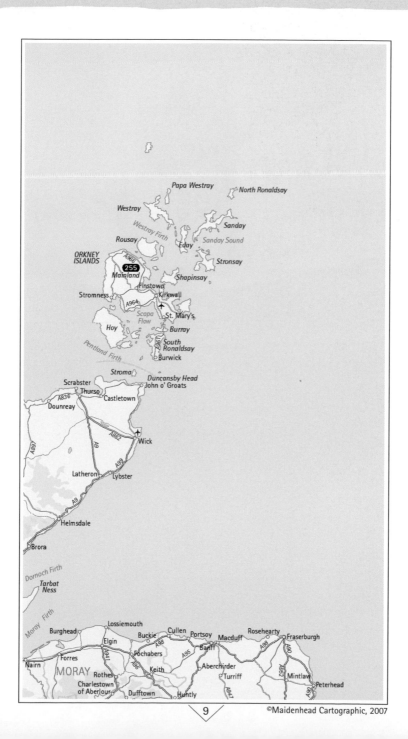

England

Bath Paradise House Hotel

You'll be hard pressed to find a better view in Bath. The views draw you out as soon as you enter the house: the magical 180-degree panorama from the garden is a dazzling advertisement for this World Heritage city. The Royal Crescent and the Abbey are floodlit at night and in summer, hot-air balloons float by low enough for you to hear the roar of the burners. Nearly all the rooms make full use of the view; the best have bay windows but all have a soft, luxurious country feel, with contemporary fabrics, wicker chairs and fabulous bathrooms. There are also two garden rooms in an extension that planners took years to approve; it's a remarkable achievement, in keeping with the original Bath stone house, and David is justly proud. The whole place has glass in all the right places, and the sitting room has lovely stone-arched French windows that pull in the light. In summer, don't miss afternoon tea in a half-acre walled garden, a perfect place to lose yourself in the vista. The occasional peal of bells comes from a nearby church. The Thermae Spa, newly opened, is a must. *Seven-minute walk down hill to centre.*

Price	£75–£175. Singles £65–£115.
Rooms	11: 4 doubles, 3 twins, 1 family, 3 four-posters.
Meals	Restaurants in Bath.
Closed	24 & 25 December.
Directions	From train station one-way system to Churchill Bridge. A367 exit from r'bout up hill; 0.75 miles, left at Andrews estate agents. Left down hill into cul-de-sac; on left.

David & Annie Lanz
86–88 Holloway, Bath,
Bath & N.E. Somerset BA2 4PX

Tel   01225 317723
Fax   01225 482005
Email   info@paradise-house.co.uk
Web   www.paradise-house.co.uk

Dorian House

A smart Victorian townhouse owned by a musician with a love of interior design. Tim is the London Symphony Orchestra's principal cellist and was once taught by the late and great Jacqueline du Pré. When he's not on stage in town, he's in Bath overseeing the smooth running of Dorian House, where the feel is more home than hotel, and the mix of traditional and contemporary design makes for a very pleasant base in the city. Everything has been beautifully restored. Step into a tiled hallway with exquisite stained glass, sink into deep sofas in the sitting room, or pop open a bottle of champagne in super bedrooms named after cellists. No surprise that the most impressive – and the most secluded – is du Pré: its huge four-poster bed is reached up a flight of stairs. Every room is decorated with beautiful fabrics and Egyptian linen. Those on the first floor are traditional, those above have a funkier feel, three have fabulous travertine marble bathrooms. The owners' art collection is everywhere, gathered from their travels abroad. Relaxation assured, and maybe some music, too. *Minimum stay two nights at weekends.*

Price	£80–£160. Singles £60–£89.
Rooms	11: 3 twins/doubles, 4 doubles, 1 family, 3 four-posters.
Meals	Pubs & restaurants within walking distance.
Closed	Never.
Directions	From Bath centre, follow signs to Shepton Mallet to sausage-shaped r'bout, then A37 up hill, 1st right. House 3rd on left, signed.

Kathryn & Tim Hugh
One Upper Oldfield Park, Bath,
Bath & N.E. Somerset BA2 3JX

Tel	01225 426336
Fax	01225 444699
Email	info@dorianhouse.co.uk
Web	www.dorianhouse.co.uk

SACO Serviced Apartments, Bath

Fabulous Bath is England's loveliest city, Georgian to its bone. It's built of mellow golden stone, so wander its streets for elegant squares, beautiful gardens, pavement cafés, delicious delis and the imperious Roman Baths (there's a spa if you want to take a dip). Close to the river, bang in the middle of town, these serviced apartments bask behind a beautifully restored Regency façade – look out for the pillared entrances. Inside you find a collection of airy studios and apartments, all of which come with sparkling kitchens that are fully stocked with ovens, dishwashers, washer/dryers, microwaves, fridges, freezers if there's room. Some are small, some are big, and if you need a bolthole for a night or a cool pad for a week, you'll find one here. You get white walls, Italian designer furniture, flat-screen TVs, CD players and big fluffy towels in spotless bathrooms. There's a lift to whisk you up and away, 24-hour reception, and high-speed broadband connection throughout. Supermarkets are close, but there are masses of great restaurants on your doorstep, too. *Minimum stay two nights at weekends.*

Price	Studios: £59–£147; 1-bed apt: £122–£197; 2-bed apt: £202–£262.
Rooms	43 studios & apartments for 2 & 4.
Meals	Full kitchen facilites. Restaurants within 0.5 miles.
Closed	Never.
Directions	In centre of town, 5-minute walk from station. Full directions on booking.

Jo Redman
SACO House, St James Parade, Bath,
Bath & N.E. Somerset BA1 1UH

Tel	01225 486540
Fax	01225 480025
Email	bath@sacoapartments.co.uk
Web	www.apartmentsbath.co.uk

The Queensberry Hotel & Olive Tree Restaurant

The Queensberry is an old favourite, grand but totally unpretentious and immensely enjoyable. It is rare to find a hotel of this size and elegance still in private hands: owners Laurence and Helen are working hard to complete their ideas, and the staff just couldn't be nicer. Those bedrooms that have had the magic treatment are excellent – contemporary and dramatic, with bold, inspirational colours and huge beds – but all have thick robes and drenching showers in large, sparkling bathrooms. If you have young children, ask for a room that's reachable by lift, and if you feel like spoiling yourself, have breakfast brought up to you: croissants, orange juice, fresh coffee, warm milk and a newspaper. At night, pop down to supper – the restaurant is renowned – and when you get back, your bed will have been turned down, your towels refreshed. As for the homemade fudge after supper... wonderful! All this in a John Wood house in the centre of Bath, a minute's walk from the Assembly Rooms, with reserved on-street parking. *Minimum stay two nights at weekends.*

Price	£120–£230. Suites £225–£420.
Rooms	29: 26 twins/doubles, 1 four-poster, 2 suites.
Meals	Breakfast £9–£14. Lunch £16.50. Dinner, à la carte, from £35.
Closed	Never.
Directions	Into Bath on A4 London Rd to Paragon; 1st right into Lansdown; 2nd left into Bennett St; 1st right into Russel St.

Laurence & Helen Beere
Russel Street, Bath,
Bath & N.E. Somerset BA1 2QF

Tel	01225 447928
Fax	01225 446065
Email	reservations@thequeensberry.co.uk
Web	www.thequeensberry.co.uk

The Bath Priory Hotel & Restaurant

An exquisite townhouse hotel, with staff who greet you by your name when you step through the front door. Spin into the drawing room while porters see to your luggage, gaze at exceptional art, warm yourself in front of the fire, then throw open the French windows and explore the four-acre garden for swimming pool, croquet lawn, kitchen garden and an ancient cedar… colour bursts through in summer, and loungers flank the pool. Back inside a Michelin star in the dining room will keep a smile on your face and may offer roasted scallops marinated in lime, slow-poached saddle of fallow deer, nougatine leaves with manuka honey and a lavender-scented truffled goats' cheese. Plush bedrooms are as you'd expect with rich fabrics, warm colours, crisp linen and Roberts radios. Those at the back have garden views, there are shelves of books, proper armchairs, a sofa if there's room. Back downstairs, fresh flowers everywhere and a spa with indoor pool, sauna, steam room, gym and treatment suites. The city is on your doorstep: stroll through the park to the Roman Baths and Royal Crescent. *Minimum stay two nights at weekends.*

Price	£245–£360.
Rooms	27: 27 twins/doubles.
Meals	Lunch from £20. Dinner £55.
Closed	Never.
Directions	From centre of Bath follow red hospital signs west for a mile. Right at far end of Royal Victoria Park. Left at T-junction into Weston Road. Hotel on left.

Sue Williams
Weston Road, Bath,
Bath & N.E. Somerset BA1 2XT

Tel	01225 331922
Fax	01225 448276
Email	mail@thebathpriory.co.uk
Web	www.thebathpriory.co.uk

The Residence

A sublime house away from the bustle of the city. The Residence is small, intimate, welcoming, with immaculate service and an effortless style. If the setting is English, the inspiration is French. There's a fountain in the front courtyard, a boules pitch in a balustraded garden, and cherubs on the wall in a conservatory/bar that opens onto a stone terrace. Breakfast is terrific. Kitchen and dining room flow from one to other, and you sit under high ceilings on ancient flagged floors listening to your sausages sizzle. This is a classical building that basks in a cool contemporary style. Light pours in, excellent art hangs on every wall, sofas wait in front of a fire in the sitting room, and there are a small sauna and a mirrored steam room too. Above, super bedrooms come crammed with luxury: old radiators, stripped floors, cow-hide rugs, fabulous beds dressed in crisp linen. You find White Company oils in Fired Earth bathrooms, digital radios, flat-screen TVs and DVD players to keep you amused. Bath is a short stroll across Victoria Park. *Minimum stay two nights at weekends.*

Price	£135-£250. Suite £300.
Rooms	6: 5 doubles, 1 suite.
Meals	Lunch from £5. Dinner, 3 courses, £40 (Thursday-Saturday only).
Closed	Never.
Directions	West out of Bath for Bristol on A4 (follow red hospital signs). 1st right after Victoria Park into Park Lane. House on north side of Weston Road at junction with Park Lane.

	David Woodwood
	Weston Road, Bath,
	Bath & N.E. Somerset BA1 2XZ
Tel	01225 750180
Fax	01225 750181
Email	info@theresidencebath.com
Web	www.theresidencebath.com

The Wheatsheaf Inn

A hidden valley, a pretty village, a gorgeous inn, three fabulous rooms. Views from the lush terraced garden stretch across to a fine ridge of trees, with the manor house and church jutting out of the woods below. In summer there are barbecues, lazy lunches, horses clopping by. This is a 15th-century farmhouse with later additions – it's all but impossible to notice the join – whose exterior comes clad in Farrow & Ball creams. Outside there are Indian benches with seagrass cushions; inside, big sofas in front of the fire. Airy interiors have neutral colours to soak up the light, sand-blasted beams, halogen spotlights and Lloyd Loom wicker dining chairs. Steps outside lead down to three deeply comfy bedrooms in a stone outbuilding. All come in contemporary rustic style with light wood furniture, flat-screen TVs, Egyptian cotton and deluge showers; there are White Company oils and bath robes too. Climb back up for seriously good food, perhaps risotto of Dorset crab, fillet of Buccleuch Scotch beef, hot raspberry soufflé. Bath is a hike across the fields. *Minimum stay two nights at weekends in summer.*

Price	£95–£110.
Rooms	3 doubles.
Meals	Lunch from £10. Dinner, 3 courses, about £35. Not Monday evenings.
Closed	Rarely.
Directions	South from Bath on A367, then left in Combe Down onto B3110. Straight ahead for 1.5 miles, then right for Combe Hay.

Ian & Adele Barton
Combe Hay, Bath,
Bath & N.E. Somerset BA2 7EG

Tel	01225 833504
Fax	01225 833504
Email	info@wheatsheafcombehay.com
Web	www.wheatsheafcombehay.com

Wheelwrights Arms

A pub for all seasons. In winter, grab the table in front of the ancient fire where the wheelwright worked his magic; in summer, skip outside for a pint on the terrace. You're in the country, two miles from Bath, so drop down to the nearby Kennet & Avon canal and cycle or walk through glorious country into the city. The Wheelwrights dates to 1750. Inside, beautiful contemporary colours mix with soft stone walls and exposed timber frames. Logs are piled high in the alcoves, there's a wonderful snug, the daily papers are left on the bar and the food is delicious, perhaps chilli mussels, rack of lamb, banana crème brûlée; in summer you can eat in the garden illuminated by lights in the trees. Airy bedrooms in what was the wheelwright's annex come in fresh, original style. Expect dark wood floors, shuttered windows, old-style radiators, flat-screen TVs. Wooden beds are covered in immaculate linen, white bathrooms come with robes and L'Occitane potions. The inn holds two season tickets for Bath Rugby Club. Guests can take them at cost price, so book early. *Minimum stay two nights at weekends.*

Price	£100-£130. Singles from £75.
Rooms	7: 5 doubles, 1 twin, 1 single.
Meals	Lunch, 2 courses, £10.
	Dinner, 3 courses, about £27.50.
Closed	Never.
Directions	A36 south from Bath for 4 miles, then right, signed Monkton Combe. Over x-roads, into village, on left.

David Phillips-White
Church Lane, Monkton Combe, Bath,
Bath & N.E. Somerset BA2 7HB

Tel	01225 722287
Fax	01225 722259
Email	bookings@wheelwrightsarms.co.uk
Web	www.wheelwrightsarms.co.uk

Entry 8 Map 2

Crown and Garter

An unreformed country local. On the night we stayed Gill was serving at the bar, her father was keeping an eye on the fire and her son was running through questions for the pub quiz. Gamekeepers and village footballers come for good beer and hearty food. Cockerels crow in the fields and in summer life spills onto a stone terrace and into the pretty garden. Inside you get wooden floors, thick red curtains and a huge settle by the fire. There's a small restaurant, so dig into homemade pies, Thai curries, lamb shank, or a fillet steak. James II is said to have visited which might account for the wooden throne by the front door. Bedrooms are in a single-storey building that looks prettier in summer when the vine is out. Rooms, however, are big and stylish. Four have painted floorboards, all have voile wall hangings. Beds are brass or wooden, linen is crisp and white, there are quilted bedspreads, coloured rugs and floral curtains; two rooms interconnect. Piping hot water flows in super little bathrooms. You can walk from the front door, try your luck at Newbury Races or watch the early morning gallops at Lambourne.

Price	£90. Singles £59.50.
Rooms	8: 6 doubles, 2 twins.
Meals	Lunch & dinner from £10. Not Mondays or Tuesday lunchtimes.
Closed	Rarely.
Directions	M4 junc. 13, then A34 south. Left onto A4 for Hungerford. After 2 miles, left for Kintbury & Inkpen. In Kintbury, left at corner shop onto Inkpen Road; follow main flow, inn on left after 2 miles.

Gill Hern
Great Common, Inkpen, Hungerford,
Berkshire RG17 9QR

Tel	01488 668325
Email	gill.hern@btopenworld.com
Web	www.crownandgarter.com

Red Roofs at Oldfield

A dazzling film set of a house and garden. Built in the 1890s, later home to the Reitlinger Museum and its Egyptian, Persian and Greek artefacts, it now houses Sandy, Colin, a canny collection of Victoriana (if something takes your fancy, you can buy it) and some deeply indulged guests. Bedrooms are packed with gleaming wood, elegant watercolours, vintage fabrics, wooden floors and old knick-knacks; one of the baths has a modesty canopy, and there are fine river views from most. There isn't a reason in the world to feel tense, but just in case you do, there's a relaxation room for massage, reiki, hot-stone therapy and a whole raft of treatments. The Great Hall is striking with its turquoise woodwork and vast windows. Communal breakfasts offer local organic sausages and bacon as well as Jack Daniels marmalade; in summer you can decamp to the garden and watch rowers and swans glide by. The river Thames idles past the bottom of the sweeping lawns. Two of England's best restaurants are close, the Fat Duck and the Waterside Inn at Bray; book a table at the latter and Colin can ferry you up in his frolic.

Price	£115–£195. Singles from £90. Family £195.
Rooms	8: 6 doubles, 2 family.
Meals	Pub/restaurant 200 yds.
Closed	Christmas.
Directions	M4 junc. 7, then A4 west towards Maidenhead. Over Maidenhead Bridge and immediately left. House on left.

Colin & Sandy Brooks
Guards Club Road, Maidenhead,
Berkshire SL6 8DN

Tel	01628 621910
Email	redroofs.oldfield@virgin.net
Web	www.redroofsatoldfield.co.uk

Simpsons

A listed Victorian villa and a Michelin star much loved by locals bring a little gastronomic theatre to the leafy streets of Edgbaston. Come for an intoxicating mix of divine food and cool design. Interiors are smart and airy with high ceilings, stripped floors and white leather armchairs, and opulent bedrooms come with buckets of style. Take your pick from: a Venetian carnival mask and mirrored antique bed; Chinese scrolls and framed tapestries; garden views in a room the size of a small swimming pool; hessian walls and colonial chic. You'll find bowls of fruit, flat-screen TVs, huge bathrooms; one with a claw-foot bath, all with enormous showers. As for the food, expect the best, served in a light-filled orangerie where French windows open onto a pretty terrace. Incredible flavour bursts from every dish, perhaps seared fois gras with coffee syrup and amaretto, venison with figs and lemon confit, then strawberry and rhubarb 'soup' with crème fraîche ice cream. An exemplary wine list has five pages for clarets alone and features a 1970 Pétrus. Well-dressed staff are friendly and attentive.

Price	£160–£225.
Rooms	4: 2 doubles, 2 twins/doubles.
Meals	Lunch from £20. Dinner from £30; à la carte about £42; 7-course tasting menu £65.
Closed	24-26 December & 1-2 January.
Directions	M6 junc. 6, then A38(M) for city centre. Thro' 1st tunnel, then left up slipway. At r'bout 2nd exit for Kidderminster (A456). Thro' underpass, then 1st left. Thro' lights, on right.

Andreas Antona
20 Highfield Road, Edgbaston,
Birmingham B15 3DX

Tel	0121 454 3434
Fax	0121 454 3399
Email	info@simpsonsrestaurant.co.uk
Web	www.simpsonsrestaurant.co.uk

Drakes

If you were to compile the definitive list of England's top ten boutique hotels, you'd include Drakes. It's small and intimate with a funky bar, a super restaurant and a heavyweight design that sets it apart from most. More than anything else, this is a hotel that stirs the adrenalin, that gives you the buzz of excitement you get when someone throws you the keys to their Ferrari and insists you drive. Bedrooms are exemplary. Eleven have free-standing baths in the room (you can gaze out to sea as you soak), while the list of must haves is as long as your arm (flat-screen TVs, monsoon showers, waffled bathrobes, White Company oils) Yet what impresses most here is the detail and workmanship. Handmade beds rest on carpets that are changed every year, contemporary plaster mouldings curl around ceilings like mountain terraces, Vi-spring mattresses come in the crispest cotton and are piled high with pillows. Don't worry if you can't afford the best rooms — all are fantastic, some are just bigger than others, and those in the attic are as cute as could be. Kylie loved hers. *Minimum stay two nights at weekends.*

Price	£120-£300. Suite £375-£475. Singles £95-£125.
Rooms	20: 17 doubles, 2 singles, 1 suite.
Meals	Breakfast £7.50-£12.50. Lunch, 2 courses, £15. Dinner, 3 courses, £32.
Closed	Never.
Directions	M23/A23 into Brighton. At seafront, with pier in front, left up hill. Hotel on left after 300 yds.

Richard Hayes
43-44 Marine Parade,
Brighton BN2 1PE

Tel	01273 696934
Email	info@drakesofbrighton.com
Web	www.drakesofbrighton.com

Paskins Town House

Paskins is neither grand nor chic, fancy nor smart, just easy-going and genuinely 'green'. And it is yards from the beach. Rambling across two graciously bow-fronted townhouses of 1810, you get four storeys of narrow winding stairs, creaking Georgian floors and much idiosyncrasy. Paint is used to mask some dilapidation, the colour schemes can be a little overwhelming and a couple of the singles are tiny, but... others are charming, with the odd four-poster, flowery fabrics and prints, cabaret posters, modern art. Most rooms are provided with irons – a thoughtful touch; bathrooms are windowless but spotless; linen is crisp and white. The Art Deco breakfast room is a delight to behold, as is breakfast: tasty tomatoes sprinkled with basil, spiced compotes, many varieties of sausage. Vegetarians are treated royally – Paskins claims to serve the best veggie breakfasts on the south coast. All the food is organic where available, from local farms if possible. The coffee is Fair Trade, the smellies are free of the taint of animal testing and you're very close to the centre of things. *Minimum stay two nights at weekends.*

Price	£70–£125. Singles £45–£55.
Rooms	19: 6 doubles, 2 twins/doubles, 7 singles, 1 triple, 3 four-posters.
Meals	Sandwiches £4.20. Restaurants nearby.
Closed	Rarely.
Directions	M23/A23 to Brighton. Left at seafront roundabout opposite pier. Hotel 13th street on left.

Roger & Susan Marlowe
18/19 Charlotte Street,
Brighton BN2 1AG

Tel	01273 601203
Fax	01273 621973
Email	welcome@paskins.co.uk
Web	www.paskins.co.uk

Neo Hotel

A groovy bohemian bolthole one block up from the seafront. Steph, a stylist, has a great eye, and has poured love and colour into her boutique empire; exquisite vintage wallpapers by Ralph Lauren, Osborne & Little and Florence Broadhurst adorn most walls. The hotel – a listed Georgian townhouse – is small but sweet with a cool little bar that comes in deep pink and a breakfast room that doubles as an art gallery. Bedrooms over three floors – some snug in the eaves, others with high ceilings – have padded headboards, silky curtains, Egyptian linen and super-comfy beds. Black mosaic bathrooms, some compact, have mirrored walls, and there are kimonos instead of bath robes. Sensational breakfasts – raspberry and banana smoothies, blueberry pancakes, the full cooked works – are served under a tear-drop chandelier while Billie Holiday and Ella Fitzgerald serenade you. Friendly staff steer you in the right direction for clubs, pubs, concerts and restaurants – pop down for a chilli chocolate martini before heading out for a night on the town. *Minimum stay two nights at weekends.*

Price	£95–£150.
Rooms	9: 5 doubles, 3 twins/doubles, 1 single.
Meals	Pubs/restaurants nearby.
Closed	Christmas.
Directions	A23 into Brighton. Down to seafront and right at pier. Pass Grand Hotel, Hilton Hotel and square on right, then 2nd right. Parking: £12 a day off-street.

Steph Harding
19 Oriental Place,
Brighton BN1 2LL

Tel	01273 711104
Fax	01273 711105
Email	info@neohotel.com
Web	www.neohotel.com

brightonwave

A small, friendly, boutique B&B hotel in the epicentre of trendy Brighton. The beach and the pier are a two-minute walk, the bars and restaurants of St James' Street are around the corner. An open-plan sitting room/dining room comes in cool colours with big suede sofas, fairy lights in the fireplace and ever-changing art on the walls. Bedrooms at the front are big and fancy, with huge padded headboards that fill the wall and deluge showers in sandstone bathrooms. Those at the back have a simpler feel (sisal matting, muted walls, local art). They're smaller, but so is the price, and they come with spotless compact shower rooms; if you're out more than in, why worry? All rooms come with fat duvets, lush linen, flat-screen TVs and DVD/CD players (there's a library of films downstairs), and the lower-ground king-size has a private garden. Shaun and Martin are open and relaxed, happy for guests to chill drinks in the kitchen (and there are corkscrews in all rooms). Shaun cooks breakfast – fresh fruit pancakes, bacon and brie croissants, the full cooked works. *Minimum stay two nights at weekends.*

Price	£90–£175. Four-poster £130–£200. Singles from £80.
Rooms	8: 2 twins/doubles, 5 doubles, 1 four-poster.
Meals	Restaurants nearby.
Closed	January.
Directions	A23 to Brighton Pier roundabout at seafront; left towards Marina; 5th street on left. On-street parking vouchers, £5 for 24 hours.

Shaun Trumble & Martin Torrens
10 Madeira Place,
Brighton BN2 1TN

Tel	01273 676794
Email	info@brightonwave.co.uk
Web	www.brightonwave.co.uk

Three Horseshoes Inn

London may only be an hour's drive, but you'll think you've washed up in the 1960s. Red kites circle a bowl of deep countryside, smoke curls from cottages that hug the hill. As for the Three Horseshoes, you find flagstones and an open fire in the tiny locals' bar, exposed timbers and pine settles in the airy restaurant. Simon, chef turned patron, has cooked in The Connaught, Chez Nico, Le Gavroche – all the best places – and dinner is a treat, the homemade piccalilli worth the trip alone. Come for lunch and dig into baked camembert with garlic and rosemary, stay for dinner and try tiger prawns, roasted sea bass and bread and butter pudding with marmalade ice cream. Guests have a private entrance, stairs lead to super-smart rooms. Expect silky quilts, goose down pillows, funky furniture, Farrow & Ball paints. Also: flat-screen TVs, deluge showers and views of the Chilterns. Breakfast indulgently, hike in the hills, walk by the Thames, hop over to Windsor. There's jazz and tapas once a month and in summer you can eat in the garden while ducks circle a sunken phone box in the pond. Only in England.

Price	£110–£120. Suite £145. Single £75.
Rooms	6: 2 doubles, 1 suite, 1 single, 2 garden rooms.
Meals	Lunch from £5. Dinner, 3 courses, £25–£30. Not Monday.
Closed	Rarely.
Directions	M40, junc. 5, A40 south thro' Stokenchurch, then left for Radnage. After 2 miles left to Bennett End. Sharp right, up hill, on left.

Simon Crawshaw & Tracey Button
Bennett End, Radnage, High Wycombe,
Buckinghamshire HP14 4EB

Tel	01494 483273
Fax	01494 485464
Email	threehorse@btconnect.com
Web	www.thethreehorseshoes.net

The Hand and Flowers

It's almost Shakespearean. Ludlow's claim to the culinary crown of England is under challenge from prosperous Marlow. Instead of arrows falling from the sky, Michelin stars are tumbling down. Chief instigator is Tom, whose incredible cooking has attracted great interest in only two years; locals now pack the place day and night. Step into these airy 18th-century cottages and find flagged floors under low beams – it's remarkably easy-going. There's no froth on the menu, no dress code in the restaurant, just ambrosial food that elates; make sure you book. Try perfectly cooked salmon with frozen horseradish, slow-cooked English veal with a succulent beetroot linguini, vanilla crème brûlée washed down by a honey-sweet beer chaser. Four stylish rooms stand 30 paces along the road in two refurbished cottages (expect a little noise). Beth, a sculptor, oversaw their creation; you get exposed beams, cow hide rugs, Egyptian cotton and flat-screen TVs. One room has a hot tub on a private terrace, another has a telescope and a window for star-gazing. The Thames is close for revitalising walks. Brilliant.

Price	£140–£190.
Rooms	4 doubles.
Meals	Lunch from £12.50. Dinner, 3 courses, about £30. Not Sunday nights.
Closed	25 & 26 December.
Directions	M4 junc. 9, A404 north, then into Marlow. Leave Marlow for Henley on A4155. On edge of town on right.

Tom & Beth Kerridge
126 West Street, Marlow,
Buckinghamshire SL7 2BP

Tel	01628 482277
Email	bbethcullen@aol.com
Web	www.thehandandflowers.co.uk

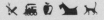

Stoke Park Club

James Bond played golf with Goldfinger here and nearly lost his head to Odd Job's bowler hat. Whether he stayed for a massage, a game of tennis, a swim in the pool or a meal in the Art Deco-style restaurant is not recorded, but if he didn't, he should have. Stoke Park is a Palladian-style mansion set in 350 acres on an estate that is noted in the Domesday Book. Matchless interiors thrill: Corinthian columns and a cupola dome in the Great Hall, the largest free-standing marble staircase in Europe, and a grand piano opposite a roaring fire. The Orangery, for late breakfasts, is also the members' clubhouse and buzzes with life (ladies in for a hand of bridge, old timers lamenting a missed putt). In summer, life spills onto a balustraded terrace for views across croquet lawn and golf course to the heritage gardens. Expect panelled bars, padded window seats, elaborate wall hangings, even a chapel. Bedrooms are the very best (Hugh Grant and Renée Zellweger stayed in *Bridget Jones's Diary*), with oak four-posters, big fat sofas and fabulous marble bathrooms. The health club, spa and golf club are yours to enjoy.

Price	£285-£345. Suites £400-£1,100. Half-board £180 p.p.
Rooms	21: 18 doubles, 3 suites.
Meals	Breakfast £15-£18. Lunch from £15. Dinner, 3 courses, £39.50
Closed	24-26 December & 1st week in January.
Directions	M4, junc. 6, A355 north, then right at 2nd r'about. On right after 1.25 miles.

Mark Fagan
Park Road, Stoke Poges,
Buckinghamshire SL2 4PG

Tel	01753 717171
Fax	01753 717181
Email	info@stokeparkclub.com
Web	www.stokeparkclub.com

The White Hart

This much-forgotten slip of England is prettier than most imagine; quiet lanes weave past wood, hill, field, village. Wash up at the White Hart and join a legion of locals who come for a lively bar and fabulous Ufford ales; they're brewed out back 50 paces from the beer tap. Farmers gather on Fridays, the cricket team drops by on Sundays, in summer life spills onto the terrace. Inside, leather sofas, fine settles, flagged floors and a crackling fire provide the traditional comforts, while railway signs, wooden pitch forks and hanging station lamps add colour. Spin through to the dining room to find an easy country elegance with flagged floors, exposed stone walls and an exquisite pitch pine window seat. You can eat simply or grandly, anything from a ploughman's at lunch to a three-course feast in the evening; there's a cheese menu, too. Bedrooms (four above the bar, two out by the microbrewery) are simple, spotless and carry an honest price. Expect seagrass matting, crisp white linen and flat-screen TVs. Burghley, Stamford and Oakham are close.

Price	£85. Singles £70.
Rooms	6: 3 doubles, 2 twins, 1 four-poster.
Meals	Lunch from £10. Dinner, 3 courses, about £25. Not Sunday night.
Closed	Rarely.
Directions	A1, then east on A47 four miles south of Stamford. Ist left, thro' Southorpe & keep right for Ufford.

Bertie Fenner
Main Street, Ufford,
Cambridgeshire PE9 3BH

Tel	01780 740250
Email	info@whitehartufford.co.uk
Web	www.whitehartufford.co.uk

The Old Bridge Hotel

A smart hotel – the best in town – with battalions of devoted locals who come for the food (delicious), the wines (exceptional) and the hugely comfortable interiors. Ladies lunch, business men chatter, all are happy. Order a glass of champagne at the bar, then sink into a winged armchair in front of the fire and study the menu. You can eat wherever you want, so lope into the muralled restaurant or grab a sofa in the lounge and feast on anything from sweet potato soup to rack of Cornish lamb (starters are available all day long). Breakfast is served in a panelled morning room with Buddha in the fireplace; in summer you decant to the terrace. Spotless bedrooms are scattered about, all in warm colours with rich fabrics, padded bedheads, crisp linen. One has a mirrored four-poster, another a sitting room/bathroom. Some overlook the river Ouse, all have spoiling extras: Molton Brown potions, Bang & Olufsen TVs, power showers and bathrobes. Kind, attentive staff deliver. As for John, he's a Master of Wine; browse and buy his stock. The A14 may pass to the front, but it doesn't matter a jot.

Price	£110–£180. Singles from £95. Half-board at weekends from £70 p.p.
Rooms	24: 13 doubles, 1 twin, 7 singles, 3 four-posters.
Meals	Lunch & dinner £7–£30.
Closed	Never.
Directions	A1, then A14 into Huntingdon. Hotel on southwest flank of one-way system that circles town.

John Hoskins
1 High Street, Huntingdon,
Cambridgeshire PE18 6QT

Tel	01480 424300
Fax	01480 411017
Email	oldbridge@huntsbridge.co.uk
Web	www.huntsbridge.com

Entry 20 Map 3

Hotel Felix

Hotel Felix is sleekly up to date, a country house with a modern twist and a mere mile (walk in, taxi back) from the historic city. Centred around a Victorian villa in three acres, two new bedroom wings have been added at right angles to the original building (just four bedrooms in the old part, popular with celebs), thus creating a courtyard with statue and plants in between. Bedrooms are sophisticated and luxurious: huge beds, plump pillows, neutral tones, silk fabrics, feather duvets, generously proportioned bathrooms lined in slate or natural stone; there are CDs and films on demand and every imaginable 'corporate' extra. Overlooking the pleasant terrace and small gardens is the light, airy, elegant Graffiti restaurant, whose chef draws on the flavoursome approach of modern British cooking... Isle of Skye scallops, roast rump of Denham venison, chilled lemon rice pudding. There's a Conran-designed health club nearby (with spa) to work off your indulgence – ask for a day pass from reception. Contemporary style without the attitude.

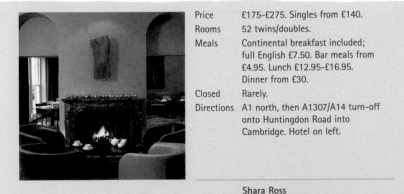

Price	£175–£275. Singles from £140.
Rooms	52 twins/doubles.
Meals	Continental breakfast included; full English £7.50. Bar meals from £4.95. Lunch £12.95–£16.95. Dinner from £30.
Closed	Rarely.
Directions	A1 north, then A1307/A14 turn-off onto Huntingdon Road into Cambridge. Hotel on left.

Shara Ross
Whitehouse Lane, Huntingdon Road,
Cambridge, Cambridgeshire CB3 0LX

Tel	01223 277977
Fax	01223 277973
Email	help@hotelfelix.co.uk
Web	www.hotelfelix.co.uk

The Anchor Inn

A real find, a 1650 ale house on Chatteris Fen. The New Bedford river streams past outside. It was cut from the soil by the pub's first residents, Scottish prisoners of war brought in by Cromwell to dig the dykes that drain the fens. These days cosy luxury infuses every corner. There are low beamed ceilings, timber-framed walls, raw dark panelling and terracotta-tiled floors. A wood-burner warms the bar, so stop for a pint of cask ale, then feast on fresh local produce: hand-dressed crabs from Cromer in spring, asparagus and Bottisham hams in summer, wild duck from the marshes in winter; breakfast is equally indulgent. Four spotless rooms above the restaurant fit the mood exactly (not posh, supremely comfy). Expect trim carpets, wicker chairs, crisp white duvets and Indian cotton throws. The suites each have a sofabed and three rooms have fen and river views. Footpaths flank the water; stroll down and you might see mallards or Hooper swans, even a seal (the river is tidal to the Wash). Don't miss Ely (the bishop comes to eat), Cambridge, and Welney for nesting swans by the thousand.

Price	£65–£95. Singles from £55. Suites £109.50–£149.50. Extra bed £20.
Rooms	4: 1 double, 1 twin, 2 suites.
Meals	Lunch, 2 courses, £10.95. Dinner, 3 courses, about £26.
Closed	26 December.
Directions	West from Ely on A142. Left in Sutton onto B1381 for Earith. On south fringes of Sutton, right signed Sutton Gault. 1 mile north on left at bridge.

Adam Pickup & Carlene Bunten
Bury Lane, Sutton Gault, Ely,
Cambridgeshire CB6 2DB

Tel	01353 778537
Fax	01353 776180
Email	anchorinn@popmail.bta.com
Web	www.anchorsuttongault.co.uk

Molesworth Manor

Geoff and Jessica are relaxed, helpful hosts, and they've done a lot to improve this place in the last four years. The house – big enough to swallow hoards of people – is filled with art and interesting antiques, cool pastel colours and restored architectural features. The huge drawing room pulls in the morning sun; the music room suits the evening. A carved staircase – no insert is the same – leads to bedrooms that vary in style and size: two at the front are grand, those in the eaves are bright and beamed. Three are in a self-catering cottage across the courtyard let to one party. The rectory garden, as you'd expect – mature, well-tended and peaceful, with a small play area for children. The delicious whiff of homemade muffins will lure you down to breakfast in the gorgeous tropical-style conservatory, and you'll eat well in the evening too – the phenomenon that is the Cornish Riviera and its attendant fresh-and-local food scene is on your doorstep. Beaches, coastal paths and great cycling are a must for heartier souls.

Price	£54–£100. Cottage £485–£820 per week. Whole house available.
Rooms	9 + 1: 7 doubles, 1 twin/double; 1 twin with separate shower. Self-catering cottage for 6.
Meals	Restaurants in Padstow.
Closed	November–January. Open off-season by arrangement for larger parties.
Directions	Off A389 between Wadebridge & Padstow. Entrance clearly signed; 300 yards from bridge in Little Petherick.

Geoff French & Jessica Clarke
Little Petherick, Padstow,
Cornwall PL27 7QT

Tel	01841 540292
Email	molesworthmanor@aol.com
Web	www.molesworthmanor.co.uk

The Well House

Silence in a blissful valley, with sprawling lawns, a swimming pool, a tennis court and lilies on the pond. A stream runs though the garden. It's fed by a well that was blessed by St Keyne in 579; those who drink from it will rule their marriage. On a lane that goes nowhere, a Victorian country house that was built by a tea magnate, hence the tea menu at breakfast. Farrow & Ball colours run throughout, there's a snug bar with busts and prints, a marble fireplace in the airy sitting room and a mirrored restaurant for fabulous food — perhaps confit of Gressingham duck, seared black bream with prawn risotto, hot coconut soufflé with warm chocolate sauce. Bedrooms are scattered about and come in a fresh country-house style. Most have garden views (go for these) and flood with light. Expect quilted bedcovers, sheets and blankets, warm colours and spotless bathrooms. There's good art on the walls and garden suites open onto a stone terrace for glorious views of the Looe Valley. You can head down to the sea at Polperro, take the ferry across to Fowey or drop in at the Eden Project.

Price	£145–£170. Suites £205. Singles from £130. Half-board £105–£135 p.p.
Rooms	9: 4 doubles, 2 twins, 3 suites.
Meals	Lunch, 3 courses, £23, by arrangement. Dinner, 4 courses, £37.50.
Closed	Rarely.
Directions	A38 to Liskard, then B3254 south for Looe. Through St Keyne, then straight on down small lane at sharp right. House on left after half a mile.

Richard Farrow
St Keyne, Nr Looe,
Cornwall PL14 4RN

Tel	01579 342001
Fax	01579 343891
Email	enquiries@wellhouse.co.uk
Web	www.wellhouse.co.uk

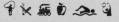

The Cormorant Hotel

A supreme position on the side of a wooded hill with the magical Fowey river curling past below. Oyster catchers swoop low across the water, sheep bleat in the fields, sail boats tug on their moorings. The hotel is one room deep and every window looks the right way, but a recent renovation has added small balconies to most of the bedrooms, so doze in the sun and listen to the sounds of the river. As for the hotel, it couldn't have fallen into better hands. Mary rescued it from neglect, poured in love and money, and now it shines: new windows, new bathrooms, new swimming pool, new everything. A terrace sweeps along the front, a finger of lawn runs below, and inside, the river follows wherever you go. You get fresh flowers in the bar, an open fire in the sitting room, wooden floors in a smartly dressed dining room. Super bedrooms come without clutter: light colours, trim carpets, walls of glass, crisp white linen. One has a claw-foot bath from which you can gaze down on the water. Swim in the pool, tan on its terrace, dine on fabulous Cornish food. Boat trips can be arranged.

Price	£90–£160. Half-board £85–£105 p.p.
Rooms	14: 10 doubles, 4 twins.
Meals	Lunch from £5.50. Dinner, 4 courses, from £34.
Closed	Rarely.
Directions	A390 west towards St Austell, then B3269 to Fowey. After 4 miles, left to Golant. Into village, along quay, hotel signed right, up very steep hill.

Mary Tozer
Golant, Fowey,
Cornwall PL23 1LL

Tel	01726 833426
Email	relax@cormoranthotel.co.uk
Web	www.cormoranthotel.co.uk

Marina Villa Hotel

The sun terrace at Marina Villa is Fowey's equivalent to the royal box at the Albert Hall: the best seat in town. You're bang on the estuary. Fishermen chug past, yachts head out to sea, gulls wheel and cry. Balconies tumble down the house (once the Bishop of Truro's summer residence), so splash out on a fancy room and spend a blissful afternoon in silent contemplation. As for the hotel, the feel is Mediterranean – small, intimate, seriously elegant – with golden interiors, teardrop chandeliers, and housekeeping armed with dusters. Bedrooms are terrific, some big, some small, some in the main house (seaside chic), others behind in Ashley House (uncluttered opulence); hope for a sea view. All are spotless and airy, you get rich fabrics, super art, swish bathrooms and a suite with a terrace by the sea. As for the food, drop down to a super-cool restaurant for some of Cornwall's best cooking. Nathan Outlaw left his Michelin star on the north coast, but his food remains ambrosial, perhaps squab pigeon with espresso and orange, venison with chocolate and thyme, rhubarb sponge with stem ginger ice cream.

Price	£134–£174. Balcony rooms £184–£248. Singles from £90.
Rooms	18: 11 doubles, 2 twins, 4 balcony rooms, 1 suite.
Meals	Lunch from £17. Dinner, à la carte, £38–£45.
Closed	Rarely.
Directions	Down hill into Fowey; right (before bottom of hill) into Esplanade; on left. Ask hotel about parking.

James Coggan
Esplanade, Fowey,
Cornwall PL23 1HY

Tel	01726 833315
Fax	01726 832779
Email	info@themarinahotel.co.uk
Web	www.themarinahotel.co.uk

The Old Quay House Hotel

The Old Quay House has everything going for it: an idyllic waterfront setting, an airy architect-designed interior, and a suite at the top of the house with huge views. Add to this owners passionate about good service and a loyal staff determined to deliver and you have a super little hotel. Stylish bedrooms spoil you all the way with goose down duvets, Egyptian cotton, Javanese cabinets and seriously indulging bathrooms (bathrobes, the odd claw-foot bath, maybe a separate shower). Eight have balconies with glittering estuary views and flood with light, those further back look over Fowey's rooftops. Stop for a drink in the bar, then settle down to delicious modern European dishes in the 'Q' restaurant, smartly decorated in neutral tones, or spill out onto the terrace overlooking the estuary; you can breakfast here in the sun and watch the ferry chug past. Fowey is enchanting, bustles with life and fills with sailors for the August regatta. Come for the best of old Cornwall — narrow cobbled streets, quaint harbour, long-lost ways. A great place to unwind. *Minimum stay two nights at weekends in high season.*

Price	£160-£220. Singles £130-£220. Suite £300.
Rooms	11: 5 doubles, 5 twins/doubles, 1 suite.
Meals	Lunch about £15. Dinner about £30.
Closed	Rarely.
Directions	Entering Fowey, follow one-way system past church. Hotel on right where road at narrowest point, next to Lloyds Bank. Nearest car park 800 yds.

	Jane & Roy Carson
	28 Fore Street, Fowey, Cornwall PL23 1AQ
Tel	01726 833302
Fax	01726 833668
Email	info@theoldquayhouse.com
Web	www.theoldquayhouse.com

Trevalsa Court Hotel

A big Edwardian country house with sprawling lawns that run down to high cliffs; steps lead down to a sandy beach or you can follow the coastal path to the lighthouse at Mevagissey, an old-fashioned fishing village with a working quay. Don't dally too long. This is the hotel the man who loves hotels bought, and he's made it the perfect seaside retreat: friendly, stylish, young at heart. Mullioned window seats come in cushioned purple, flowers float in a bowl on the wood-burner and polished American oak sparkles in the panelled dining room. Bauhaus clocks and lamps add style, black-and-white photos adorn the walls, a bowl of lemons sits on an oak chest. In fine weather, sip drinks on the stone terrace amid beds of colour or hide away with a good book in the summer house. Bedrooms are harmonious and varied, some big, others snug; all but two have sea views. Expect happy colours, crisp linen, Art Deco lamps, perhaps a sofa. Delicious food doesn't try to be too fancy (perfect pastry on a lemon tart), there's no rush in the morning and the Lost Gardens of Heligan and the Eden Project are close.

Price	£98–£150. Singles £65–£90. Suites £150–£200.
Rooms	11: 6 doubles, 2 twins, 1 single, 2 suites.
Meals	Dinner from £29.
Closed	December–January.
Directions	From St Austell, B3273, signed Mevagissey, for 5.5 miles past beach caravan park, then left at top of hill. Over mini-r'bout. Hotel on left, signed.

Klaus Wagner & Matthew Mainka
School Hill Road, Mevagissey,
Cornwall PL26 6TH

Tel	01726 842468
Fax	01726 844482
Email	stay@trevalsa-hotel.co.uk
Web	www.trevalsa-hotel.co.uk

Wisteria Lodge

Is it a small, elegant hotel or a posh B&B? The building is 70s modern in a small residential street – and inside, charming interior designer Sally has created a pampering space. Nothing is too much trouble: food can be cooked to order by the resident chef, beauty treatments and massages will be smoothly arranged, you can laze around the lush garden all day or leap in the hot tub. There are enough staff to pander to a small army; this would be great for a house party. Bedrooms (some with whirlpool baths) are neatly dressed in saffrons, mustards and reds, mattresses are huge and expensive, towels are madly fluffy and the Wisteria Room, which is the most private, has its own terrace. There's nothing quirky or unusual, just seamless service, delicious food at tables for two in the conservatory dining room and a comfortable sitting room to slump in. For the idle it is fine and dandy – but you could, possibly, rouse yourself to walk the mile to the Eden Project, or hop in the car for art at the Tate, theatre at the Minack, great surfing or a visit to Rick Stein's.

Price	£90–£160.
Rooms	5: 3 doubles, 2 twins/doubles.
Meals	Light suppers from £7.
Closed	Rarely.
Directions	A390 2 miles east of St Austell, turning to Tregrehan opp. St Austell Garden Centre. First turning on left marked Boscundle Close, just off on right hand side.

Sally Wilkins
Boscundle, Tregrehan, St Austell,
Cornwall PL25 3RJ

Tel	01726 810800
Email	info@wisterialodge.co.uk
Web	www.wisterialodgehotel.co.uk

The Lugger Hotel

A smugglers' inn dipping its toes in the cool waters of Portloe Cove, where pirate ships once sheltered after a good night's haul. These days three fishermen work from the village and you can watch from the restaurant as they carry their cargo straight to the kitchen — lobsters and crabs fresh from the sea offering scope for gluttony of the very best kind. The hotel is supremely cosy: low ceilings and a log fire in the snug sitting room, a couple of decked terraces for lunch in the sun, whitewashed walls, fabulous views and Wellington boots waiting at the back door. The hotel stands on the Cornish coastal path, so order a picnic and spend a day on the top of wild cliffs. Fine bedrooms and bathrooms may not be huge, but all swim in seaside elegance and have super-comfy beds, power showers that knock you flat, bath robes, fresh flowers and flat-screen TVs. Five have sea views, but from many you can hear the sea beating out its message: relax, unwind, let the world hurtle on without you for a while. Bliss. *Minimum stay two nights at weekends in high season.*

Price	£160–£270. Suites & cottage £220–£370. Half-board from £105 p.p.
Rooms	22: 12 doubles, 7 twins/doubles, 2 suites, 1 cottage.
Meals	Lunch, 3 courses, £19.50. Dinner, 3 courses, £37.50.
Closed	Never.
Directions	West from St Austell on A390, then B3287 to Tregony. Left onto A3078 for St Mawes. After 2 miles fork left for Portloe; left at T-junc. In village, by sea.

	Ben Young Portloe, Truro, Cornwall TR2 5RD
Tel	01872 501322
Fax	01872 501691
Email	office@luggerhotel.com
Web	www.luggerhotel.com

Driftwood Hotel

Cape Cod meets Cape Cornwall. This is a superb place, perfectly positioned, refreshingly understated. It's said the original owner of this 1930s beach villa wandered all over the Roseland Peninsula looking for the right spot and chose here. The views are out of this world: the sun rises over Nare Head, Portscatho village peeks from a small inlet, boats criss-cross the bay. Fiona and Paul are charming and make the place feel like home. The driftwood theme is everywhere, the colours are restful, the light pours in from every angle. There's a bar with comfy window seats and a lounge with handsome driftwood lamps, deep sofas, piles of books, a log fire. And the food is brilliant, often from the sea, masterminded by a chef who has cooked in top London places; the restaurant is an expanse of white and wooden floor. Mind your head as you go upstairs; bedrooms, including four new, have fabulous linen and sea views from most. Bathrooms are immaculate. Sit on the decked balcony for breakfast and drinks before dinner, or take a hamper to the private beach – you may see a hairy snail. *Minimum stay two nights at weekends.*

Price	£180–£220.
Rooms	15: 11 doubles, 3 twins, 1 cabin.
Meals	Dinner £39.
Closed	January.
Directions	From St Austell, A390 west. Left on B3287 for St Mawes; left at Tregony on A3078 for about 7 miles. Signed left down lane.

Paul & Fiona Robinson
Rosevine, Portscatho,
Cornwall TR2 5EW

Tel	01872 580644
Fax	01872 580801
Email	info@driftwoodhotel.co.uk
Web	www.driftwoodhotel.co.uk

Halzephron

An opera singer serving real ale in an ancient smuggler's inn: only in Cornwall. But Halzephron (cliffs of hell) is more than that; Harry, Angela's late husband, ran the inn for many years, a much-loved landlord, and a picture of him, pipe in hand, claims its rightful place on the mantelpiece. Come for low ceilings, stone walls, coal fires and polished brass. There are sea views from the roadside terrace, a lively courtyard for summer afternoons, and a small garden overlooking the fields. Lunch on hearty homemade food – perhaps seafood chowder, boeuf bourguignon or Armenian lamb – then walk it all off on cliff-top coastal paths; you can strike out for the Lizard and Church Cove, then catch the bus home. Bedrooms above the bar are country cosy, with antique dressers, quilted eiderdowns, bowls of fruit and restful florals. Both are at the back and come with long views across the fields. One has a bath, one has a shower, and there are books galore, Dickens to Alan Coren. Breakfast is cooked to order and comes with marmalade made by Angela and her niece.

Price	From £84. Singles £48.
Rooms	2 doubles.
Meals	Lunch & dinner: main courses £9–£17.50.
Closed	Christmas Day.
Directions	From Helston, A3083, signed The Lizard. Pass Culdrose air base, then right, signed Gunwalloe. 2 miles and inn on left after houses.

Angela Thomas
Gunwalloe, Helston,
Cornwall TR12 7QB

Tel	01326 240406
Fax	01326 241442
Email	halzephroninn@gunwalloe1.fsnet.co.uk
Web	www.halzephron-inn.co.uk

The Old Coastguard Hotel

The sea spumes over the rocks a hundred yards from your window. To the right is the shelter of the little harbour, where tiny fishing boats and pleasure craft jostle for a place under the kindly gaze of the village. On a calm day the palm trees in the garden and the limpid sea lend a Mediterranean mood; to the left is the distant St Michael's Mount, the Lizard occupying much of the horizon. Neither thoughts of the Spanish sacking the village in 1595, nor of tourists sacking it today, can detract from the beauty of it all. The hotel is easy-going and generous, the dining room airy, the meals among Cornwall's best. The produce is sourced locally, as is proper with Newlyn's fishing fleet round the corner: scallops, crab, monkfish, hake, chargrilled sirloin, honey-roast tomatoes, roasted garlic and potato purée. There is even Cornish wine. The bedrooms are simple, fresh and modern: no vast beds, no flounces, but great duvets and some of the best views in Britain. Staff are delightful, the bar is a mix of wood and steel, the village is two minutes by foot. *Minimum stay two nights at weekends in high season.*

Price	£90-£170. Single from £45. Half-board from £75 p.p.
Rooms	21: 20 doubles, 1 single.
Meals	Lunch, 2 courses, from £18. Table d'hôte dinner £28-£35.
Closed	Christmas Day.
Directions	Follow A30 to Penzance & signs to Mousehole. Hotel on left as you enter the village. Limited parking on first come first served basis or public car park next door, £2 on departure.

Bill Treloar
The Parade, Mousehole,
Cornwall TR19 6PR

Tel	01736 731222
Fax	01736 731720
Email	bookings@oldcoastguardhotel.co.uk
Web	www.oldcoastguardhotel.co.uk

The Summer House Restaurant with Rooms

A glittering find just off the harbour: stylish, imaginative, bustling, informal, and so, so colourful. In an elegant Georgian house, sunshiny yellows and strong Tuscan shades bring a dreamy sense of the Mediterranean to the bustling industry of Penzance. Linda and Ciro, English and Italian respectively, run the place with energy and warmth. And food is a celebration – dishes are fresh, simple and cooked with flair, "a gentle meander through Provence and Italy", with fish bought daily from nearby Newlyn market. Clusters of shells decorate tables in the restaurant, local artists' work hangs on the walls. Outside, a walled garden of stone pots and swishing palm trees is a magical setting for candlelit dinners; alfresco breakfasts when the sun shines are just as good. Unwind on squashy sofas in a high-ceilinged, wooden-floored drawing room with big mirrors and art to die for, and chat to other guests – most do. Bedrooms combine chunky wooden antiques and family pieces with resourceful dabs of peppermint or lemon stripe; bathrooms are beach-house style. A happy, atmospheric place.

Price	£95–£120. Singles from £90.
Rooms	5: 4 doubles, 1 twin/double.
Meals	Dinner £29.50.
	Not Monday-Wednesday.
Closed	November-February.
Directions	With sea on left, along harbourside, past open-air pool, then immediate right after Queens Hotel. House 30 yds up on left. Private carpark.

Linda & Ciro Zaino
Cornwall Terrace, Penzance,
Cornwall TR18 4HL

Tel	01736 363744
Fax	01736 360959
Email	reception@summerhouse-cornwall.com
Web	www.summerhouse-cornwall.com

The Abbey Hotel

The Abbey is a rare gem, a hotel that refuses to enter the modern world, choosing instead to linger in its serenely elegant past. The feel is of a smart country house, and the drawing room – roaring fire, huge gilt mirror, walls of books, rugs on stripped floors – is hard to beat. Drinks are brought to you, there's a bust of Lafayette, exquisite art and huge arched windows that rise to the ceiling and open onto the loveliest walled garden; step out in summer for afternoon tea or a breakfast to remember. The house dates to 1660 and has views to the front of Penzance harbour and St Michael's Mount. Country-house bedrooms are grandly quirky (in one you pull open a cupboard to find an en suite shower). Sink into big comfy beds wrapped up in crisp white linen and woollen blankets. There are chandeliers, quilted bedspreads, French armoires, plump-cushioned armchairs. You breakfast indulgently in a panelled dining room with a fire crackling and assorted busts and statues for company. Kind staff don't act the part, they simply go the extra mile. The Abbey restaurant next door has a Michelin star. Exceptional.

Price	£105–£180. Suite £150–£190. Singles from £70. Flat £105–£130.
Rooms	7 + 1: 4 doubles, 1 twin, 1 family, 1 suite. 1 self-catering flat (sleeps 4).
Meals	Restaurants nearby.
Closed	Rarely.
Directions	Follow signs to town centre. Up hill (Market Jew St). Left at top, then fork left & 3rd on the left.

Jean & Michael Cox
Abbey Street, Penzance,
Cornwall TR18 4AR

Tel	01736 366906
Fax	01736 351163
Email	hotel@theabbeyonline.co.uk
Web	www.theabbeyonline.co.uk

The Gurnard's Head

The coastline here is utterly magical and the walk up to St Ives is hard to beat. Secret beaches appear at low tide, cliffs tumble down to the water and wild flowers streak the land pink in summer. As for the hotel, you couldn't hope for a better base. It's earthy, warm, stylish and friendly, with airy interiors, colourwashed walls, stripped wooden floors and fires at both ends of the bar. Logs are piled up in an alcove, maps and art hang on the walls, books fill every shelf; if you pick one up and don't finish it, take it home and post it back. Rooms are warm and cosy, simple and spotless, with VI-sprung mattresses, crisp white linen, throws over armchairs, Roberts radios. Downstairs, super food, all homemade, can be eaten wherever you want: in the bar, in the restaurant or out in the garden in good weather. Snack on rustic delights — pork pies, crab claws, half a pint of Atlantic prawns — or tuck into more substantial treats, maybe fresh asparagus with a hollandaise sauce, fish stew with new potatoes, rhubarb crème brûlée. Picnics are easily arranged and there's bluegrass folk music in the bar most weeks.

Price	£72.50–£125. Singles from £50.
Rooms	7: 4 doubles, 3 twins/doubles.
Meals	Lunch from £4.50.
	Dinner, 3 courses, about £25.
Closed	New Year.
Directions	West from St Ives on B3306. On right at head of village.

Charles & Edmund Inkin
Treen, Zennor, St Ives,
Cornwall TR26 3DE

Tel	01736 796928
Email	enquiries@gurnardshead.co.uk
Web	www.gurnardshead.co.uk

Primrose Valley Hotel

No need to bang on about the wonderful beach or fabulous St Ives and its winding streets, the New Tate and the Barbara Hepworth Garden; you know you're in for a treat. The place is humming in summer, so this calm hotel is a godsend. A spade's throw from the beach, the crisp Edwardian townhouse with large windows has a cool, contemporary interior of gleaming wooden floors, modern prints and photographs, fresh flowers and uncluttered walls with bold bamboo wallpaper. Some of the bedrooms are not large but half have great sea views, and the suite – red leather armchair, slipper bath, deluge shower – is enormous. All rooms have hand-stitched mattresses, fluffy towels, sleek blond wood floors and an unstuffy feel. The owners are environmentally aware, particularly over marine conservation and sustainable tourism: the breakfast menu lists where all the food comes from, while Cornish platters of charcuterie, cheese and smoked salmon are on tap through the day. Grab a paper and relax at the bar with something lively from the wine list served in a Riedel glass for maximum oomph. *Minimum stay two nights at weekends.*

Primrose Valley is heavily involved in sustainable tourism and a raft of initiatives shows how small gestures can make a difference. Suppliers are asked to reduce packaging, 60% of all waste is recycled, eco wood floors come from Sweden and vegetable-based inks are used on recycled paper. Much Cornish food makes the table, with suppliers featured on the website; honey, soaps, jams and meat come from the county. Fish is sourced from sustainable stocks, £4,000 has been raised for the Marine Conservation Society. Jute beach bags are sold for £5, with £2.50 going to the Cornwall Wildlife Trust. Come by train – from London, Penzance, St Ives.

Price	£90-£225.
Rooms	10: 6 doubles, 2 twins, 1 suite, 1 family.
Meals	£7.50.
Closed	December & January.
Directions	From A3074 Trelyon Avenue; before hospital sign slow down, indicate right & turn down Primrose Valley; under bridge, left, then back under bridge; signs for hotel parking.

Andrew Biss
Porthminster Beach, St Ives,
Cornwall TR26 2ED

Tel	01736 794939
Fax	01736 794939
Email	info@primroseonline.co.uk
Web	www.primroseonline.co.uk

SPECIAL
GREEN ENTRY
see page 17

Blue Hayes

No expense has been spared in the restoration of this 1922 manse with glittering views of the sea. Having retired from a computer software career, Malcolm has thrown himself into masterminding a small private hotel. Lights come on as if by magic, sensing your presence as you saunter down your corridor, and high-tech showers blast from multiple angles in state-of-the-art bathrooms. Bedrooms have raw silk curtains, thick cotton sheets and (in four) views to the sea; the suite has the best outdoor space with a huge balcony that feels suspended above the sea. A harmonious sea-blue and oatmeal palette holds court – even the cocktails are colour coordinated: enjoy yours on the large terrace as the sunset inches round the bay. Dinners are good with fresh local fish and meat presented with mouthwatering sauces and the wine list is diverse. Friendly, attentive staff want you to enjoy yourself and are there for your every need; retire to the intimate lounge and meet the other guests over coffee and cognac. Truly cossetting.

Price	£140–£190. Singles £120–£145.
Rooms	6: 4 doubles, 1 four-poster, 1 triple.
Meals	Dinner £20–£25.
Closed	December & January.
Directions	From A30 past Hayle, A3074 to St Ives through Lelant and Carbis Bay. After mini-r'bout (Tesco on left) down hill. At bottom, right immed. after garage on right.

Malcolm Herring
Trelyon Avenue, St Ives,
Cornwall TR26 2AD

Tel	01736 797129
Fax	01736 799098
Email	bluehayes@btconnect.com
Web	www.bluehayes.co.uk

Boskerris Hotel

A quietly swanky hotel with glass everywhere framing huge views of ocean and headland. Step inside and drift into the sitting room, then float onto the decked terrace and gaze at Godrevy lighthouse twinkling to the right, St Ives slipping into the sea to the left and the wide sands of Cabris Bay, Lelant and Gwithian lying in between. Back inside you find creamy walls to soak up the light. There are bleached boards and smart sofas in the sitting room, fresh flowers and blond wood in the dining room. Airy bedrooms are uncluttered, with silky throws, padded headboards, crisp white linen, flat-screen TVs and DVD players. Eleven rooms have the view, all have fancy bathrooms, some have deep baths and deluge showers. You get White Company lotions, Designer Guild fabrics, and in one room you can soak in the bath whilst gazing out to sea. Take the coastal path to St Ives and follow the mazy streets to the Tate; spin back for delicious locally sourced food in the restaurant or stop at Porthminster Café for the fanciest nosh in town.

Price	£90-£200. Singles from £65.
Rooms	15: 12 doubles, 3 twins.
Meals	Dinner, 3 courses, about £25.
Closed	Christmas & New Year.
Directions	A30 past Hayle, then A3074 for St Ives. After 3 miles pass brown sign for Carbris Bay, then third left. Down hill, on left.

Jonathan & Marianne Bassett
Boskerris Road,
Carbis Bay, St Ives,
Cornwall TR26 2NQ
Tel   01736 795295
Email   reservations@boskerrishotel.co.uk
Web   www.boskerrishotel.co.uk

Hell Bay

Magical Bryher. In winter, giant rollers crash against high cliffs; in summer, sapphire waters sparkle in the sun. There are sandy beaches, passing sail boats, waders and wild swans, absolute peace. The hotel lazes on the west coast with sublime watery views – there's nothing between you and America – so grab a drink from the bar and wander onto the terrace to watch a vast sky blush at sunset. Inside, you get stripped floors, coastal colours, excellent art and airy interiors that look out to sea. Step outside and find a heated pool in the garden and a courtyard stocked with rosemary and lavender; castaways would refuse rescue. Bedrooms offer beach-house heaven, all with terraces or balconies, most with views of sand and sea. You get tongue and groove panelling, walls of windows, crisp fabrics, super bathrooms. In summer dig into crab and lobster straight from the ocean, fresh asparagus and succulent strawberries from neighbouring Tresco (don't miss its world-famous gardens). There's a sauna, a PlayStation for kids, golf for the hopeful. Low-season deals are exceptional.

Price	Half-board £130–£275 p.p.
Rooms	25 studios & suites.
Meals	Half-board only. Lunch £5–£15.
Closed	3 January–10 February.
Directions	Ship/helicopter from Penzance, or fly to St Mary's from Bristol, Southampton, Exeter, Newquay or Land's End; boat to Bryher. Hotel can arrange.

Philip Callan
Bryher, Isles of Scilly,
Cornwall TR23 0PR

Tel	01720 422947
Fax	01720 423004
Email	contactus@hellbay.co.uk
Web	www.hellbay.co.uk

Crosby Lodge

Restful, opulent, blissfully detached from the outside world, Crosby Lodge welcomes all. Come to elope (Gretna is close) or just to escape. Patricia is everywhere, always impeccably dressed, never seeming to stop, but never seeming to hurry, either. She used to be a banker – the considerate kind, what else! – and this original 'country-house hotel' remains a laid-back family affair. Michael and Patricia fell in love with the house long before it came on the market – 30-odd years ago now – and the chef has been here since the start; the dining is elaborate and classical. All is warm and cosy within: open fires, polished banisters, family portraits, a wonderful antique chaise-longue, a stunning bay window with shutters. Bedrooms are (mostly) big, bright and fun, with flowery fabrics lovingly chosen – even the shower curtains have two layers of ruffles. You get arches and alcoves, ornate lamps and candlesticks, a huge antique wardrobe or a lovely gnarled half-tester. Outside you might sip a pre-prandial glass in the walled garden, or chance upon an artist sketching a pastoral view.

Price	£130–£180. Singles £85–£95.
Rooms	11: 2 doubles, 5 twins/doubles, 1 single, 3 family.
Meals	Lunch from £5. Dinner, 4 courses, £38–£40.
Closed	Christmas–mid-January.
Directions	M6 junc. 44, A689 east for 3.5 miles, then right to Low Crosby. Through village. House on right.

Michael & Patricia Sedgwick
High Crosby, Carlisle,
Cumbria CA6 4QZ

Tel	01228 573618
Fax	01228 573428
Email	enquiries@crosbylodge.co.uk
Web	www.crosbylodge.co.uk

Swinside Lodge

A short stroll takes you to the edge of the Queen of the Lakes. Immediately behind, fells rise and spirits soar. Swinside – a small-scale model of English country-house elegance – sits at the foot of Cat Bells. Inside, all is in classic style: pretty sofas, oriental rugs, pictures, an open fire. In the dining room, deep reds are reflected in candlelight and glasses shine. Eric has exacting standards – join him on his 6am run! – and a repertoire of jokes; Irene fills the house with books and flowers. Every tiny detail has been well thought out, not least in the bedrooms where beds excel: linen is double-pressed by the laundry, country-style eiderdowns grace firm mattresses, pillows are soft. Expect Molton Brown toiletries for non-slip baths, pastel colours, fabric headboards, sash windows and uplifting views; watch the weather change. An award-winning young chef stars in the kitchen, the food is local, fresh, outstanding, and the evening is pure theatre. In the gardens are flowers for the butterflies and herbs for the chef. *Children over 12 welcome. Minimum stay two nights at weekends in high season.*

Price	Half-board £88–£120 p.p.
Rooms	7: 5 doubles, 2 twins.
Meals	Half-board only. Dinner for non-residents, £35.
Closed	Rarely.
Directions	M6 junc. 40. A66 west past Keswick, over r'bout, then 2nd left, for Portinscale & Grange. Follow signs to Grange for 2 miles. House signed on right.

Eric and Irene Fell
Grange Road, Newlands, Keswick, Cumbria CA12 5UE

Tel	01768 772948
Fax	01768 773312
Email	info@swinsidelodge-hotel.co.uk
Web	www.swinsidelodge-hotel.co.uk

The Pheasant

A 15th-century coaching inn with Sale Fell and Whythop Woods rising behind. A wonderfully English country-cottage garden (apple blossom, climbing roses, the trimmest lawn) looks the right way and is for guests only, so grab a deck chair on the lawn and settle in for an early evening drink. Interiors are no less spoiling; this is an extremely comfortable country-house inn, with open fires in elegant sitting rooms and a low beamed ceiling in the bright and breezy dining room. The snug bar, a treasured relic of times past, has a ceiling coloured by 300 years of tobacco smoke and polish, 40 malts, and a couple of Thompson sketches hanging on the wall (he exchanged them for drink). Cosseting bedrooms, warm in yellow, come with pretty pine beds, thick fabrics, Roberts radios, flat-screen TVs, and robes in spotless bathrooms. Most are in the main house, two are in a nearby garden lodge. Wander the corridors and meet Housekeeping armed with feather dusters. There's a kennel for visiting dogs, Skiddaw to be scaled, and Bassenthwaite — the only lake in the Lake District — is close. *Minimum stay two nights at weekends.*

Price	£150–£160. Singles from £85. Suites £176–£186. Half-board from £102 p.p. (min. 2 nights).
Rooms	15: 11 twins/doubles, 1 single, 3 suites.
Meals	Light lunch from £7. Dinner, à la carte, around £30.
Closed	Christmas Day.
Directions	From Keswick, A66 north-west for 7 miles. Hotel on left, signed.

Matthew Wylie
Bassenthwaite Lake, Cockermouth,
Cumbria CA13 9YE

Tel   01768 776234
Fax   01768 776002
Email   info@the-pheasant.co.uk
Web   www.the-pheasant.co.uk

New House Farm

A sublime position in the Vale of Lorton; Swinside rises on one side, Low Fell on the other, huge views shoot down the valley to Melbreak looming afar. Lie in a claw-foot bath and gaze on it all while planning your next ascent: you can from one room. This is a warm, chic, farmhouse B&B set in 17 lush acres. Horses graze in the fields, one the granddaughter of Nijinsky. There's a tearoom in summer for walkers, and grass paths in the garden lead up through an orchard to a small lake. Back at the house – 1650 at the front, 1820 at the back – are a stone-flagged entrance hall, a wood-burner in the dining room, warm reds and greens in snug sitting rooms. Bedrooms are fabulous – the feel of home, the style of a hotel – with bowls of fruit, smart red carpets, old beams, exposed stones. Both rooms in the converted stables have four-posters, all have exquisite bathrooms – claw-foots, an enormous shower, perhaps a bath for two. Hazel's delicious cooking – chicken liver pâté, roast Lakeland lamb, crème brûlée – is rounded off with a plate of local cheeses. Loweswater, Crummock Water and Buttermere are all close.

Price	£148. Singles £75–£105.
Rooms	5: 2 doubles, 1 twin/double. Stables: 2 four-posters.
Meals	Lunch from £6 (April–November). Dinner, 3 courses, £23.
Closed	Never.
Directions	A66 to Cockermouth, then B5289 for Buttermere. Signed left 2.5 miles south of Lorton.

Hazel Thompson
Lorton, Cockermouth,
Cumbria CA13 9UU

Tel	01900 85404
Fax	01900 85478
Email	hazel@newhouse-farm.co.uk
Web	www.newhouse-farm.co.uk

White Moss House

This is the epicentre of Wordsworth country: walk north a mile to his home at Dove Cottage or south to his house at Rydal Mount. The paths are old and you can follow his footsteps up fell and through wood. He knew White Moss; he bought it for his son and came here to escape. The Dixons have lived here for a quarter century and have kept the feel of a home: deep armchairs, heaps of books, flowers on sofas and in vases, a cosy woodburning stove. There's a small bar in an old linen cupboard, and after-dinner coffee in the sitting room brings out the house-party feel. Bedrooms range in size but not comfort and all have good views; those at the back, away from the main road, are the quietest. Expect pretty chintz, a sprinkling of books, Radox in bathrooms to soothe fell-worn feet. The cottage is in a quiet, beautiful spot further up the hill, with fine views across Rydal Water. Then there's the small matter of food, all cooked by Peter — five courses of famed indulgence await, and superb wines. *Free use of local leisure centre. Children over five welcome. Minumim stay two nights at weekends.*

Price	£79-£129.
Rooms	6: 2 doubles, 3 twins/doubles, 1 cottage for 2-4.
Meals	Lunch, 3 courses, £25. Dinner, 5 courses, £39.50. Both by arrangement.
Closed	December-mid-February.
Directions	From Ambleside, north on A591. House signed on right at far end of Rydal Water.

Susan & Peter Dixon
Rydal Water, Grasmere,
Cumbria LA22 9SE

Tel	015394 35295
Fax	015394 35516
Email	sue@whitemoss.com
Web	www.whitemoss.com

Old Dungeon Ghyll

One of England's most famous walking hotels; if you're looking for a night in frontier land, you'll find it here. It's an old favourite of hardy mountaineers – Tenzing and Hilary stayed before scaling Everest – and it stands at the foot of Raven Cragg, surrounded by spectacular peaks. The house was given over to the National Trust in 1928 and has been leased as a hotel/pub ever since. Hikers pour off the mountains, ruddy from the day's exertions, full of stories of courage in the face of adversity – mist, driving rain, mobile phone failure and the like. They head for the Walkers' Bar, with cattle-stall seating and a big fire, and feast on decent grub, mugs of tea, and God's own beer: Yates. In wild weather old stone walls keep the wind at bay; when it's fine there are tables outside with Tolkeinian views in every direction. Next door is the hotel, with a crackling fire in the residents' lounge and a dining room for great breakfasts. Bedrooms are simple, not all have their own bathrooms; if you don't mind that, you'll find thick bedspreads, brass beds, good mattresses and fat pillows. *Minimum stay two nights at weekends.*

Price	£99–£104. Singles £49.50.
Rooms	13: 6 twins/doubles all ensuite; 5 singles sharing 1 bath & 1 shower; 2 family rooms each with separate bath.
Meals	Bar meals from £7.75.
Closed	Christmas.
Directions	From Ambleside, A593 for Coniston, right on B5343. Hotel on right after 5 miles, signed, past Great Langdale campsite.

Neil Walmsley
Great Langdale, Ambleside,
Cumbria LA22 9JY

Tel	015394 37272
Fax	015394 37272
Email	neil.odg@lineone.net
Web	www.odg.co.uk

Drunken Duck Inn

Afternoon tea can be taken in the garden, where lawns run down to Black Tarn and Greek gods gaze upon jumping fish. You're up on the hill, away from the crowds, cradled by woods and highland fell. Huge views from the terrace shoot off for miles to towering Lakeland peaks. Roses ramble on the veranda, stone walls double as flower beds and burst with colour. As for the Duck, she may be old, but she sure is pretty, so step into a world of airy interiors — stripped floors in a beamed bar, timber-framed walls in the inspired restaurant. Wander at will and find open fires, grandfather clocks, rugs on the floor, exquisite art. They brew their own beer and have nine bitters on tap. Bedrooms are dreamy, smartly dressed in crisp white linen, with colours courtesy of Farrow & Ball and peaty water straight off the fell. Rooms in the main house are snug in the eaves; those across the courtyard are crisply uncluttered and indulgent. Some have private terraces, one comes with a balcony, several have walls of glass to frame the mighty mountains. Don't miss Duck Tarn for blue heron and brown trout.

Price	£120–£250. Singles from £90.
Rooms	16: 14 doubles, 2 twins.
Meals	Lunch from £5. A la carte dinner about £40.
Closed	Never.
Directions	West from Ambleside on A593, then left for Hawkshead on B5285. After 1 mile, left, signed. Up hill to inn.

Stephanie Barton
Barngates, Ambleside,
Cumbria LA22 0NG
Tel   015394 36347
Fax   015394 36781
Email info@drunkenduckinn.co.uk
Web   www.drunkenduckinn.co.uk

Holbeck Ghyll

A turretted, mullioned hunting lodge set in eight acres of sublime hillside gardens with Lake Windermere shimmering majestically below. Holbeck may have one of the 15 "top views in the world" but step inside and find luxury to match it. Curved window seats overlook the lush sloping lawns, smart armchairs laze in front of luxuriant fires, an Arts & Crafts style glows courtesy of golden oak panelling and stout polished floors. Sitting rooms are grandly furnished in country-house style, there's an elevated sun terrace overlooking the lake and a Michelin star in the west-facing dining room; sunsets are unbeatable, as is the food. Bedrooms have an overdose of elegance and style, delicious bathrooms come with thick robes and towels. All but a couple of rooms in the main house have fine lake views, while the Potter suite has a hot tub on its terrace, and Madison House and the Shieling are perfect for families. Any excesses in the dining room can be assuaged by the spa, staff know every guest by name, the warmth and care is deeply personal. Luxurious, intimate, delightful. *Minumum stay two nights at weekends.*

Price	Half-board from £140 p.p.
Rooms	23: 4 doubles, 12 twins/doubles, 6 suites, 1 cottage.
Meals	Lunch from £22.50. Dinner £49.50.
Closed	First two weeks in January.
Directions	M6 junc. 36, A591 to Windermere. Continue towards Ambleside, pass Brockhole Visitor Centre, then right towards Troutbeck (Holbeck Lane). Half a mile on left.

David & Patricia Nicholson
Holbeck Lane, Windermere,
Cumbria LA23 1LU

Tel	015394 32375
Fax	015394 34743
Email	stay@holbeckghyll.com
Web	www.holbeckghyll.com

Linthwaite House Hotel & Restaurant

The view here is simply magnificent with Windermere sparkling half a mile below and a chain of peaks rising beyond; no great surprise to discover the terrace acts as a *de facto* sitting room in summer. Linthwaite is a grand Lakeland country house run in informal style. Everything is a treat: wonderful bedrooms, gorgeous interiors, glorious food and attentive staff. The house dates from 1900 and is sound-proofed by 15 acres of trim lawns, formal gardens and wild rhododendrons. Totter up through a bluebell wood to find a small lake surrounded by fields where you can fish, swim or retreat to the summer house and fall asleep in the sun. The house is no less alluring with logs piled high by the front door, fires smouldering, sofas everywhere and a clipped colonial elegance in the conservatory sitting room. Sublime food is served in elegant dining rooms (one is decorated with nothing but mirrors) and Keith Floyd occasionally comes to perform an act or two of culinary theatre. Gorgeous bedrooms are uncluttered and airy; those at the front have lake views. *Minimum stay two nights at weekends.*

Price	Half-board £95–£185 p.p. Singles from £128.
Rooms	27: 21 doubles, 4 twins/doubles, 1 single, 1 suite.
Meals	Half-board only. Lunch from £5.50. Dinner for non-residents, £45.
Closed	Rarely.
Directions	M6 junc. 36. Take A590 north, then A591 for Windermere. At roundabout, left onto B5284. Past golf course; hotel signed left after 1 mile.

Mike Bevans
Crook Road, Windermere,
Cumbria LA23 3JA

Tel	015394 88600
Fax	015394 88601
Email	stay@linthwaite.com
Web	www.linthwaite.com

Gilpin Lodge

One of the loveliest places to stay in the country. Staff are delightful, the house is a treasure trove, and the food, Michelin-starred, is heavenly. Run by two generations of the same family, Gilpin delivers at every turn. Clipped country-house elegance flows throughout: smouldering coals, Zoffany wallpaper, gilded mirrors, flowers everywhere. Afternoon tea, served wherever you want it, comes on silver trays. You're in 20 acres of silence, so throw open doors and sit on the terrace surrounded by pots of colour or stroll through the garden for magnolias, rhododendrons, cherry blossom or climbing roses and a fine copper beech. Bedrooms are predictably divine with crisp white linen, exquisite fabrics, delicious art; nothing is left to chance. Some have French windows that open onto the garden, others have private terraces complete with hot tub, all have sofas or armchairs. As for Chris Meredith's food — the foie gras with a Sauternes jelly was faultless, while a three-page breakfast menu includes nine different teas and strawberry sorbet served with pink champagne. *Minimum stay two nights at weekends.*

Price	Half-board £125–£180 p.p. Singles from £175.
Rooms	20: 4 doubles, 4 twins/doubles, 12 suites.
Meals	Half-board only. Lunch £10–£27. Dinner for non-residents, £47.
Closed	Never.
Directions	M6 junc 36, A591 north, then B5284 west for Bowness. On right after 4 miles.

John, Christine, Barnaby & Zoe Cunliffe
Crook Road, Windermere,
Cumbria LA23 3NE

Tel	015394 88818
Fax	015394 88058
Email	hotel@gilpinlodge.co.uk
Web	www.gilpinlodge.co.uk

The Punch Bowl Inn

You're away from Lake Windermere in a small village encircled by a tangle of lanes that defeat most tourists. A church stands next door; the odd bride ambles out in summer, bell ringers practise on Friday mornings. But while the Punch Bowl sits in a sleepy village lost to the world and doubles up as the local post office, it is actually a seriously fancy inn. It was rescued from neglect by Paul and Steph, who own the impeccable Drunken Duck, and after a top-to-toe renovation it now sparkles. Outside, honeysuckle climbs on old stone walls, inside four fires keep you warm in winter. A clipped elegance runs throughout: leather sofas in a beamed sitting room, Farrow & Ball colours on the walls, candles in vases on dining room tables, an old farmhouse table in the restaurant crammed with brandies and malts. Bedrooms are delightful. Expect crisp white linen, super bathrooms, Roberts radios, flat-screen TVs. All are dressed in lovely fabrics, four have huge views down the Lyth valley and the fabulous suite, with double baths, is enormous. Don't miss the lakes and the hills. Wonderful.

Price	£110–£195. Suite £225–£280. Singles from £82.50.
Rooms	9: 1 twin/double, 5 doubles, 2 four-posters, 1 suite.
Meals	Lunch from £5. Dinner, 3 courses, about £30.
Closed	Never.
Directions	M6 junc. 36, then A590 for Newby Bridge. Right onto A5074, then right for Crosthwaite after 3 miles. Pub on southern flank of village.

Jenny Sisson
Crosthwaite, Kendal,
Cumbria LA8 8HR

Tel	015395 68237
Fax	015395 68875
Email	info@the-punchbowl.co.uk
Web	www.the-punchbowl.co.uk

The Mason's Arms

A perfect Lakeland inn tucked away two miles inland from Lake Windermere. You're on the side of a hill with huge views across lush fields to Scout Scar in the distance. In summer, all pub life decants onto a spectacular terrace – a sitting room in the sun – where window boxes and flowerbeds tumble with colour. The inn dates from the 16th century and is impossibly pretty. The bar is properly traditional with roaring fires, flagged floors, wavy beams, a cosy snug… and a menu of 70 bottled beers to quench your thirst. Rustic elegance upstairs comes courtesy of stripped floors, country rugs and red walls in the first-floor dining room – so grab a window seat for fabulous views and order delicious food, anything from a sandwich to Cumbrian duck. Self-catering cottages and apartments are a steal and come with fancy kitchens (breakfast hampers can be arranged). You get cool colours, fabulous beds, gleaming bathrooms and Bang & Olufsen TVs. Best of all, you have your own private terrace; order a meal in the restaurant and they'll bring it to you here. Brilliant. *Minimum stay two nights at weekends.*

Price	£55–£125. Cottages £115–£175.
Rooms	5: 3 suites. 2 cottages (1 for 4, 1 for 6).
Meals	Self-catering. Breakfast hampers £15–£25. Lunch & dinner £5–£30.
Closed	Never.
Directions	M6 junc. 36; A590 west, then A592 north. 1st right after Fell Foot Park. Straight ahead for 2.5 miles. On left after sharp right-hand turn.

John & Diane Taylor
Strawberry Bank, Cartmel Fell,
Cumbria LA11 6NW

Tel	015395 68486
Fax	015395 68780
Email	info@masonsarmsstrawberrybank.co.uk
Web	www.strawberrybank.com

L'Enclume

Cartmel is idyllic, a tiny village that stands in the shadow of its magnificent 800-year-old priory. It is one of those spots that lifts the soul, nowhere more so than the garden at L'Enclume – paradise by the river with the priory's tower rising beyond. Not that you'll linger. This is one of Europe's most lauded restaurants, and a stream of pilgrims arrive each day for Simon's tantalizing Michelin-starred cooking. You eat amid a gleaming world of whitewashed walls, sandstone floors, beamed ceilings and contemporary art. Tasting menus bring course after course, each one listed by flavour and texture: fois gras served with fois gras ice cream, local venison with barley and banana, beef rib accompanied by watermelon and liquorice. Puddings are equally intriguing and exciting, perhaps coffee praline with green tea and apple, or parmesan cake with white chocolate and cardamom. Retire to the silence of princely rooms. One has bedside lights on plinths, another opens onto the garden; you get designer wallpapers, silky throws and robes in super bathrooms.

Price	£98–£158.
Rooms	10 doubles.
Meals	7-course tasting menu £50; 11-course tasting menu £70. (No lunch Monday-Wednesday; no dinner Monday.)
Closed	Occasionally.
Directions	M6 junc. 36, then A590 west. Pass turn-off for Grange-Over-Sands, then left for Cartmel. In village.

Simon Rogan & Penny Tapsell
Cavendish Street, Cartmel,
Cumbria LA11 6PZ

Tel	015395 36362
Email	info@lenclume.co.uk
Web	www.lenclume.co.uk

Entry 53 Map 5

Aynsome Manor Hotel

A small country house with a big heart. It may not be the grandest place in the book but the welcome is genuine, the peace is intoxicating and the value is unmistakable. Stand at the front and a long sweep across open meadows leads south to Cartmel and its priory, a view that has changed little in 800 years. The house, a mere pup by comparison, dates to 1512. Step in to find red armchairs, a grandfather clock and a coal fire in the hall. There's a small bar at the front and a cantilever staircase with cupola dome that sweeps you up to a first-floor drawing room and panelled windows framing the view. Downstairs you eat under an ornate tongue-and-ball ceiling with Georgian colours and old portraits on the walls, so come for delicious cooking, perhaps cream of tomato and red pepper soup, roast leg of Cumbrian lamb, then rich chocolate mousse served with white chocolate sauce. Bedrooms are warm, cosy, simple, spotless, colourful. Some have views over the fields, one may be haunted, another has an avocado bathroom suite. Windermere and Coniston are both close. *Minimum stay two nights at weekends.*

Price	£70–£115. Singles from £60. Half-board £65–£86 p.p.
Rooms	12: 5 doubles, 4 twins, 1 four-poster, 2 family.
Meals	Dinner, 4 courses, £27.
Closed	25 & 26 December; January.
Directions	From M6 junc. 36 take A590 for Barrow. At top of Lindale Hill, follow signs left to Cartmel. Hotel on right 3 miles from A590.

Christopher & Andrea Varley
Cartmel, Grange-over-Sands,
Cumbria LA11 6HH

Tel	015395 36653
Fax	015395 36016
Email	aynsomemanor@btconnect.com
Web	www.aynsomemanorhotel.co.uk

Augill Castle

No uniforms, no rules, just Wendy, Simon and their staff to ply you with delicious food, scented hot water bottles, big pillows and massive tubs. Augill Castle is an early Victorian folly in Cumbria's beautiful Eden Valley, and was completed in 1841 for John Bagot Pearson, the eldest of two brothers, determined to build a bigger and better house overlooking the family pile at Park House after a sibling row. The result is wonderfully over the top, with turrets, arched fairytale windows, a castellated tower and monstrously large rooms. It's grand but intimate too and guests feel quite at home in the music room with tumbling curtains, well-loved antiques, old rugs on polished floors and significant African touches (Wendy once lived there). Bedrooms, too, are historic but homely: four-posters, roll top baths, swagged curtains, maybe a turret wardrobe or a piano. Relax in the elegant drawing room with honesty bar; banquet around a huge table in the dining room beneath a panelled ceiling of stunning blues. Perfect for big house parties and weddings, with seating for up to 40 or roaming feasts for 60.

Price	£140. Singles £100.
Rooms	10: 4 doubles, 4 twins/doubles, 2 four-posters.
Meals	Dinner, 4 courses, £40 (Fridays & Saturdays). Supper, 2 courses, £20 (Monday, Tuesday, Thursday).
Closed	Never.
Directions	M6 junc. 38; A685 through Kirkby Stephen. Just before Brough, right for South Stainmore; signed on left after 1 mile.

Simon & Wendy Bennett
Brough, Kirkby Stephen,
Cumbria CA17 4DE

Tel	01768 341937
Fax	01768 342287
Email	enquiries@stayinacastle.com
Web	www.stayinacastle.com

Entry 55 Map 6

Lovelady Shield

Remote, unspoilt, beguiling – if you want to leave the world behind, the High Pennines is a fine spot to do it. At Lovelady, the River Nent runs through the garden; you can follow it up to Alston, then come home over the fell. The house, hidden down a long and suitably bumpy drive, was rebuilt in 1832, but the cellars date from 1690 and the foundations stretch back to the 14th century when a religious order stood here. No noise, save for sheep in the fields, birds in the trees and the burbling river that you can hear if you sleep with your window open. Peter and Marie run the place with a hint of eccentricity and a relaxed country-house feel: log fires in the sitting room, a well-stocked library in the hall and a snug rag-rolled bar. Long windows bring in the views, but doors fly open in summer for Pimms on the veranda or croquet on the lawn. Dine on super food amid gilt mirrors, sash windows and fresh flowers, then retire to bright, uncluttered bedrooms that come in stylish yellows and whites. You'll find TVs and Scrabble, a sofa if there's room, and most have gorgeous views. Hadrian's Wall is close.

Price	Half-board £110–£145 p.p.
Rooms	12: 9 doubles, 2 twins, 1 four-poster.
Meals	Half-board only. Lunch by arrangement. Dinner for non-residents, £37.50.
Closed	Rarely.
Directions	From Alston, A689 east for 2 miles. House on left at junction of B6294, signed.

Peter & Marie Haynes
Nenthead Road, Alston,
Cumbria CA9 3LF

Tel	01434 381203
Fax	01434 381515
Email	enquiries@lovelady.co.uk
Web	www.lovelady.co.uk

Fischer's at Baslow Hall

Ambrosial food and country-house elegance combine in spades to make Fischer's a must for those in search of a welcoming bolthole in the Derbyshire Dales. The house was built in 1913, but you'll think it belongs to the 17th century. It stands at the top of its own hill in lightly wooded grounds on the northern flank of town, with Baslow Edge running above – walk up for magnificent views. Inside you find grandeur on a small scale: plaster-moulder ceilings, old oak doors, mullioned windows through which the sun pours, a fire roaring in the half-panelled sitting room. Bedrooms in the main house come in country-house style (warm florals, smart fabrics, crisp white linen), while large garden rooms are more contemporary and have Italian marble bathrooms. Best of all is the Michelin-starred food. Max has been cooking all his life and coaxes incredible flavours from his ingredients, some of which he grows in the garden. Try pan-fried scallops with ginger milk, Gressingham duck with a sauternes sauce, blood orange soufflé with a sorbet to match. Chatsworth is close. Fabulous.

Price	£140–£180. Singles £100–£130.
Rooms	11: 5 doubles, 5 garden rooms, 1 suite.
Meals	Continental breakfast included; cooked extras £3–£9.50. Lunch, 2 courses, £20–£24. Dinner, à la carte, around £65. Menu de Jour (not Sat) £30–£35. Tasting menu £60.
Closed	25 & 26 December.
Directions	Leave Baslow to the north on A623. Signed on right on edge of town.

Max & Susan Fischer
Calver Road, Baslow,
Derbyshire DE45 1RR
Tel   01246 583259
Fax   01246 583818
Email reservations@fischers-baslowhall.co.uk
Web   www.fischers-baslowhall.co.uk

The Peacock at Rowsley

The Peacock began in 1652. It was once the dower house to Haddon Hall and stands by the bridge in the middle of the village. It opened as a coaching inn 200 years ago and its lawns sweep down to the river Derwent. Fishermen come to try their hand, but those who want to walk can follow the river up to Chatsworth, then sweep back over gentle hills and return for a night at this warmly contemporary hotel. Inside, the old and the new mix harmoniously. Expect mullioned windows, hessian rugs, open fires, fresh flowers everywhere and good art on the walls. The feel is light and airy. French windows in the restaurant open in summer onto a pot-festooned terrace; the fire in the bar smoulders all year. Rooms come in different shapes and sizes, all with a surfeit of style: crisp linen, good beds, Farrow & Ball paints, the odd fine antique. Drop down for dinner and nip into the restaurant for imaginative seasonal dishes, perhaps Dorset crab, breast of duck, green apple brûlée. Six circular walks start from the front door, so you can walk off any excess in the hills that surround you. *Minumum stay two nights at weekends.*

Price	£165–£210. Singles £85–£105. Half-board from £118 p.p.
Rooms	16: 6 doubles, 7 twins, 1 four-poster, 2 singles.
Meals	Breakfast buffet included; cooked dishes £3.50–£6.25. Lunch £21.50. Dinner, à la carte, about £45. Sunday lunch £18.50–£23.
Closed	Rarely.
Directions	A6 north through Matlock, then to Rowsley. On right in village.

Jenni MacKenzie
Bakewell Road, Rowsley, Matlock,
Derbyshire DE4 2EB

Tel	01629 733518
Fax	01629 732671
Email	reception@thepeacockatrowsley.com
Web	www.thepeacockatrowsley.com

St Vincent House & Restaurant

A hidden gem on the north Devon coast. Everything here is wonderful: owners, décor, food and price. Jean-Paul and Lin do their own thing brilliantly; boundless kindness and fabulous food are the hallmarks. Daisies grow on the lawn, a 100-year-old wisteria spreads its wings at the front, Jean-Paul's herbs lie hidden in pots and beds. Inside this charming house, built by Captain Green with monies from the battle of Cape St Vincent, you find stripped floors, warm rugs, gilt mirrors and polished brass in front of an open fire. Turn left for the sitting room, right for the restaurant. Spotless bedrooms upstairs are a delight. Expect good beds, warm colours and super little bathrooms. Aperitifs are served in the front garden in summer; you're in the middle of town, but lush plants screen you from it. Hop back into the restaurant for fabulous food: scallops cooked in butter and lemon; filet mignon with roasted garlic; lavender and vodka ice cream. John-Paul is Belgian, so are his beers, chocolate and waffles; the latter are served at breakfast with free-range eggs and local sausages. Moor and coast wait for walkers.

Price	£70-£75.
Rooms	5 twins/doubles.
Meals	Dinner £24-£27.
Closed	November to Easter.
Directions	In Lynton, ignore 1st sign to left; follow signs for carparks. Up hill, see car park on left, thatched house on right; on left after car park, next to Exmoor Museum.

Jean-Paul Salpetier & Lin Cameron
Market Street, Castle Hill, Lynton,
Devon EX35 6JA

Tel	01598 752244
Fax	01598 752244
Email	welcome@st-vincent-hotel.co.uk
Web	www.st-vincent-hotel.co.uk

Entry 59 Map 2

The Old Rectory

As you quietly succumb to the spiritual calm, it's hard to conceive that one field away the land skids to a halt and spectacular cliffs drop 800 feet. The Exmoor plateau meets the sea abruptly at the village of Martinhoe – 'hoe' being Saxon for high ground – creating a breathtaking view as you approach. This lovely understated hotel stands next to an 11th-century church in three acres of mature garden. Nurtured by clergy past, the garden now occupies the affection of Chris and Stewart; birdsong, waterfalls, scented azaleas and wild gunnera make it a wonderful spot for afternoon tea. Inside, warm interiors are restful and stylish: an open fire in the snug sitting room, a 200-year-old vine shading the conservatory and a big airy dining room for Stewart's delicious cooking. Homemade bread, Exmoor lamb and West country cheeses fill the table, and the water, filtered and purified, is from a local spring. Airy bedrooms come in fresh colours with trim carpets, pressed white linen, fresh garden flowers and bowls of fruit that include grapes from the vine in season. *Minimum stay two nights at weekends.*

Price	Half-board (breakfast, dinner, afternoon tea) £97.50-£127.50 p.p.
Rooms	8: 2 doubles, 6 twins/doubles.
Meals	Half-board only. Dinner for non-residents, £35.
Closed	November-February.
Directions	M5 junc. 27, A361 to South Molton, then A399 north. Right at Blackmore Gate onto A39 for Lynton. Left after 3 miles, signed Matinhoe, just past Woody Bay Station. In village, next to church.

Stewart Willis & Chris Legg
Martinhoe, Exmoor National Park,
Devon EX31 4QT

Tel	01598 763368
Fax	01598 763567
Email	info@oldrectoryhotel.co.uk
Web	www.oldrectoryhotel.co.uk

Broomhill Art Hotel & Sculpture Gardens

Broomhill is a one off and anyone with the slightest interest in art will love it here. Owner-run and owner-loved, Rinus and Aniet, both wonderfully easy-going, came to fulfil a generous dream: to make art more accessible in the country. Ten years on and you find original pieces on every wall, and a dazzling sculpture garden that's floodlit at night and which defies overstatment; huge bronzes lurk behind trees, paths cut through ten acres of glorious woodland. Back at the hotel, a ten-foot-high red stiletto on the front lawn gives some idea of what to expect, but step inside and find galleries all around (no guest sitting room, just sofas in the galleries). The whole place elates, so even if you don't come to stay, pop in and take a look. Simple bedrooms, now refurbished, are good value for money. One has a sleigh bed, some overlook the garden, all have pretty linen and original art. Slow food in the Broomhill kitchen has a Mediterranean touch and mixes organic produce, local seafood, fair trade goods and fresh vegetables from neighbouring farms. *Minimum stay two nights half-board at weekends.*

Price	£70. Singles from £45. Weekends (Fri & Sat) half-board only, £205 per room.
Rooms	6: 4 doubles, 2 twins.
Meals	Lunch from £5 (Wed-Sun). Dinner Fri & Sat only.
Closed	20 December-mid-January.
Directions	From Barnstable, A39 north towards Lynton, then left onto B3230 for Ilfracombe. On left 2 miles after NDD Hospital.

Rinus & Aniet Van de Sande
Muddiford, Barnstable,
Devon EX31 4EX

Tel	01271 850262
Fax	01271 850575
Email	info@broomhillart.co.uk
Web	www.broomhillart.co.uk

Heasley House

A Georgian dower house in a sleepy hamlet on the southern fringes of Exmoor. Paul and Jan escaped London armed with paint brushes, dispatching the chintz in favour of an airy elegance, and you now get stripped floors, open fires, Farrow & Ball paints and an eclectic collection of art. Best of all is Paul's food – Heasley is pretty much a restaurant with rooms – so come for fresh Devon asparagus, marinated leg of local lamb, then roasted pears with marsala and crème fraîche. Whatever can be is locally sourced, with beef from Exmoor and game from nearby estates, while herbs come from a kitchen garden that will soon supply vegetables and soft fruits. Breakfast is a long lazy affair with freshly squeezed juice, fresh kippers and no time limits, so dig into bacon and eggs, then set off for the beach at Croyde, imperious walks on Exmoor or a canter across the gallops. Super-comfy rooms have big beds dressed in Egyptian cotton, extra-wide baths or power showers. There are gardens back and front, the sound of running water, and Paul's collection of brandy or armagnac is not to be missed.

Price	From £98. Suite £120. Singles from £75.
Rooms	8: 7 twins/doubles, 1 suite.
Meals	Dinner, 3 courses, £21.50.
Closed	Christmas Day, Boxing Day & February.
Directions	From junc. 27 of M5, A361 to Barnstaple. Turn right at sign for North Molton, then left for Heasley Mill.

Paul & Jan Gambrill
Heasley Mill, North Molton,
Devon EX36 3LE

Tel	01598 740213
Fax	01598 740677
Email	enquiries@heasley-house.co.uk
Web	www.heasley-house.co.uk

Northcote Manor

If you're in need of sanctuary then follow the footsteps of those wise 15th-century monks who chose to come to Northcote. The long drive climbs lazily through thick woodland with emerald green valleys and stunning views; the elegant wisteria-clad house with tall chimneys has been lounging here for hundreds of years. The gardens are gorgeous and beautifully kept: good specimen trees, gravel paths, a glassy pond and a newly restored water garden are a must for a gentle stroll. The soundtrack is pure L P Hartley; loud bird song punctuated by the thwack of a tennis ball or crack of a croquet mallet. Cheryl will quietly and professionally show you through the studded oak doors to large, light, comfortable rooms with big windows, cosy chairs, fires in winter. The colours are creams, yellows and blues; some chintzes mixed with stripes and tapestries on deep window seats. Old-fashioned bedrooms with dark antique furniture are a good size, all have lovely views, fresh flowers in tall vases and warm, spotless bathrooms. Eat well in the formal dining room with its hand-painted wall murals.

Price	£155–£250. Singles from £90. Half-board (min. 2 nights) from £100 p.p.
Rooms	11: 4 doubles, 2 twins/doubles, 1 four-poster, 4 suites.
Meals	Dinner £38.
Closed	Rarely.
Directions	M5 junc. 27, A361 to S. Molton. Fork left onto B3227; left on A377 for Exeter. Entrance 4.1 miles on right, signed.

Cheryl King
Burrington, Umberleigh,
Devon EX37 9LZ

Tel	01769 560501
Fax	01769 560770
Email	rest@northcotemanor.co.uk
Web	www.northcotemanor.co.uk

Bark House Hotel

The comfort of a country hotel – a cosy lounge with books and magazines, a candlelit dining room serving fabulous food – yet here you have the personal touch. The service is superb for a place this size: Alastair takes your luggage and ushers you in, Justine offers irresistible homemade cake and tea. These are people who love what they do and their old-fashioned courtesy is reassuring and hugely appreciated. Behind the wisteria-strewn façade all is pristine: pale velvety sofas, candles and fresh flowers, crisp flowered chintz. Proper-sized bedrooms have floral covers on firm beds, a touch of noise from the road, but nothing to worry about, vases of garden flowers and sweet meadow views, and exquisite new showers in most rooms. As for the food, you'll be bowled over by it. Alastair orchestrates it all, from the canapés to the truffles. There are 50 bins from the old and new worlds, while breakfast here is as good as it gets, one of the best in Britain. A garden to relax in, seats for afternoon tea, and bird tables to coax the locals out of the woods for a bite of lunch. Wonderful.

Price	£95–£119. Singles £50–£57.50. Half-board from £76 p.p.
Rooms	5: 3 doubles, 2 twins/doubles.
Meals	Dinner £29.50.
Closed	Occasionally.
Directions	From Tiverton, A396 north towards Minehead. Hotel on right, 1 mile north of junction with B3227.

Alastair Kameen & Justine Hill
Oakfordbridge, Bampton,
Devon EX16 9HZ

Tel	01398 351236
Email	bark.house.hotel@btinternet.com
Web	www.barkhouse.co.uk

Combe House Hotel & Restaurant

A sensational setting: 3,500 acres with a 'lost' arboretum and a long, meandering approach; darting pheasants and galloping Arabian horses add to the romance. Globe-trotting hoteliers Ruth and Ken Hunt have made this mullion-windowed Grade I manor into a very special place without giving it a hotel look or atmosphere and the staff are delightful. The Georgian Kitchen where private parties dine by the glow of the Tilley lamps and candles is celebrated in a Richard Adams picture called 'Making Jam'. Here, and in the charmingly frescoed, award-winning dining room, you will be treated to fabulous food with the emphasis on the best Devon produce. Bedrooms are a good size, the master suites sport silk-hung wallpapers, antiques and large beds, and the Linen suite in the restored laundry has a huge round copper bath. Most atmospheric of all is the entrance hall with its carved fireplace, oak panelling, worn slate flagstones and ancestral portraits – grab a book and settle here on one of the many comfy sofas. Or head for the coast; it's nearer than you might think. *Minimum stay two nights at weekends.*

Price	£164–£254. Singles from £134. Suites £308. Half-board from £115 p.p.
Rooms	15: 10 twins/doubles, 1 four-poster, 4 suites.
Meals	Lunch £20–£26. Dinner £39.50. Private parties in Georgian kitchen from £39.50 p.p. plus room hire.
Closed	Rarely.
Directions	M5 junc. 28 or 29 to Honiton, then Sidmouth. A375 south for a mile. House signed right through woods.

Ruth & Ken Hunt
Gittisham, Honiton, Exeter,
Devon EX14 3AD

Tel	01404 540400
Fax	01404 46004
Email	stay@thishotel.com
Web	www.thishotel.com

Blagdon Manor

You'll have the warmest of welcomes from Steve and Liz in their supremely comfortable country house in the middle of nowhere – actually, in 20 acres of woodland and moor – with huge views stretching to Yes Tor. There are doors that open onto the garden in the stone-flagged library, an open fire in the sitting room, a panelled bar in what was the 16th-century kitchen, and a conservatory for breakfast where you can watch the birds flit by. Bedrooms are equipped to spoil. Come for decanters of sherry and fresh flowers, warm country florals and bathrobes. Colours are bold: blues, yellows, lilacs and greens; one room has a fine purple carpet. You get small sofas if there's room, the odd beam, a bit of chintz and comfortably snug bathrooms. All rooms are the same price; the first to book gets the biggest, but none are small. Steve's cooking is not to be missed, perhaps smoked duck breast, local lamb in a rosemary jus, a trio of citrus puddings. Blagdon is dog-friendly (a couple of labradors sleep in front of the fire) and there are towels, blankets, bowls, treats and toys.

Price	£125. Singles £85.
Rooms	7: 5 doubles, 2 twins/doubles.
Meals	Lunch from £17 (Wed–Sun). Dinner from £31.
Closed	2 weeks in January; 2 weeks in October; New Year.
Directions	A30, then north from Launceston on A388. Ignore signs to Ashwater. Right at Blagdon Cross, signed. Right; right again; house signed right.

Steve & Liz Morey
Ashwater,
Devon EX21 5DF

Tel	01409 211224
Fax	01409 211634
Email	stay@blagdon.com
Web	www.blagdon.com

Entry 66 Map 2

Percy's Country Hotel

Percy's is a way of life. Tony and Tina came west not merely to cook, but also to grow the food and rear the meat they serve at the table. These days their 130-acre organic estate teems with life: pigs – Large Blacks – roam freely through 60 acres of woodland, 150 Jacob sheep graze the open pasture, geese, ducks and chickens supply eggs for breakfast. There's a huge kitchen garden that's planted seasonally and serves the kitchen throughout the year, and much is harvested wild from the woods – a natural larder of mushrooms, juniper, crab apples and elderflower. At the house Tina turns her ingredients into soups and salads, terrines and sausages. She also cures her own bacon and delicious hams; a meal at Percy's is no ordinary event. Bedrooms in the converted granary are smart, with big comfortable beds, chic leather sofas, flat screen TVs and harlequin-tiled spotless bathrooms (some with whirlpools)… but Percy's is about more than just a bed. Grab a pair of wellies and lose yourself in the estate: woodpeckers and kingfishers, deer and badger, old hedgerows, wild flowers and a huge sky wait.

Price	£150–£210. Singles £155–£185. Half-board £115–£155 p.p.
Rooms	8 twins/doubles.
Meals	Dinner, 3 courses, £40.
Closed	Never.
Directions	From Okehampton, A3079 for Metherell Cross. After 8.3 miles, left. Hotel on left after 6.5 miles.

Tina & Tony Bricknell–Webb
Coombeshead Estate, Virginstow,
Okehampton, Devon EX21 5EA

Tel	01409 211236
Fax	01409 211460
Email	info@percys.co.uk
Web	www.percys.co.uk

Lewtrenchard Manor

A thrilling, historical pastiche set in a Jacobean mansion; only Edwardian radiators and soft-towelled bathrobes belie the fact you're not in 16th-century England. One fabulous room follows another until you reach the 1602 gallery, with the salvaged, honeycombed, plaster-moulded ceiling, grand piano and 1725 Bible – one of the most beautiful rooms you will see in this book. The ornamental friezes in the dining room are extraordinary and there's a good library too. Bedrooms are large – Queen Henrietta Maria's four-poster sits in one of the more traditional bedrooms in the main house; there's a more contemporary feel to the new North Wing rooms, but all have bowls of fruit and flowers from the garden. Follow breakfast with a stroll round the newly restored walled garden, or 6th-century St Petroc's church next door. A pretty inner courtyard is great for summer Sunday lunches (with jazz) and the food is as local and seasonal as possible – modern British style with a Mediterranean and Asian twist. Try salt cod sausage with Cornish crab, or turbot with samphire – delicious.

Price	£150–£250. Singles from £125.
Rooms	14: 9 doubles, 5 suites.
Meals	Lunch £15–£19 (not Monday). Dinner from £40.
Closed	Rarely.
Directions	From Exeter, exit A30 for A386. At T-junc., right, then 1st left for Lewdown. After 6 miles, left for Lewtrenchard. House signed left after 0.75 miles.

Jason Hornbuckle
Lewdown, Okehampton,
Devon EX20 4PN

Tel	01566 783222
Fax	01566 783332
Email	info@lewtrenchard.co.uk
Web	www.lewtrenchard.co.uk

The Dartmoor Inn

There aren't many inns where you can sink into Zoffany-clad winged armchairs in the dining room, snooze on a pink silk bed under a French chandelier, or shop for rhinestone brooches and Provençal quilts while you wait for the wild sea bass to crisp in the pan. Different rules apply at the Dartmoor. This is the template of deep-country chic, a fairytale inn dressed up as a country local. True, there is a snug bar at the front where you can perch on a stool and knock back a glass of ale, but then again the walls are coated in textured wallpaper, gilded mirrors sit above smouldering fireplaces and upstairs a shimmering velvet throw is spread out across a sublimely upholstered sleigh bed. Come for stripped wood floors, timber-framed walls, sand-blasted settles and country-house rugs. Add to this wonderful staff and Philip's ambrosial food (corned beef hash for breakfast, ham hock terrine for lunch, free-range duck for dinner) and you have a very special place. Triple-glazed bedroom windows defeat road noise and ensure a good night's rest. The moors are on your doorstep, so walk in the wind, then eat, drink and sleep.

Price	£100–£115.
Rooms	3 doubles.
Meals	Lunch from £5. Dinner from £15.
Closed	Occasionally.
Directions	North from Tavistock on A386. Pub on right at Lydford turnoff.

Karen & Philip Burgess
Lydford, Okehampton,
Devon EX20 4AY

Tel	01822 820221
Fax	01822 820494
Email	info@dartmoorinn.co.uk
Web	www.dartmoorinn.com

The Arundell Arms

A tiny interest in fishing would not go amiss, though the people here are so kind they welcome everyone. Anne has been at the helm for 45 years; her MBE for services to tourism is richly deserved. This is a *very* settled hotel, with Mrs VB, as staff call her fondly, quietly presiding over all; during a superb lunch – St Enodoc asparagus, scallops, homemade chocs – she asked after an 80th birthday party, ensuring their day was memorable. Over the years the hotel has resuscitated buildings at the heart of the village: the old police station and magistrates court is a pub, the old school a conference centre. Pride of place is the funnel-roofed cock-fighting pit, one of only two left in England; now it's the rod room, where local knowledge is shared generously every morning. Anne's late husband wrote about fly-fishing for *The Times* and it's no surprise to discover that this is one of the best fishing hotels in England – or that they own 20 miles of the Tamar. Come to try your luck or merely to search for otter and kingfisher on its banks. As for the hotel: it's newly refurbished, divine from top to toe.

Price	£160–£190. Singles from £99.
Rooms	21: 9 doubles, 7 twins, 3 singles, 2 suites.
Meals	Bar meals £7–£15. Dinner from £38.
Closed	Christmas.
Directions	A30 south-west from Exeter, past Okehampton. Lifton 0.5 miles off A30, 3 miles east of Launceston & signed. Hotel in centre of village.

Anne Voss-Bark
Lifton,
Devon PL16 0AA

Tel	01566 784666
Fax	01566 784494
Email	reservations@arundellarms.com
Web	www.arundellarms.com

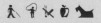

Tor Cottage

At the end of the track, a blissful valley lost to the world. This is an indulging hideaway, wrapped up in 28 acres of majestic country, and those who like to be pampered in peace will find heaven. Hills rise, cows sleep, streams run, birds sing. Bridle paths lead onto the hill, wild flowers carpet a hay meadow. Big rooms in converted outbuildings are the lap of rustic luxury, each with a wood-burner and private terrace. All are impeccable, one filled with Art Deco, one straight out of *House and Garden*, one whitewashed with ceilings open to the rafters. Best of all is the cabin in its own valley – a wonderland in the woods – with hammocks hanging in the trees and a stream passing below. You can self-cater here and eat on the deck while deer wander in the trees. Breakfasts served in the conservatory promise homemade muesli, local sausages and farm-fresh eggs, but if you get peckish later in the day, wash down smoked salmon sandwiches with a glass of sangria while sunbathing by the pool. Staff couldn't be nicer, guests return. *Minimum stay two nights. Special deals available.*

Price	£140–£150. Singles £94. Self-catering from £66 (min. 3 nights).
Rooms	5: 2 doubles, 1 twin/double, 1 suite; 1 woodland cabin for 2 (B&B or self-catering).
Meals	Supper, 3 courses, £24. On request.
Closed	B&B: Christmas & New Year. Self-catering: Never.
Directions	In Chillaton keep pub & PO on left, up hill towards Tavistock. After 300 yds, right down bridleway (ignore No Access signs).

Maureen Rowlatt
Chillaton, Tavistock,
Devon PL16 0JE
Tel   01822 860248
Fax   01822 860126
Email info@torcottage.co.uk
Web   www.torcottage.co.uk

Browns Hotel

This is a popular spot. The Romans came first and left a well: you can stand on a sheet of glass in the conservatory and peer into it. Then came the Benedictines, who built an abbey: old carved stones are on show in the bar. If tradition holds they'll find Roberts radios and leather sofas when they rebuild in 200 years. Helena swept in armed with ideas and has already made her mark: Lloyd Loom wicker sits in the courtyard, a hidden terrace is being brought back to life. The house dates to 1700 and was Tavistock's first coaching inn. It's still the best place to stay in town, with armchairs in front of the fire, wood floors in the restaurant, and a stone-flagged conservatory for delicious breakfasts. Clutter-free bedrooms have a clipped elegance: Farrow & Ball colours, Egyptian cotton, latticed windows and comforting bathrobes. Some in the coach house are huge, with cathedral ceilings. Dine under beams on Cornish scallops, roast loin of lamb, rhubarb and custard crumble. Tavistock is an old market town, its famous goose fair takes place in October. Don't miss Dartmoor for uplifting walks.

Price	£110–£220. Singles from £70.
Rooms	20: 11 doubles, 3 twins, 6 singles.
Meals	Continental breakfast included. Cooked dishes £6.00–£12.50. Lunch from £9. Dinner £32–£37. 5-course tasting menu £45.
Closed	Never.
Directions	Leave A386 for Tavistock. Right, at statue, for town centre. Left at T-junction, them immediately left into West Street. Hotel on right. Ask about parking.

Helena King & Phil Biggin
80 West Street, Tavistock,
Devon PL19 8AQ

Tel	01822 618686
Fax	01822 618646
Email	enquiries@brownsdevon.co.uk
Web	www.brownsdevon.co.uk

The Horn of Plenty

This country-house hotel has been thrilling guests for 40 years. It's won just about every award going and the food is glorious, so if you're looking for somewhere very special, you'll find it here. You get fabulous rooms, jaw-dropping views, exceptional service. Staff come to meet you on arrival – with an umbrella if it's wet – then escort you into this impeccable house. Airy interiors are the essence of graceful simplicity with stripped floors, gilt mirrors, exquisite art and flowers everywhere. Bedrooms elate wherever you go, some with terraces that look down on the Tamar, others with painted wooden floors, shimmering throws or crushed velvet headboards. All come fully armed with an excess of hi-tech gadgetry, bathrooms are predictably divine. As for the food, well, just don't miss it. Try fois gras crème brûlée, loin of venison with spiced pear, then chocolate truffle mousse with raspberry sauce. In summer you can eat on the terrace with views of the Tamar cutting through the valley below. You're in five acres of silence. Tavistock is close, as is Dartmoor.

Price	£160–£250. Singles £150–£240.
Rooms	10 twins/doubles.
Meals	Lunch, 3 courses, £26.50.
	Dinner, 3 courses, £45.
Closed	25 & 26 December.
Directions	A386 north to Tavistock. Turn left onto A390, following signs to Callington. After 3 miles, right at Gulworthy Cross. Signed.

Paul Roston & Peter Gorton
Gulworthy, Tavistock,
Devon PL19 8JD

Tel	01822 832528
Fax	01822 834390
Email	enquiries@thehornofplenty.co.uk
Web	www.thehornofplenty.co.uk

Lydgate House

You're in 36 acres of heaven, so come for the sheer wonder of Dartmoor: deer and badger, fox and pheasant, kingfisher and woodpecker. A 30-minute circular walk takes you over the East Dart, up to a wild hay meadow where rare orchids flourish, then back down to a 12th-century clapper bridge; sensational. Herons dive in the river by day; you may get a glimpse from the conservatory as you dig into your bacon and eggs. The house is a dream, a nourishing stream of homely comforts: a drying room for walkers, deep white sofas, walls of books, a wood-burner and a cat in the armchair. Cindy, a classics teacher, and Peter, a surveyor, somehow find time to double up as host and hostess extraordinaire: expect a good chat, delicious home cooking and peace when you want it. Bedrooms — two are huge — are warmly cossetting: crisply floral with comfy beds and Radox in the bathrooms. Rescued sheep live in the top field and are partial to a slice of toast, while moonwort grows in the hay meadow. Legend says if gathered by moonlight it unleashes magical properties; clearly someone has.

Price	£110–£140. Singles £50–£65.
Rooms	7: 4 doubles, 1 twin/double, 2 singles.
Meals	Dinner, 3 courses, £28.50.
Closed	January.
Directions	From Exeter A30 west to Whiddon Down, A382 south to Moretomhampstead, B3212 west to Postbridge. In village, left at pub. House signed straight ahead.

Cindy & Peter Farrington
Postbridge, Dartmoor,
Devon PL20 6TJ

Tel	01822 880209
Fax	01822 880202
Email	lydgatehouse@email.com
Web	www.lydgatehouse.co.uk

Gidleigh Park

Gidleigh is a perfect place, ten out of ten on all counts. It stands in 45 acres of lush silence with the North Teign river pottering through and huge views shooting off to Meldon Hill. Inside, you find a faultless country house. A fire smoulders in the oak-panelled hall, ferns tumble from silver champagne bowls, sofas come crisply dressed in dazzling fabrics. Bedrooms are divine, impeccably presented with hand-stitched linen, woollen blankets, upholstered headboards and polished wooden furniture; the panelled suite comes with an enormous bathroom that opens onto a private balcony. Back downstairs, beautiful art adorns the walls, while summer life spills onto a view-filled terrace. As for the food, Michael Caines brings two Michelin stars to the table, so expect the best, perhaps terrine of fois gras with rhubarb and lemon grass jelly, Cornish duckling with roast garlic and honey, poached peach with vanilla mousse and nectarine sorbet. Breakfast offers porridge with whisky among other delicacies. Best of all is sublime service from the loveliest staff. Matchless. *Minimum stay two nights at weekends.*

Price	Half-board £220–£290 p.p. Suites £300–£600 p.p.
Rooms	24: 3 suites, 15 twins/doubles, 6 doubles.
Meals	Half-board only. Lunch £27–£41. Dinner for non-residents, £75–£85.
Closed	Never.
Directions	A30 west from Exeter to Whiddon Down. A382 south, then B3206 into Chagford. Right in square, right at fork. Signed straight across at x-roads.

Susan Kendall
Chagford,
Devon TQ13 8HH

Tel	01647 432367
Fax	01647 432574
Email	gidleighpark@gidleigh.co.uk
Web	www.gidleigh.com

Sandy Park Inn

A small thatched pub in a tiny village on Dartmoor. The river Teign runs through the valley, so follow its path for views that lift the soul. Those of a more sedentary disposition can sit in the beer garden and take in the view while sampling local delicacies. This is a cracking country boozer, loved by locals, and with food that punches above its weight; Barry the butcher brings in slow-grown pork off the moor, the cod comes battered in beer, the cheeses are all local. It's snug, with low ceilings, flagged floors, country rugs and huge knots of wood crackling in an old stone fire. Standing room only at the bar at weekends; local musicians occasionally drop in to play on Sunday nights. Bedrooms sparkle with unexpected treats – flat screen TVs, CD players, padded headboards, colourful throws – but the bar is lively, and a night here will only suit those who want to have some fun. Most rooms have pretty views over the village; some are en suite, others not, so come to practise the dying art of smiling at strangers on the landing. Also: kippers at breakfast, maps for walkers and dog biscuits behind the bar.

Price	£92. Singles £59.
Rooms	5: 1 twin, 1 double, both en suite; 3 doubles each with separate bath or shower.
Meals	Lunch from £5. Dinner from £8.
Closed	Never.
Directions	A30 west from Exeter to Whiddon Cross. South 2 miles to Sandy Park. Pub on right at x-roads.

Nick Rout
Sandy Park,
 Chagford,
Devon TQ13 8JW

Tel	01647 433267
Email	sandyparkinn@aol.com
Web	www.sandyparkinn.co.uk

Kingston House

It's hard to know where to begin with this stupendous house – the history in one bathroom alone would fill a small book. "It's like visiting a National Trust home where you can get into bed," says Elizabeth, your gentle, erudite host. Set in a flawless Devon valley, Kingston is one of the finest surviving examples of early 18th-century English architecture. Arrive down a long country lane and at the brow of the last hill the house comes into view… along with the Great Danes that bound out to greet you. Completed in 1735 for a wealthy wool merchant, original features remain including numerous open fires, murals peeling off the walls, a sitting room in the old chapel (look for the drunken cherubs) and 24 chimneys. The craftsman who carved the marble hallway later worked on the White House, the marquetry staircase is the best in Europe, and the magnificent bed in the Green Room has stood there since 1830. The cooking is historic, too – devilled kidneys, syllabub and proper trifle. Flowers by the thousand in various gardens and a small pool with a jet stream so you can swim 20 miles.

Price	£160–£180. Singles £100–£110.
Rooms	3: 2 doubles, both en suite; 1 double with separate bath.
Meals	Lunch from £18.50. Dinner, 3 courses, £35. On request.
Closed	Christmas & New Year.
Directions	From A38, A384 to Staverton. At Sea Trout Inn, left fork for Kingston; halfway up hill right fork; at top, ahead at x-roads. Road goes up, then down to house; right to front of house.

Michael & Elizabeth Corfield
Staverton, Totnes,
Devon TQ9 6AR

Tel	01803 762235
Fax	01803 762444
Email	info@kingston-estate.co.uk
Web	www.kingston-estate.co.uk

Bickley Mill

A small inn full of good things. David and Tricia recently orchestrated a total refurbishment and their stylishly cosy interiors are just the ticket. Come for wood floors, stone walls, hessian rugs, cushioned sofas. Three fires burn in winter, there are Swedish benches, colourful art and a panelled breakfast room in creamy yellow. Everywhere you look something lovely catches the eye, be it a huge sofa covered with mountainous cushions, old black and white photos hanging on the walls or a decked terrace at the side for a pint or two in the summer sun. Bedrooms have a simple beauty in warm colours, pretty pine, trim carpets, crisp white linen – and with reasonable prices they're an absolute steal. Downstairs you'll find helpful staff, local ales and loads to eat (light bites to a three-course feast) perhaps devilled kidneys, salmon fishcakes, banana and toffee pancakes; there's a menu for children and baby chairs, too. You're in the lush Stoneycombe valley with Dartmouth, Dartmoor and the south Devon coast all close. A very generous place, so don't delay.

Price	£70-£80. Singles £55.
Rooms	8: 5 doubles, 2 twins, 1 family.
Meals	Lunch from £5. Dinner from £11.
Closed	Rarely.
Directions	South from Newton Abbot on A381. Left at garage in Ipplepen. Left at T-junc. after 1 mile. Down hill, left again, pub on left.

David & Tricia Smith
Stoneycombe, Kingskerswell,
Devon TQ12 5LN

Tel	01803 873201
Fax	01803 875129
Email	info@bickleymill.co.uk
Web	www.bickleymill.co.uk

Browns Hotel

Bang in the centre of bustling Dartmouth, this painted Georgian townhouse with pretty windows appears unremarkable. But inside is a large, airy space with vibrant James Stewart paintings on otherwise unadorned cream and lilac walls, cast-iron fireplaces, squashy sofas, books and magazines and no reception desk – it's very friendly, very relaxed, and there are loads of places to sit and sip something delicious while you ponder which of the fresh tapas dishes to order. James has his pick of Devon's finest fish, meat and veg, so your taste buds will be thrilled. Bedrooms vary in size – none are huge – but all have pocket-sprung mattresses, plain colours with the odd funky headboard or zebra-striped screen, super snazzy bathrooms and modern art. Gorgeous breakfasts, fantastic cocktails, board games for rainy days, sailing for sunny ones. There are arduous walks too, great beaches and all the shops and restaurants of pretty Dartmouth. Check their website before you come: it's packed with good advice about what you can do. One night may not be enough. *Minimum stay two nights at weekends.*

Price	£85–£170. Singles £65 (Sunday–Thursday).
Rooms	10: 8 doubles, 1 twin, 1 four-poster.
Meals	Tapas £3.50–£8 (Thurs-Sat only).
Closed	January.
Directions	From M5, A38 for Plymouth; A385 for Totnes then to Dartmouth. There, 3rd right (Townstal Road) & down into town. On right hand side. Free parking permit (small doubles exempt).

James & Clare Brown
27-29 Victoria Road, Dartmouth,
Devon TQ6 9RT

Tel	01803 832572
Email	enquiries@brownshoteldartmouth.co.uk
Web	www.brownshoteldartmouth.co.uk

Entry 79 Map 2

Fingals

Richard runs Fingals with flair, generosity, a sense of fun and a rare informality. Sheila, behind every scene, is impossibly kind and helpful. The place is an expression of Richard's personality, so you need to be in tune to enjoy it. It is not so much a hotel, more a big house with lots of bedrooms. Guests, many of whom are old fans, wander around as if at home. Children and dogs mill about, tennis is played on the lawn, punctuality at dinner time is not an issue (the bar clock only has one hand). This laid-back atmosphere has its benefits: breakfast is served until 11am. You will make friends, laugh, stay up too late, have long conversations at dinner, get to know Richard and Sheila and their friends. Some see it as a handsome, country-house hotel with indoor pool, panelled dining room, log fires and some very comfortable bedrooms. But it is not for the over fastidious; the occasional spider web may be overlooked and rooms are a mix of gorgeous, interesting and traditional. It is more an experience than a hotel; not everybody will love it – but we do, and so do hundreds of others. *Minumum stay two nights at weekends.*

Price	£75–£160. Barn £500–£800 per week.
Rooms	10 + 1: 8 doubles, 1 twin, 1 family. Self-catering barn for 4.
Meals	Dinner £30.
Closed	2 January–26 March.
Directions	From Totnes, A381 south; left for Cornworthy. Right at x-roads for Cornworthy; right at ruined gatehouse for Dittisham. Down steep hill, over bridge. Signed on right.

Richard Johnston
Dittisham, Dartmouth,
Devon TQ6 0JA

Tel	01803 722398
Fax	01803 722401
Email	richard@fingals.co.uk
Web	www.fingals.co.uk

Hazelwood House

Crest the hill, drop down the drive and dive into a hidden valley. If you are looking to escape the outside world, you can here. Sixty-seven wild acres wrap around you with a river galloping through. You'll find native woodlands, ancient rhododendrons, fields of wild flowers, a shepherdess grazing her flock. Hazelwood isn't your standard hotel or B & B, it's a country venue with accommodation for all who wish to rest, retreat and recoup — you may occasionally find yourself among guests on a residential course. It's a comfy, no frills house with open fires, sublime peace and a large drawing and dining room. Bedrooms are homely with an assortment of furniture, some have huge views over the valley, some face the back, others have brass beds and quilted bedcovers or big mirrors and a Victorian fireplace. Cream teas on the wisteria-shaded veranda are wonderful and you get lectures, exhibitions, courses, even recitals. Wellington boots wait at the front door. Pull on a pair, pick up a map, lope past a Frederick Frank sculpture in the garden and a boathouse on the river.

Price	£70–£150. Singles £47–£112.
Rooms	15: 4 doubles, 2 twins, 1 family room, all en suite; 2 doubles, 2 twins, 2 family rooms, 1 single, sharing 4 baths.
Meals	Lunch £14. Dinner £30–£35.
Closed	Never.
Directions	From Exeter, A38 south; A3121 south. Left onto B3196 south. At California Cross, 1st left after petrol station. After 0.75 miles, left.

Janie Bowman, Gillian Kean & Anabel Watson
Loddiswell, Kingsbridge,
Devon TQ7 4EB

Tel	01548 821232
Fax	01548 821318
Email	info@hazelwoodhouse.com
Web	www.hazelwoodhouse.com

Buckland Tout-Saints

Tiny lanes lead up to this William and Mary manor house. It stands in four acres of parkland gardens with views at the front sweeping across an ancient quilt of field and copse. The land was listed in the Domesday book, the current house dates to the 17th century, its dovecote is one of England's oldest. Inside you find grandly panelled reception rooms dressed in shimmering Russian pine. Old oils adorn the walls, flames leap in the marble fireplace, there are scattered sofas, bowls of fruit, vast displays of flowers. There's a bar in red leather that resembles a gentleman's club, a ceiling rose in the stately dining room, a terrace with big views for afternoon tea. First-floor bedrooms come in country-house style: high ceilings, warm colours, thick fabrics, fine views. Those above in the eaves are smaller but funkier, with padded headboards, neutral colours, flat-screen TVs, comfy beds. Excellent food is often organic, perhaps fish terrine with horseradish cream, rack of lamb with a black olive sauce, ginger crème brûlée with plum chilli sorbet. Salcombe and Dartmouth are both close.

Price	£135–£225. Suites from £245. Singles from £95.
Rooms	16: 12 doubles, 2 twins, 2 suites.
Meals	Lunch from £7.50. Dinner, 3 courses, about £35.
Closed	Never.
Directions	A381 south from Totnes for Kingsbridge. Hotel signed right three miles south of Halwell. Follow signs up narrow lanes to hotel.

Howard Turner
Goveton, Nr. Kingsbridge,
Devon TQ7 2DS

Tel	01548 853055
Fax	01548 856261
Email	buckland@tout-saints.co.uk
Web	www.tout-saints.co.uk

Seabreeze

A Mediterranean-style beach café at the end of Slapton Sands: the sea laps ten paces from the front door, the rolling hills of Devon soar behind. Seabreeze is a treat, small, cute and nicely relaxed, a little piece of homespun magic. It's not grand, but what you get is priceless. Andrew organises kite surfing, Charlotte runs the café. There are kayaks and bikes for intrepid adventures, cliff walks for fabulous views. Those who want to stay put can soak up the sun on the terrace at the front and tuck into homemade smoothies and grilled paninis while seaside life ambles by. Inside, airy interiors are just as they should be: colourful and comfy. You get stripped floors, halogen lighting, sky-blue tongue and groove panelling. You can buy sun cream and kites, there are sofas, candles and a fire in the café. Airy bedrooms are perfect for the price: crisp linen, seaside colours, flat-screen TVs, super bathrooms. Two have huge sea views; padded window seats oblige. Fabulous seafood at the Start Bay Inn is yards away. There's a surf school at Bigbury and sailing at Salcombe. *Minimum stay two nights at weekends.*

Price	£60–£100. Singles from £40.
Rooms	3: 1 double, 1 twin/double, 1 family.
Meals	Lunch (March-October) from £5. Restaurants in village.
Closed	Rarely.
Directions	A379 south from Dartmouth to Torcross. House on seafront in village.

Andrew & Charlotte Barker
Torcross, Kingsbridge,
Devon TQ7 2TQ

Tel	01548 580697
Email	info@seabreezebreaks.com
Web	www.seabreezebreaks.com

Burgh Island

Burgh is unique — grand English Art Deco trapped in aspic. Noel Coward loved it, Agatha Christie wrote here. It's much more than a hotel — you come to join a cast of players — so bring your pearls and come for cocktails under a stained-glass dome. By day you lie on steamers in the garden, watch gulls wheeling above, dip your toes into Mermaid's pool or try your hand at a game of croquet. At night you dress for dinner, sip vermouth in a palm-fringed bar, then shuffle off to the ballroom and dine on delicious organic food while the sounds of swing and jazz fill the air. Follow your nose and find flowers in vases four-feet high, bronze ladies thrusting globes into the sky, walls clad in vitrolite, a 14th-century smugglers inn. Art Deco bedrooms are the real thing: Bakerlite telephones, ancient radios, bowls of fruit, panelled walls. Some have claw-foot baths, others have balconies, the Beach House suite juts out over rocks. There's snooker, tennis, massage, a sauna. You're on an island; either sweep across the sands at low tide or hitch a ride on the sea tractor. *Minimum stay two nights at weekends.*

Price	Half-board £320-£340 per room. Suites £380-£500.
Rooms	24: 10 doubles, 3 twins, 12 suites.
Meals	Half-board only. Lunch £10-£38. Dinner for non-residents, 3 courses, £55.
Closed	Rarely.
Directions	Drive to Bigbury-on-sea. At high tide you are transported by sea tractor, at low tide by Landrover. Walking takes three minutes.

Deborah Clark & Tony Orchard
Bigbury-on-Sea,
Devon TQ7 4BG

Tel	01548 810514
Fax	01548 810243
Email	reception@burghisland.com
Web	www.burghisland.com

Hotel

The Henley

A small house above the sea with fabulous views, super bedrooms and some of the loveliest food in Devon. Despite such credentials, it's Martyn and Petra who shine most brightly, and their kind, generous approach makes this a memorable place to stay. Warm Edwardian interiors come with stripped wood floors, seagrass matting, Lloyd Loom wicker chairs, the odd potted palm. Beyond, the Avon estuary slips out to sea: at high tide surfers ride the waves; at low tide you can walk on the sands. There's a pretty garden with a path down to the sea, binoculars in each room, a wood-burner in the snug and good books everywhere. Bedrooms are a steal, not large but in warm yellows with crisp linen, tongue-and-groove panelling and robes in super little bathrooms. As for Martyn's table d'hôte dinners, expect something special. Fish comes daily from Kingsbridge market, you might have cream of parsnip, apple and potato soup, roasted monkfish with king prawns and a garlic and butter sauce, then hot chocolate soufflé with fresh raspberries. Gorgeous Devon is all around. Don't miss it. *Minimum stay two nights at weekends.*

Price	£100–£120. Singles from £60.
Rooms	5: 3 doubles, 2 twins/doubles.
Meals	Dinner £29.
Closed	November–March.
Directions	From A38, A3121 to Modbury, then B3392 to Bigbury-on-Sea. Hotel on left as road slopes down to sea.

Martyn Scarterfield & Petra Lampe
Folly Hill,
Bigbury-on-Sea,
Devon TQ7 4AR

Tel	01548 810240
Fax	01548 810240
Web	www.thehenleyhotel.co.uk

Entry 85 Map 2

Stapleton Arms

An inn with a big heart. There are no pretensions here, just kind, knowledgeable staff committed to running the place with informal panache. A recent face-lift has brought a streak of glamour back to this old coaching inn, infusing it with a warm colourful style. Downstairs there are sofas in front of the fire, a piano for live music in the bar and a restaurant in Georgian blue with shuttered windows and candles in the fireplace. You can eat wherever you want. Pork pies, Serrano ham and Tête de Moine cheese all wait at the bar, but if you want a bowl of soup or a three-course feast you can have it; try salmon and crab fishcakes, home-baked Dorset ham, banana tarte tatin. There's a beer menu (ale matters here), on Sundays groups can order their own joint of meat, and there's always a menu for kids. Rooms above are sound-proofed to ensure a good night's sleep. They're comfy-chic with Egyptian linen, fresh flowers, happy colours, perhaps a claw-foot bath. Also: maps and picnics, wellies if you want to walk, games for children, DVDs for all ages. Wincanton is close for the races.

Price	£72–£120. Singles £72–£96.
Rooms	4: 1 twin/double, 3 doubles.
Meals	Lunch & dinner £5–£20.
Closed	Rarely.
Directions	A303 to Wincanton. Into town, right after fire station, signed Buckhorn Weston. Left at T-junc. after 3 miles. In village, left at T-junc. Pub on right.

Kaveh Javvi
Church Hill,
Buckhorn Weston, Gillingham,
Dorset SP8 5HS

Tel	01963 370396
Email	relax@thestapletonarms.com
Web	www.thestapletonarms.com

Plumber Manor

Best of all at Plumber is the family triumvirate of Brian in the kitchen, Richard behind the bar and Alison, who is simply everywhere. They know exactly how to make you feel at home. This has been *their* family home for 300 years, though ancestors have lived "in the area" since they arrived with William the Conquerer. Outside, a large, sloping lawn, a white bridge over the river and deckchairs scattered about the well-groomed garden. Inside, more home than hotel with huge family portraits crammed on the walls, endless sitting rooms with vast fireplaces and comfortable old chairs, dining rooms with an English club feel and food generous and unpretentious. In the main house huge bedrooms are decorated with fresh colours and fabrics; those in the converted outbuildings are as big but with a younger feel. The stone path between them came from a local river bed and kept one guest amused for hours looking for dinosaur fossils… The enormous old sofa on the landing may be the most uncomfortable ever made – but this is the *only* discomfort you'll find. *Pets by arrangement.*

Price	£110–£170. Singles from £95.
Rooms	16: 2 doubles, 13 twins/doubles, all en suite; 1 twin/double with separate bath.
Meals	Dinner, 3 courses, £27.50.
Closed	February.
Directions	From Sturminster Newton, follow signs to hotel & Hazlebury Bryan for 2 miles. Entrance on left, signed.

Richard, Alison & Brian Prideaux-Brune
Sturminster Newton,
Dorset DT10 2AF

Tel   01258 472507
Fax   01258 473370
Email   book@plumbermanor.com
Web   www.plumbermanor.com

Bridge House Hotel

Beaminster — Emminster in Thomas Hardy's *Tess* — sits in a lush Dorset valley. From the hills above, rural England goes on show: quilted fields lead to a country town, the church tower soars towards heaven. At Bridge House stone flags, mullioned windows, old beams and huge inglenooks sweep you back to a graceful past. This is a comfortable county hotel — intimate, friendly, quietly smart. There are rugs on parquet floors, a beamed bar in a turreted alcove, a sparkling dining room with Georgian panelling. In summer, French windows in the conservatory open for breakfast on the terrace, so watch the gardener potter about as you scoff your bacon and eggs. Delicious food — local and organic — is a big draw, perhaps seared scallops, Gressingham duck, champagne sorbet. And so to bed. Rooms in the main house are bigger and smarter, those in the coach house are simpler and less expensive; all are pretty, their traditional florals being gradually replaced by chic fabrics, flat-screen TVs and stylish bathrooms. There are river walks, antique shops and Dorset's Jurassic coast. *Minimum stay two nights at weekends.*

Price	£116–£170. Four-poster £180. Singles from £90. Half-board (min. 2 nights) from £85 p.p.
Rooms	13: 7 twins/doubles, 1 four-poster, 1 single. Coach House: 3 doubles, 1 family room.
Meals	Lunch, 2 courses, £10. Dinner, 3 courses, £31.50.
Closed	Never.
Directions	From Yeovil, A30 west; A3066 for Bridport to Beaminster. Hotel at far end of town, as road bends to right.

Mark & Joanna Donovan
3 Prout Bridge, Beaminster,
Dorset DT8 3AY

Tel	01308 862200
Fax	01308 863700
Email	enquiries@bridge-house.co.uk
Web	www.bridge-house.co.uk

The Priory Hotel

Come for a slice of old England. The lawns of this 16th-century priory run down to the river Frome. Behind, a church rises, beyond, a neat Georgian square; in short, a little bit of time travel. A stone-flagged courtyard leads up to the hotel, where comfortable country-house interiors include a first-floor drawing room with views of the garden and a stone-vaulted dining room in the old cellar. Best of all is the terrace; 200 yards of dreamy English gardens front the river, so sit in the sun and watch yacht masts flutter. Bedrooms in the main house come in different sizes, some cosy under beams, others grandly adorned in reds and golds. Also: mahogany dressers, padded window seats, bowls of fruit, the odd sofa. Bathrooms – some new, some old – come with white robes. Eight have river views, others look onto the garden or church. Rooms in the boathouse, a 16th-century clay barn, are opulent, with oak panelling, stone walls, the odd chest and sublime views. Four acres of idyllic gardens have climbing roses, a duck pond and banks of daffs. Wonderful. *Minimum two nights at weekends in summer.*

Price	£215–£290. Suites from £315. Half-board (obligatory at weekends) from £122.50 p.p.
Rooms	18: 14 twins/doubles. Boat House: 4 suites.
Meals	Lunch from £25. Dinner from £35.
Closed	Never.
Directions	West from Poole on A35, then A351 for Wareham and B3075 into town. Through lights, 1st left, right out of square, then keep left and entrance on left beyond church.

Jeremy Merchant
Church Green, Wareham,
Dorset BH20 4ND

Tel	01929 551666
Fax	01929 554519
Email	reservations@theprioryhotel.co.uk
Web	theprioryhotel.co.uk

🚶 ✕ 🐾 🚲

Lord Bute Hotel

Tucked behind the original entrance lodges to Highcliffe Castle (itself worth a visit), a hotel that stands head and shoulders above the rest. The restaurant is glamorous – black carpets, white linen – and you book in advance for its award-winning menu. Settle back with a pre-dinner drink in the relaxing conservatory-orangery for blissful garden views – oriental pots sprout bamboo and colourful acers sit on well-groomed terraces leading to a pretty grassed area. Air-conditioned, double-glazed bedrooms are smartly contemporary with big suede headboards and subtle colours (oatmeals, beiges, a touch of mustard or crimson). The bridal suite and Garden suite are sumptuous and bathrooms are awash with Molton Brown goodies; the family suite has a kitchenette. Best of all: Gary and Simon, full of enthusiasm for this place and working hard to give you a good time; there are monthly cabaret evenings with famous names and live music on most weekends. If you have any energy left over, take the path down to the beach behind the castle, or head for the New Forest. Bournemouth is nearby for shopping.

Price	From £98. Singles from £65. Suites from £120.
Rooms	13: 8 doubles, 1 twin, 3 suites. Coach House: 1 family suite.
Meals	Lunch from £8. Dinner £29.95 & à la carte. Sunday lunch £19.95. Closed Monday.
Closed	Never.
Directions	From Christchurch, A337 towards Lymington to Highcliffe. Hotel 200 yds past castle.

Gary Payne & Simon Box
Lymington Road, Highcliffe,
Christchurch, Dorset BH23 4JS

Tel	01425 278884
Fax	01425 279258
Email	mail@lordbute.co.uk
Web	www.lordbute.co.uk

Rose and Crown

An idyllic village of mellow stone where little has changed in 200 years. The Rose and Crown dates from 1733 and stands on the green, next to the village's Saxon church. Roses ramble above the door in summer, so pick up a pint and search out the sun on the gravelled forecourt. Inside is just as good. You can sit at settles in the tiny locals' bar and roast away in front of the fire while reading the *Teesdale Mercury*, or seek out sofas in the peaceful sitting room and tuck into afternoon tea. Bedrooms are lovely. Those in the converted barn have padded headboards and tumble with colour; those in the main house come with antique pine, padded window seats and warm country colours. All have crisp white linen, Bose sound systems and quietly fancy bathrooms. Fabulous food can be eaten informally in the brasserie (smoked salmon soufflé, confit of duck, sticky toffee pudding) or grandly in the panelled dining room (farmhouse ham with fresh figs, grilled sea bass, honey and whisky ice cream). High Force waterfall and Hadrian's Wall are close and there's a drying room for walkers. *Minimum stay two nights at weekends.*

Price	£130–£159. Singles from £80. Suites £170–£184.
Rooms	12: 6 doubles, 4 twins, 2 suites.
Meals	Bar meals from £6. Dinner, 4 courses, £28.
Closed	Christmas.
Directions	From Barnard Castle, B6277 north for 6 miles. Right in village towards green. Inn on left.

Christopher & Alison Davy
Romaldkirk, Barnard Castle,
Durham DL12 9EB

Tel	01833 650213
Fax	01833 650828
Email	hotel@rose-and-crown.co.uk
Web	www.rose-and-crown.co.uk

The Bell Inn & Hill House

A 600-year-old timber-framed coaching inn, as busy today with happy locals as it was when pilgrims stopped on their way to Canterbury. Everything here is a treat: hanging lanterns in the courtyard, stripped boards in the bar, smartly dressed staff in the restaurant, copious window boxes bursting with colour. This is a proper inn, warmly welcoming, with thick beams, country rugs, panelled walls and open fires. Stop for a pint of cask ale in the lively bar, then potter into the restaurant for sensational food, perhaps Stilton ravioli, grilled Dover sole, orange and passion fruit tart. Christine grew up here, John joined her 35 years ago; both are much respected in the trade, as is Joanne, their loyal manager of many years and Master Sommelier. An infectious warmth runs throughout this ever-popular inn. As for the bedrooms, go for the suites above the shop: cosy, traditional, individual, rather wonderful. In the morning stroll up the tiny high street to breakfast with the papers at elegant Hill House, then head north into Constable country or east to the pier at Southend. London is close.

Price	£50–£60. Suites £85.
Rooms	15: 7 doubles, 3 twins, 5 suites.
Meals	Breakfast £4.50–£9.50. Bar meals from £8.50. Dinner, à la carte, around £27. No food bank holidays.
Closed	Christmas Day & Boxing Day.
Directions	M25 junc. 30/31. A13 towards Southend for 3 miles, then B1007 to Horndon-on-the-Hill. On left in village.

Christine & John Vereker
High Road, Horndon-on-the-Hill,
Essex SS17 8LD

Tel	01375 642463
Fax	01375 361611
Email	info@bell-inn.co.uk
Web	www.bell-inn.co.uk

The Sun Inn

An idyllic village made rich by mills in the 16th century. These days you can hire boats on the river, so order a picnic at the inn, float down the glorious Stour, then tie up on the bank for lunch al fresco. You're in the epicentre of Constable country; the artist attended school in the village and often returned to paint St Mary's church with its soaring tower; it stands directly opposite. As for the Sun, you couldn't hope to wash up in a better place. Step in to find open fires, stripped floors and an easy elegance. A panelled lounge comes with sofas and armchairs, the bar is made from a slab of local elm and the dining room is beamed and airy, so settle in for fresh seafood, wild boar, slow-cooked lamb and English cheeses. Rooms are gorgeous: creaking floorboards, a panelled four-poster, timber-framed walls, decanters of sherry. You get Farrow & Ball colours on the walls, crisp Egyptian linen on the beds, super little power-showered bathrooms. There's afternoon tea on arrival, a garden for summer barbecues and the inn owns a traditional grocer's next door.

Price	£80–£130. Singles from £60.
Rooms	5: 4 doubles, 1 four-poster.
Meals	Continental breakfast included. Lunch & dinner £5–£25.
Closed	25-27 December.
Directions	A12 north past Colchester. 2nd exit, marked Dedham. On High St.

Piers Baker
High Street, Dedham,
Colchester,
Essex CO7 6DF
Tel   01206 323351
Email info@thesuninndedham.com
Web   www.thesuninndedham.com

The Mistley Thorn

In Constable country: an unexpectedly chi-chi village with some red-bricked and some painted Georgian cottages gathered around the river estuary with its wide, light views of water, bobbing boats and green hills beyond. David and Sherri (who have a cookery school next door) run the place beautifully: staff are young and very good, there are plenty of locals tossed into the mix downstairs and some impeccably behaved children too. The mood is laid-back city wine bar rather than country pub. Colours are soft and easy, the tables are of various shapes, candles flicker, modern art rubs along well with the odd antique and food is taken seriously but with no grim reverence. There's lots of good local fish and seafood – perhaps cooked with an Italian or Asian twist – and a pudding list that includes cheesecake from Sherri's mum. Bedrooms are calm with cream carpets, big beds, pale green paintwork and some have views over the water. Bathrooms have a Turkish feel with tiny beige and cream tiles, spotless white baths and overhead showers. It's all entirely charming.

Price	From £80.
Rooms	5: 3 doubles, 2 twins/doubles.
Meals	Dinner, 2 courses, £12.80–£25.90.
Closed	Christmas Day.
Directions	From A12 take Hadleigh/East Bergholt exit north of Colchester. Go through East Bergholt to A137. Follow signs to Manningtree, drive through to Mistley High Street.

	David McKay & Sherri Singleton
	High Street, Mistley, Colchester, Essex CO11 1HE
Tel	01206 392821
Fax	01206 390122
Email	info@mistleythorn.co.uk
Web	www.mistleythorn.co.uk

The Pier at Harwich

Built in the style of a Venetian palazzo, the Pier stands handsomely on the historic quayside. The owners took over the adjoining pub six years ago and have carved out a stylish and cosy lounge: black beams, white brick walls, brown leather sofas and large travel posters. Upstairs is strikingly contemporary: a polished pewter bar, spotlights on ceiling and in floor, bucket seats at round pewter tables, an elegant restaurant – with food to match – and the pick of the harbour views. Fresh fish is, of course, what you should eat; Chris and Vreni Oakley – he's the seafood expert, she, his charming Swiss-born wife, does front of house – have been here for years. They clearly love the place and run a happy ship. Informal eating takes place in the Ha'penny Bistro (don't miss the fish and chips) and on the buzzing quayside. Bath and shower rooms are perfect, bedrooms have been delightfully modernised – seagrass floors and restful colours, washed beech and quirky touches. Splash out on the Mayflower Suite for the most exciting views.

Price	£97.50–£117.50. Suite £170. Singles £72.50–£92.50. Half-board (min. 2 nights) from £80 p.p.
Rooms	14: 13 doubles, 1 suite.
Meals	Lunch £17.50. Dinner, à la carte, £25–£35.
Closed	Never.
Directions	M25 junc. 28, A12 to Colchester bypass, then A120 to Harwich. Head for quay. Hotel opposite pier.

Chris & Vreni Oakley
The Quay, Harwich,
Essex CO12 3HH

Tel	01255 241212
Fax	01255 551922
Email	pier@milsomhotels.com
Web	www.milsomhotels.com

Three Choirs Vineyards

A fondness for cooking and wine-making will equip you for the full-bodied and very English experience of Three Choirs. Thomas has run the pesticide-free vineyard with thoughtful and gentle reserve for over a decade. There are 100 acres of grounds of which 75 grow 16 varieties of grape; the rest have been left to encourage wildlife, including birds of prey. The wine from here went to the wedding of Charles and Diana and still lubricates British embassies; the hotel and restaurant evolved more recently as an addition to the winery; weddings are welcomed. The bedrooms are in a purpose-built building and are crisply clean and comfortable, each with French windows opening to a small patio with cast-iron furniture: relax with a glass of wine and enjoy the peaceful views that produced it. At breakfast, don't be embarrassed to ask for more wine with your smoked salmon and scrambled eggs – it's a house special. Chef Darren cooks like a dream, has won many accolades and runs monthly cookery courses. Dick Whittington was born up the road – you may wonder why he ever left. *Minimum stay two nights at weekends.*

Price	£95–£125. Singles £75–£115. Half-board from £82.50 p.p. (min. 2 nights).
Rooms	8 twins/doubles.
Meals	Lunch from £21. Dinner, à la carte, around £35.
Closed	Christmas & New Year.
Directions	From Newent, north on B4215 for about 1.5 miles, follow brown signs to vineyard.

Thomas Shaw
Newent,
Gloucestershire GL18 1LS

Tel	01531 890223
Fax	01531 890877
Email	info@threechoirs.com
Web	www.threechoirs.com

Corse Lawn House Hotel

Old-fashioned values win out at Corse Lawn. It may not be the fanciest place in the book, but excellent service, delicious food and generous prices make it a must for those in search of an alternative to contemporary minimalism. This impeccable Queen Anne manor house was built on the ruins of a Tudor inn where Cromwell is thought to have slept before the battle of Worcester (1651); it is now the hub of a small community. The Rotary Club dine once a week, shooting parties lunch here in winter, locals bring the family for birthdays. At the front a willow dips its branches into the country's last surviving coach-wash; in summer you can sit out under parasols and dig into a cream tea while ducks glide by. Inside, slightly eccentric furnishings prevail. There are palms in the swimming pool, a sofa'd bistro for light meals, an open fire in the sitting room and a paddock at the back for visiting horses. Big bedrooms may be chintzy, but they're eminently comfortable, with crisp white linen, bowls of fruit, fresh milk and leaf tea. As for the food, it's all homemade, utterly delicious, and breakfast is a treat.

Price	£145–£165. Suites £185. Singles £90. Half-board from £97.50 p.p.
Rooms	19: 14 twins/doubles, 2 four-posters, 2 suites, 1 single.
Meals	Lunch & dinner £10–£35.
Closed	Christmas Day & Boxing Day.
Directions	West from Tewkesbury on A438 for Ledbury. After 3 miles left onto B4211. Hotel on right after 2 miles.

Baba Hine
Corse Lawn,
Gloucestershire GL19 4LZ

Tel	01452 780771
Fax	01452 780840
Email	enquiries@corselawn.com
Web	www.corselawn.com

Hotel on the Park

Symmetry and style to please the eye in the centre of the spa town of Cheltenham. The attention to detail is staggering – everything has a place and is just where it should be. The style is crisp and dramatic, a homage to the Regency period in which the house was built, but there's plenty of good humour floating around, not least in Darryl and Jo, who are brilliant at encouraging people to dive in and enjoy it all. There are lovely touches too: piles of fresh hand towels in the gents' cloakroom, where there's a sink with no plug hole – you'll work it out; newspapers hang on poles, grab one and head into the drawing room where drapes swirl across big windows. Lose yourself in Scrabble (on the rotating games table) in the library, tuck into pan-fried scallops, noisette of lamb or red mullet escabèche on the terrace or in the brasserie: wooden tables, planked floor, modern dishes. Upstairs, bedrooms are fabulous, crisp and artistic, all furnished to fit the period. One has an infinity bath, others aromatherapy baths, jacuzzis and walk-in showers. A huge treat.

Price	£129.50–£189.50. Singles £99–£106.50. Suite £159.
Rooms	12: 7 doubles, 4 twins/doubles, 1 suite.
Meals	Breakfast £7.95–£11.95. Starters from £5.95; main courses from £13.95.
Closed	Never.
Directions	From town centre, join one-way system, & exit signed Evesham. On down Evesham Road. Hotel on left opposite park, signed.

Darryl Gregory
Evesham Road, Cheltenham,
Gloucestershire GL52 2AH

Tel	01242 518898
Fax	01242 511526
Email	stay@hotelonthepark.co.uk
Web	www.hotelonthepark.com

Thirty Two

A magnificent regency townhouse on Cheltenham's loveliest square. Strictly speaking this is simply a B&B, but nothing here is simple and those who come find divine interiors on a grand scale, a match for any design hotel. The building doubles up as a showroom for Jonathan Parkin's predictably successful interior design company, and anything that can move is for sale. Climb up stairs clad in smart red carpet and find a first-floor sitting room to beat most others. French windows soar to the ceiling and open onto a small balcony; when the jazz festival comes to town, cool tunes float in. You get varnished wooden floors, candles everywhere, the odd Thai deity carved in stone, beautifully upholstered armchairs. Bedrooms are just as you'd expect: sublime to behold and kitted out with all the best names: Cole & Son wallpaper, Whites of London linen, natural travertine marble bathrooms and the same showers as Buckingham Palace. Delicious breakfasts are eaten communally or brought up to your room, and Cheltenham's restaurants lie outside the door. Exceptional. *Minimum stay two nights at weekends July-September.*

Price	£139-£189. Singles from £123.
Rooms	4: 2 twins/doubles, 2 doubles.
Meals	Restaurants nearby.
Closed	Rarely.
Directions	A40 west into Cheltenham. Left onto one-way system. Swing right, heading east; 3rd left; hotel on the left.

	Jonathan Parkin & Jonathan Sellwood
	32 Imperial Square, Cheltenham,
	Gloucestershire GL50 1QZ
Tel	01242 771110
Fax	01242 771119
Email	stay@thirtytwoltd.com
Web	www.thirtytwoltd.com

Wesley House

Wesley House, a 15th-century half-timbered townhouse, entices you off the street and seduces you once inside. Old timber-framed white walls, a terracotta-tiled floor, an inviting log fire and a cosy-smart bar were made for lazy afternoons flicking through the papers. Food plays a big part here, and will have you purring with pleasure. Meat is local, fruits come from the farm down the road and the formal dining area stretches back in search of the gentle countryside. French windows lead out to an atrium-ed terrace where breakfast and lunch and dinner are enjoyed – ideal for private parties. Bedrooms, each with a little shower room, are small but cosy, very well decorated and sympathetically lit. Whitewashed, timber-framed walls, good wooden beds, comfy mattresses, plump pillows, new carpets and the occasional head-cracking door; the best has a little balcony. Indulge, if you prefer, in breakfast in bed, with home-baked bread, croissants, pains au chocolat... even kumquat, orange and whisky marmalade. There's a tapas bar next door, too. *Children over seven & babies welcome. Half-board only on Saturday nights.*

Price	£80–£95. Half-board (obligatory Saturdays) £75–£100 p.p.
Rooms	5 doubles.
Meals	Lunch £15.50. Dinner £29.50–£39.50. Tapas bar & grill from £6.50.
Closed	25 & 26 December.
Directions	From Cheltenham, B4632 to Winchcombe. Restaurant on right. Drop off luggage, parking nearby.

Matthew Brown
High Street, Winchcombe,
Gloucestershire GL54 5LJ

Tel	01242 602366
Fax	01242 609046
Email	enquiries@wesleyhouse.co.uk
Web	www.wesleyhouse.co.uk

Lower Brook House

The village is a Cotswold jewel, saved from the tourist hordes by roads too narrow for coaches. Lower Brook is no less alluring. It was built in 1624 to house workers from one of the 12 silk mills that made Blockley rich. Step inside to find country rugs on flagged floors, Farrow & Ball paints on timber framed walls, mullioned windows, vases of flowers and piles of vintage luggage. Winter logs smoulder in a huge inglenook in the sitting room – slide onto the leather sofa and roast away. Bedrooms are crisply stylish with beautiful fabrics, pristine linen, bowls of fresh fruit and handmade soaps in super little bathrooms. All but one overlooks the garden; views fly up the hill. Outside, colour bursts from the beds in summer and a small lawn runs down to a shaded terrace for afternoon tea in good weather. Walks start from the door: you can be deep in the country within half a mile. Come back to Anna's delicious cooking, perhaps mustard and cress soup, roast loin of lamb, rhubarb crumble; breakfast treats include smoothies, croissants and freshly squeezed juice. *Minimum stay two nights at weekends.*

Price	£95-£175.
Rooms	6: 3 doubles, 2 twins, 1 four-poster.
Meals	Dinner, 3 courses, £25.
Closed	Christmas.
Directions	A44 west from Moreton-in-Marsh. At top of hill in Bourton-on-the-Water, right signed Blockley. Down hill to village, on right.

Julian & Anna Ebbutt
Lower Street, Blockley,
Gloucestershire GL56 9DS

Tel	01386 700286
Fax	01386 701400
Email	info@lowerbrookhouse.com
Web	www.lowerbrookhouse.com

Horse and Groom

You're at the top of the hill, so grab the window seats for views that pour over the Cotswolds. This is a hive of youthful endeavour, with brothers at the helm; Will cooks, Tom pours the ales, and a cheery conviviality flows throughout. Recently refurbished interiors mix the old (open fires, stone walls, beamed ceilings) with the new (halogen lighting, crisp coir matting, a cool marble bar), making this a fine place in which to hole up for a night or two. There are settles and boarded menus in the bar, stripped wooden floors and old rugs in the dining room. Tuck into homemade soups, Cornish sardines, Cotswold lamb, then sinful chocolate puddings. In summer you can eat in the back garden under the shade of damson trees and watch the chefs raid the kitchen garden for raspberries and strawberries, onions, fennel, broad beans and herbs. Bedrooms are nicely plush, smart but uncluttered, and those at the front are sound-proofed to minimise noise from the road. The red room is huge and comes with a sofa, while the garden room has doors that open onto the terrace. *Minimum stay two nights at weekends April-September.*

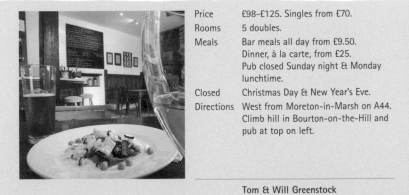

Price	£98–£125. Singles from £70.
Rooms	5 doubles.
Meals	Bar meals all day from £9.50. Dinner, à la carte, from £25. Pub closed Sunday night & Monday lunchtime.
Closed	Christmas Day & New Year's Eve.
Directions	West from Moreton-in-Marsh on A44. Climb hill in Bourton-on-the-Hill and pub at top on left.

Tom & Will Greenstock
Bourton-on-the-Hill, Moreton-in-Marsh,
Gloucestershire GL56 9AQ

Tel	01386 700413
Fax	01386 700413
Email	info@horseandgroom.info
Web	www.horseandgroom.info

The Cotswold House Hotel

Cotswold House is no ordinary hotel. It may be expensive, but it is also dazzling, one of those rare hotels that sets the trends that others follow. As if to prove the point, everywhere you go something wonderful looms into view, be it idyllic gardens, a fancy bar in Ferrari red leather, or huge Italian stone baths in some of the suites. Bedrooms are divine – you could write a book about them – all presented in Sunday-best fabrics, with cashmere throws on giant beds and contemporary art hanging on the walls (one has a leather jacket framed behind glass). There are pillow menus, coffee machines, flat-screen TVs, breakfast in bed. Suites are astonishing, some with open fires in the room, others with hot tubs on private terraces. As for the bathrooms, expect the best, maybe a steam room, a shower for two, fibre-optic coloured lights hanging in bunches above free-standing baths. Tear yourself away – no mean feat – to discover smouldering fires, light sculptures in the cocktail bar, a stone terrace for afternoon tea, and a brasserie and restaurant for seriously good food. *Minimum stay two nights at weekends.*

Price	£245–£295. Cottage rooms £385. Suites £450–£725. Singles from £150.
Rooms	30: 20 doubles, 7 suites, 3 cottage rooms.
Meals	Brasserie meals from £10. Dinner £49.50
Closed	Never.
Directions	From Oxford, A44 north for Evesham. 5 miles after Moreton-in-Marsh, right on B4081 to Chipping Campden. Hotel in square by town hall.

Ian & Christa Taylor
The Square, Chipping Campden,
Gloucestershire GL55 6AN

Tel	01386 840330
Fax	01386 840310
Email	reception@cotswoldhouse.com
Web	www.cotswoldhouse.com

The Malt House

In the middle of a refreshingly untouched Cotswold village, a place that so echoes to the past you almost expect the vicar to call for tea. Still much in evidence is that very English ritual of sipping gin in a lovely setting: the garden has its own 'gin and tonic' bench! And a thatched summer house for afternoon tea, a walled kitchen garden that grows figs and soft red fruits, and a perfect croquet lawn by a sweet stream. The house has a mellow grandeur: polished wooden floors, walls of shimmering gold and an inglenook fireplace at its heart. Bedrooms, all enticing, have mullioned windows, sloping floors, gilt mirrors, elegantly refurbished bathrooms, a collection of exotic *objets trouvés* and… perhaps a fireplace or doors onto the garden. This is a quintessential English country house with a personal feel – everything ticks over beautifully, Judi's smile is warm and her breakfasts will keep you smiling for days. For lunch and dinner you can't do better than the Churchill Arms at Paxford, two miles up the road. *Minimum stay two nights at weekends April-October.*

Price	£128-£135. Singles from £85. Suite from £150.
Rooms	7: 1 double, 4 twins/doubles, 1 four-poster, 1 suite.
Meals	Pub 1 mile. Dinner by arrangement (min. 12 people).
Closed	Christmas.
Directions	From Oxford, A44 through Moreton-in-Marsh; right on B4081 north to Chipping Campden. Entering village, 1st right for Broad Campden. Hotel 1 mile on left.

Judi Wilkes
Broad Campden, Chipping Campden , Gloucestershire GL55 6UU

Tel	01386 840295
Fax	01386 841334
Email	info@malt-house.co.uk
Web	www.malt-house.co.uk

The Dial House

Bourton — Venice of the Cotswolds — is bisected by the river Windrush; willow branches bathe in its waters, the odd duck preens for tourists. Dial House is equally alluring, a sublime retreat set back from the high street. It dates to 1698, but skip past the trim lawns and hanging baskets and find the old world made new. Mullioned windows and stone fireplaces shine warmly, the fire crackles with glee, armchairs are dressed in Zoffany colours, Cole & Son wallpaper sparkles on some walls. You're in the heart of the village with a peaceful garden at the back in which to escape the summer hordes. You can eat here in good weather or just pull up a deckchair and read in the sun. There are stripped floors in the restaurant, cool colours in the bar, old oils on the walls. Bedrooms come in different shapes and sizes. Try for those in the main house (rich colours, teardrop chandeliers, chunky four-posters, perhaps a claw-foot bath), or the coach house (airy and colourful with silky quilts and the odd exposed stone wall). There's fabulous food, too, so don't come to diet. Heaven. *Minimum stay two nights at weekends.*

Price	£110–£180. Suite £190.
	Half-board (min. 2 nights) from £72 p.p.
Rooms	13: 9 doubles, 3 four-posters, 1 suite.
Meals	Lunch, 2 courses, from £10.50.
	Dinner, 3 courses, from £30.
	Packed lunch available.
Closed	Never.
Directions	From Oxford, A40 to Northleach, right on A429 to Bourton. Hotel set back from High St opp. main bridge.

Jane & Adrian Campbell-Howard
The Chestnuts, Bourton-on-the-Water,
Gloucestershire GL54 2AN

Tel	01451 822244
Fax	01451 810126
Email	info@dialhousehotel.com
Web	www.dialhousehotel.com

Bibury Court Hotel

A Jacobean mansion that stands next to the church in one of Gloucestershire's loveliest villages. The six-acre garden is reason enough to come; it's utterly English, with croquet on the lawn, clipped yew hedges, a rose arbour flanked by beds of lavender and the serene river Coln ambling past on one side. You can fish from its banks or follow the footpath into glorious country; just wonderful. A very friendly place, grand, but not stuffy. There's a panelled drawing room for afternoon teas, a conservatory for indulgent breakfasts and a smart dining room for serious dinners; in summer, life spills out onto the stone terrace for sundowners in a scented garden. Antiques are scattered about: oak chests, mahogany dressers, writing desks and oil paintings by the score. A refurbishment is underway to remove all trace of the 1980s, but it wouldn't matter if it wasn't; what wins here is the relaxed atmosphere and the kind staff. Bedrooms tend to be large, with mullioned windows, old radiators, parkland views, crisp linen, the odd four-poster and a grand piano in the suite. *Minumum stay two nights at weekends April-September.*

Price	£150–£190. Suite £230. Singles from £125.
Rooms	18: 5 four-posters, 1 suite, 12 twins/doubles.
Meals	Lunch from £12.50. A la carte dinner from £30.
Closed	Never.
Directions	West from Burford on B4425. Cross bridge in village and house signed right along high street.

Robert Johnston
Bibury,
Gloucestershire GL7 5NT

Tel	01285 740337
Fax	01285 740660
Email	info@biburycourt.com
Web	www.biburycourt.com

The Peat Spade

Hampshire is as lovely as any county in England, deeply rural with lanes that snake through glorious countryside. As if to prove the point, the Peat Spade serves up a menu of boundless simplicity and elegance. First there's this dreamy thatched village in the Test valley, then there's the inn itself, packed to the gunnels with lip-licking locals for Sunday lunch in early February (and there's a 4pm sitting to satisfy demand). A Roberts radio on the bar brings news of English cricket, gilt mirrors sparkle above smouldering fires, fishing rods hang from the ceiling (fish the Test while you're here) and a pith helmet sits in an alcove. There's a horseshoe bar, flowers everywhere, varnished wood floors and claret walls. Upstairs, a snug residents' sitting room, a roof terrace for summer breakfasts and a couple of bedrooms above the bar. Others are in next-door Peat House, all are as lovely as you'd expect. Fired Earth colours, sisal matting, big wooden beds, Roberts radios, crisp white linen – the works. There's no space left to describe how utterly wonderful the food is, but be assured it is.

Price	£110.
Rooms	6 doubles.
Meals	Lunch & dinner £5–£25.
Closed	Christmas Day.
Directions	A3057 north from Stockbridge, then left after a mile for Longstock. In village.

Lucy Townsend & Andy Clarke
Longstock, Stockbridge,
Hampshire SO20 6DR

Tel	01264 810612
Fax	01264 811078
Email	info@peatspadeinn.co.uk
Web	www.peatspadeinn.co.uk

The Greyhound

There's a Michelin star in the restaurant, an easy elegance in the bedrooms and jumping brown trout in the river Test, which flanks one side of the garden. It's one of the loveliest chalkstreams in the country, a site of pilgrimage for those who like to cast a fly on lazy afternoons. The inn has a couple of rods on its 300-yard stretch; have some luck and they'll smoke your catch or cook it for supper. No hot food in the garden; instead, wonderful hampers of terrine, charcuterie, salad and wine that are brought to you with crisp white napkins and proper crockery. Chef John Howe offers year-round treats, perhaps black bream, Gressingham duck or fillet of beef – the best of English perfectly cooked. Open fires smoulder under low beamed ceilings, so pick up a newspaper and flop into a sofa. Bright and airy bedrooms upstairs fit the bill perfectly: exposed brick and timber walls, crisp Egyptian cotton, mohair blankets, beautifully upholstered armchairs and smart monsoon showers. Stockbridge is a delight, the sort of country town you find in a Jane Austen novel.

Price	£85-£120. Singles from £65.
Rooms	8: 4 twins, 3 doubles, 1 single.
Meals	Lunch & dinner £6-£36.
Closed	Christmas Day & New Year's Day.
Directions	A303, A34 south, then A30 into Stockbridge. Pub on right on west end of high street.

John Howe
31 High Street, Stockbridge,
Hampshire SO20 6EY

Tel	01264 810833
Fax	01264 810833
Email	enquiries@thegreyhound.info
Web	www.thegreyhound.info

Chewton Glen

Chewton Glen is one of England's loveliest country-house hotels. It opened in 1964 with eight bedrooms; now it has 58. Despite this growth it still remains wonderfully intimate and hugely welcoming, and, with a ratio of two staff to every guest, there's sublime service too. As for the hotel, it has everything you could ever want: a pillared swimming pool, a hydrotherapy spa, plunge pools and treatment rooms, a small golf course, a tennis centre and vast parkland gardens. Beauty at every turn, be it in the fabric of a sofa in one of the sitting rooms or afternoon tea served on the croquet terrace. Bedrooms are exemplary, as their price demands. Some come in warm country-house style, others bask in contemporary flair. Expect the best: marble bathrooms, private balconies, designer fabrics, faultless housekeeping. Fires burn, Wellington boots wait at the front door, five gardeners work minor miracles. Exquisite food, too, and a pianist who plays at dinner each evening. The beach is a 20-minute walk, and you can ride in the New Forest. Hard to beat. *Minimum stay two nights at weekends.*

Price	£290–£467. Suites £467–£1,250.
Rooms	58: 35 twins/doubles, 23 suites.
Meals	Lunch £17.50–£24.50. Dinner, 3 courses, £62.50. Light meals available throughout the day.
Closed	Never.
Directions	A337 west from Lymington. Through New Milton for Christchurch. Right at r'about, signed Walkford. Right again; hotel on right.

Andrew Stembridge
Christchurch Road, New Milton, Hampshire

Tel	01425 275341
Fax	01425 272310
Email	reservations@chewtonglen.com
Web	www.chewtonglen.com

Westover Hall

A small-scale country house by the sea with levels of service that surpass most others. Views from the back stretch across the Solent to the Isle of Wight, so sip champagne cocktails in the sunroom before supper, spill out into the garden for afternoon tea or follow the path down to the beach – and the private beach hut. Inside, oak panelling astounds, not least in the hall, which soars up to a minstrels' gallery. A fire burns in an opulent sitting room, tartan curtains mix with leather stools in the bar, and a huge bay window in the restaurant looks out to sea (though excellent food holds your attention and you may not notice). Bedrooms upstairs may be pricey but they're lavish too. Go for the bigger rooms (two are small); those at the front have long views across to the Needles. Enjoy gilt mirrors, antique beds, grand armoires and smart sofas – and crisp linen, marble bathrooms, waffle bathrobes and flat-screen TVs. Excellent art hangs on the walls. There's great walking, too; drop down to the sea and follow the fabulous coastal path. *Minimum stay two nights at weekends.*

Price	£200-£260. Half-board from £135 p.p.
Rooms	12: 8 doubles, 2 twins, 1 family, 1 suite.
Meals	Light lunch £15-£20. Dinner, 3 courses, £40. Tasting menu £60.
Closed	Rarely.
Directions	A337 west from Lymington, then B3058 to Milford-on-Sea. Through village; house on left.

Christine & David Smith
Park Lane, Lymington,
Hampshire SO41 0PT

Tel	01590 643044
Fax	01590 644490
Email	info@westoverhallhotel.com
Web	www.westoverhallhotel.com

Master Builder's House Hotel

By the river Beaulieu, in timeless, end-of-the-road, postcard-pretty Buckler's Hard, the Master Builder's has the feel of a well-heeled yacht club. The hotel shares this blissful spot with two rows of cottages still lived in by workers of the nearby Montagu Estate, and was the modest home of Master Shipwright Henry Adams who built many of the warships that fought at Trafalgar. The ancient slipways that launched the ships still survive; now yachts and sailing boats glide past on their way to the Solent following the route taken by Nelson's fleet two centuries before. Bedrooms in the modern wing are lavish; pricier rooms in the older, more characterful part of the hotel have river views (bring the binoculars). There's a traditional pub full of yachties in summer, a hall that seems to tumble down to the water, a restaurant with a view and a terrace for summery meals. The staff are excellent and the food is quite something. Work off lunch with a one-hour walk upstream past marshland and birdlife to Beaulieu. Wonderful.

Price	£175–£235. Singles from £130.
Rooms	25 twins/doubles.
Meals	Lunch from £19.95; bar lunch from £4.95. Dinner from £32.50.
Closed	Rarely.
Directions	From Lyndhurst, B3056 south past Beaulieu turn, then 1st left, signed Bucklers Hard. Hotel signed left after 1 mile.

Sally Elcoate
Bucklers Hard, Beaulieu,
Hampshire SO42 7XB

Tel	01590 616253
Fax	01590 616297
Email	res@themasterbuilders.co.uk
Web	www.themasterbuilders.co.uk

The Bridge at Wilton

Built in 1740, the large white-painted house with partially walled gardens slopes down to the river with views of Ross-on-Wye and an abundance of trees. At the front, a fairly busy road – but once inside you won't notice it. Mike and Jane have worked hard over the last two years and have (almost) rid the place of woodchip. Now there are wide elm planks and newly-laid slate on the floor, leather sofas and cheery yellow walls hung with modern oils. A small conservatory overlooks the garden – two acres with a mainly cottage feel and a well-kept lawn and tables with parasols running down to the river where you can fish. The food here is superb: lamb from the next village, Herefordshire beef, Gloucester Old Spot belly and cheek, and vegetables and fruit, home or locally grown. Smart (but not swish) bedrooms over two floors of rather wonky walls and beams have some antique beds, new mattresses, patchwork quilts, easy chairs and pristine slate-floored bath and shower rooms. There are endless outdoor water sports to hurl yourself into, lovely walks and delightful snoops around town. Then back for tea and cakes.

Price	£96–£120.
Rooms	9 twins/doubles.
Meals	Lunch & dinner, 3 courses, £30.
Closed	Never.
Directions	End of M50, follow A40. At 3rd roundabout take left marked Ross-on-Wye. Approx 150 yds on left.

Michael & Jane Pritchard
Wilton, Ross-on-Wye,
Herefordshire HR9 6AA

Tel	01989 562655
Email	info@bridge-house-hotel.com
Web	www.bridge-house-hotel.com

Wilton Court

A Grade-II listed stone house with a Grade-I listed mulberry tree; in season, its berries are turned in sorbets and pies. The house dates to 1510 and looks out across the river to Wye; herons dive, otters swim, kingfishers nest. Roses ramble on the outside, happy guests potter within. This may not be the fanciest place in the book, but Roger and Helen go the extra mile, and, with good prices, a pretty position on the river and a restaurant popular with locals, Wilton Court has won itself a devoted following. Bedrooms upstairs come in different shapes and sizes. Splash out on the more expensive ones for watery views, William Morris wallpaper, lots of space, perhaps a four-poster. A couple of rooms are small, but so are their prices and you can lose yourself in the rest of the hotel. Drop down for a drink in the smart panelled bar, then nip across to the airy conservatory/dining room for super food, perhaps tiger prawns in garlic butter or rack of Welsh lamb with rosemary mash. A small garden across the lane drops down to the river for summer sundowners. *Minimum stay two nights at weekends.*

Price	£90–£140. Suite £120–£160. Singles from £75. Half-board from £65 p.p. (min 2 nights).
Rooms	10: 3 doubles, 5 twins/doubles, 1 four-poster, 1 family suite.
Meals	Lunch from £9.75. Dinner, 3 courses, about £30. Sunday lunch £14–£17.50.
Closed	Never.
Directions	South into Ross at A40/A49 roundabout. 1st right into Wilton Lane. Hotel on right.

Roger & Helen Wynn
Ross on Wye,
Herefordshire HR9 6AQ

Tel	01989 562569
Email	info@wiltoncourthotel.com
Web	www.wiltoncourthotel.com

Glewstone Court Country House Hotel & Restaurant

Grand, yet relaxed enough to have no rule book. Bill does front of house, Christine cooks brilliantly, both are charming and fun. There's faded elegance and an easy conviviality in the drawing room bar, with squashy sofas and an open log fire in front of which resident dogs lie. The centre of the house is early Georgian, with a stunning staircase that spirals up to a galleried and porticoed landing; some of Christine's award-winning textile art pieces are on display here, as well as in the art gallery restaurant. Good-sized bedrooms are warm, comfortable and traditional with pleasant furniture and excellent lighting. The Rose Room is wonderful, the Victoria Room is magnificent. All look over fruit orchards to the Wye Valley and the Forest of Dean beyond, while in the garden an ancient cedar of Lebanon shades the croquet lawn and an antique fountain quietly serenades. Dine in the art gallery restaurant or outside in good weather. Most food is locally sourced – the Hereford beef is exceptional – some organic, some from the potager garden. Heaven for those in search of the small and friendly.

Price	£115-£132. Singles £58-£99.
Rooms	8: 5 doubles, 1 four-poster, 1 single, 1 suite.
Meals	Lunch & dinner à la carte. Sunday lunch £18.
Closed	25-27 December.
Directions	From Ross-on-Wye, A40 towards Monmouth, right 1 mile south of Wilton r'bout, for Glewstone. Hotel on left after 0.5 miles.

Christine & Bill Reeve-Tucker
Glewstone, Ross-on-Wye,
Herefordshire HR9 6AW

Tel	01989 770367
Fax	01989 770282
Email	glewstone@aol.com
Web	www.glewstonecourt.com

Moccas Court

Glorious Moccas. Sweep down the drive, plunge into ancient parkland, pass a 12th-century Norman church and discover this thrilling mansion. The river Wye flows past serenely behind; you can fish from its banks, or follow a path down to the red cliffs and spy on peregrine falcons. As for the interiors, enormous stately rooms come in classical design: stripped wood floors and a Broadwood piano forte in the music room; library steps and a moulded marble fireplace for open fires in the sitting room; original wallpaper in the circular dining room. Windows open onto balustraded terraces that lead down to the river. Bedrooms (two big, three huge) have Zoffany wallpapers, Jane Churchill fabrics, gigantic beds, mahogany dressers, padded window seats, the original 1785 shutters... the very best. Those at the front look towards the deer park where an enclosed fallow herd have run since Norman times (now they eat the garden) and the Moccas beetle is found nowhere else. Ben's cooking hits the spot: perhaps goat's cheese salad, rack of lamb, lemon tart. Exceptional.

Price	£140–£195.
Rooms	5: 4 twins/doubles, 1 double.
Meals	Dinner, 3 courses, £35.
	Picnic lunch £7, by arrangement.
Closed	Christmas and New Year.
Directions	South from Hereford on A465, then west on B4352 to Moccas. Right by stone cross in village, 200 yds to drive, signed.

Ben & Mimi Chester-Master
Moccas, Hereford, Herefordshire HR29LH

Tel	01981 500019
Fax	01981 500095
Email	info@moccas-court.co.uk
Web	www.moccas-court.co.uk

Priory Bay Hotel

Medieval monks thought Priory Bay special, so did Tudor farmers and Georgian gentry; all helped to mould this tranquil landscape. Parkland rolls down from the main house and tithe barns to a ridge of trees. The land then drops down to a long, clean sandy beach and a shallow sea, ideal for families; fishermen land their catch here for the freshest grilled seafood. Huge rooms in the house mix classical French and contemporary English styles. The sun-filled drawing room has tall windows; exquisite rococo-style chairs obligingly face out to sea, and afternoon cream teas by the winter log fire are a treat. There's a lovely brasserie for breakfast — tall windows, old parquet floors, fine murals on the wall. Bedrooms in the main house are luxurious; some have a fresh and modern feel, others oak panelling, maybe a crow's nest balcony and telescope. Bedrooms in the outbuildings are less enticing but less pricey. Andrew is a humorous host, and a supporter of the organic movement. The swimming pool is floodlit and the grounds support falcon and red squirrel, and the odd golfer. *Minimum stay two nights at weekends.*

Price	£90–£270. Singles from £50. Half-board £70–£160 p.p.
Rooms	25: 16 twins/doubles, 2 family, 7 cottages for 2, 4 or 6.
Meals	Lunch £18.50. Dinner £29.50. Picnic hampers available.
Closed	Rarely.
Directions	From Ryde, B3330 south through Nettlestone, then left up road, signed to Nodes Holiday Camp. Entrance on left, signed.

Andrew Palmer
Priory Drive, Seaview,
Isle of Wight PO34 5BU

Tel	01983 613146
Fax	01983 616539
Email	enquiries@priorybay.co.uk
Web	www.priorybay.co.uk

Seaview Hotel

Everything here is a dream. You're 50 yards from the water in a small seaside village that sweeps you back to a nostalgic past. Locals pop in for a pint, famished yachtsmen step ashore for a meal, those in the know drop by for a luxurious night in indulging rooms. This small hotel manages to be all things to all men, making it one of the most inclusive places in this book. The pitch pine bar has a roaring fire and every conceivable nautical curio nailed to its walls, the terrace buzzes with island life in summer, the restaurants hum with the contented sighs of happy diners. The whole show is orchestrated by Andrew and a battalion of kind staff, who book taxis, carry bags, send you off in the right direction. Interior designer Graham Green oversaw the fabulous refurbishment; some rooms come in super-smart country-house style (upholstered four-posters, padded headboards), others are more contemporary (Farrow & Ball colours, very fancy bathrooms). Don't miss the food; the crab ramekin is an island institution, and the fish comes fresh from the sea. *Minimum stay two nights at weekends.*

Price	£120–£199.
Rooms	Main house: 14 twins/doubles, 3 four-posters. Seaview Modern: 4 doubles, 3 twins/doubles.
Meals	Lunch & dinner £5–£30.
Closed	Never.
Directions	From Ryde, B3330 south for 1.5 miles. Hotel signed left.

Andrew Morgan
High Street, Seaview,
Isle of Wight PO34 5EX

Tel	01983 612711
Fax	01983 613729
Email	reception@seaviewhotel.co.uk
Web	www.seaviewhotel.co.uk

The Hambrough

You look out on a carpet of sea rolling off towards France. Splash out on the best rooms and you get a balcony – the Hambrough's equivalent of the royal box. There are loungers and tables and they'll bring up your breakfast, freshly juiced oranges and a plate of peeled fruits, then bacon and eggs with coffee and toast. Rooms are exquisite with huge beds, high ceilings, espresso machines and LCD TVs. Mosaic bathrooms are faultless (underfloor heating, thick white bathrobes, the deepest baths); from those on the top floor you can gaze out to sea as you bathe. Despite all this the Hambrough's chief passion is its food. Come down for champagne cocktails at the bar, then dig into seared scallops with a pea bavoise, fillet of pork with a ravioli of braised cheek, chocolate clafoutis with white chocolate ice cream. Back upstairs you'll find your bed turned down and a bowl of popcorn in case you want to watch a movie. Ventnor, an old-fashioned English seaside town, is worth exploring. Don't miss the botanic gardens or Osborne House, Queen Victoria's favourite home. *Minimum stay two nights at weekends.*

Price	£130–£200.
Rooms	7 doubles.
Meals	Lunch from £7. Dinner from £25. 8-course tasting menu £45.
Closed	Never.
Directions	A3055 into Ventnor. On western edge of town, south into Hambrough Rd, following blue sign to police station. House on left overlooking sea.

Jo dos Santos
Hambrough Road, Ventnor,
Isle of Wight PO38 1SQ

Tel	01983 856333
Fax	01983 857260
Email	info@thehambrough.com
Web	www.thehambrough.com

The George Hotel

The position is fabulous, with the old castle on one side, the sea at the end of a lovely lawn dotted with umbrellas, and the centre of the island's oldest town just beyond the front door. Handy if you're a corrupt governor intent on sacking passing ships: Admiral Sir Robert Holmes moved here for that very reason in 1668, demolishing a bit of the castle to improve his view. The house has been rebuilt since Sir Robert's day but a grand feel most definitely lingers: the entrance is large, light and stone-flagged, the drawing room is beautifully traditional – tapestry cushions, velvet drapes, big old oils, a stag's head, a roaring fire. Bedrooms refurbished in Colefax and Jane Churchill are smartly panelled and immaculate; one has a huge four-poster, two have timber balconies with views out to sea. You dine in the brasserie – busy, bright and with wonderful views of the Solent. Dig even deeper into your pocket and charter a private boat to take you to lunch at their other hotel on the mainland. A gracious and atmospheric hotel, perfectly run. *Minimum stay two nights at weekends.*

Price	£180–£255. Singles from £130.
Rooms	15 twins/doubles.
Meals	Brasserie lunch & dinner from £25. Dinner, 3 courses, £46.50. Restaurant closed Sundays & Mondays.
Closed	Rarely.
Directions	Lymington ferry to Yarmouth, then follow signs to town centre.

Jeremy Wilcock
Quay Street, Yarmouth,
Isle of Wight PO41 0PE

Tel	01983 760331
Fax	01983 760425
Email	res@thegeorge.co.uk
Web	www.thegeorge.co.uk

The Bell Hotel

Sandwich is a gem – if you've never been, come and see why. It's tiny, dates to the 12th century, was prosperous in Tudor times and has timber-framed houses dotted all over town. The Bell stands opposite the old town gate, the river Stour running past to one side on its way to sea. You can follow it down to Sandwich Bay (there's a shortcut across Royal St George's golf course). Oak revolving doors swing you through into a grand world of shimmering golden hues, logs smouldering on the fire and vintage luggage piled up in a corner. Open-plan interiors flow from restaurant to conservatory to bar. All are smart and airy, with blond wood floors and halogen lighting giving a warm feel; doors open onto a terrace in summer. Delightfully stylish bedrooms come in different sizes; the bigger ones with river views are fabulous, but all have the same cool colours, crisp white linen, sparkling bathrooms, digital radios and wireless internet access. Canterbury and its cathedral is a 20-minute drive. Don't miss Broadstairs, a pretty seaside town preserved in an elegant past. *Minimum stay two nights at weekends May-October.*

Price	£109–£135. Suites £165–£195. Singles from £85.
Rooms	34: 22 twins/doubles, 4 family, 6 suites, 2 singles.
Meals	Lunch & dinner £5–£25.
Closed	Never.
Directions	A2, M2, A299, then A256 south. Follow signs into Sandwich. Over bridge, under gatehouse, & hotel on left by river.

Matt Collins
The Quay, Sandwich,
Kent CT13 9EF

Tel	01304 613388
Fax	01304 615308
Email	reservations@sandwich.theplacehotels.co.uk
Web	www.bellhotelsandwich.co.uk

Wallett's Court Country House Hotel & Spa

Wallett's Court is *old*. Odo, half-brother of William the Conqueror, lived on the land in Norman times, then Jacobeans left their mark in 1627 but it still retains the feel of a small country house without any pretension. Gorgeous architectural features have been retained; ancient red-brick walls in the drawing room, an oak staircase with worn, shallow steps in the hall and a huge log fire on chilly days. Bedrooms in the main house are big with four-posters and heaps of character, those in the barn and cottages are smaller and quiet. Above the spa complex — indoor pool, sauna, steam room and massage, aromatherapy and treatment suite — four excellent, contemporary suites have been added. There are tennis, a terrace with views towards a distant sea and white cliffs within a mile for breezy walks, rolling mists and wheeling gulls. First class cooking from Steven Harvey is a delight; try caramelised Rye Bay scallops with medallions of wild rabbit or Folkestone-landed sea bass. Walk it off with a stroll around the lovely garden. *Minimum stay two nights at weekends half-board.*

Price	£129–£169. Singles £109–£139.
Rooms	16: 12 twins/doubles, 4 suites.
Meals	Sunday lunch £23. Dinner £40.
Closed	Christmas.
Directions	From Dover, A2/A20, then A258 towards Deal, then right, signed St Margaret's at Cliffe. House 1 mile on right, signed.

Chris, Lea & Gavin Oakley
Westcliffe, St Margaret's at Cliffe,
Dover, Kent CT15 6EW

Tel	01304 852424
Fax	01304 853430
Email	stay@wallettscourt.com
Web	www.wallettscourt.com

The Place Camber Sands

A boutique motel, a 'diner with rooms' – friendly, stylish, very well priced. Across the road, enormous dunes tumble down to Camber Sands for two miles of uninterrupted beach, so watch the kite-surfing or walk west to the river Rother and follow it up to Rye (three miles). Back at The Place there's lots to enjoy. Comfy bedrooms come in light colours, with crisp white linen, digital radios, big mirrors, a sofa if there's room; spotless bathrooms provide for a good soak after a hard day on the beach. Doors in the airy brasserie open onto a dining terrace in summer, where monthly changing menus offer local and organic food when possible, with Dover sole and mackerel sourced from a sustainable fishing fleet in Hastings. Try Rye Bay scallops, Romney Marsh lamb's liver with bacon, treacle tart with crème Anglaise. There's a good DVD library at reception; great photography on the walls; big family rooms (busy in summer); and body boards and beach towels for those who want to ride the waves. Lympne Castle is close, as is Dungeness; Derek Jarman's Prospect Cottage is worth a look. *Minimum stay two nights at weekends.*

Price	£80–£120. Family £99–£140.
Rooms	18: 15 doubles, 3 family.
Meals	Lunch & dinner £5–£30.
Closed	Never
Directions	A259 east from Rye, then B2075 for Camber & Lydd. On left after 2 miles.

Morné Potgieter
New Lydd Road, Camber Sands,
Camber, Rye, Kent TN31 7RB

Tel	01797 225057
Fax	01797 227003
Email	enquiries@theplacecambersands.co.uk
Web	www.theplacecambersands.co.uk

Romney Bay House

The library look-out upstairs has a telescope so you can spy France on a clear day. Designed by Clough Williams-Ellis – creator of Portmeirion – for American film star Hedda Hopper, this ethereal dreamscape is as stunning as the photograph suggests. Inside, the whole place has a lingering 1920s house-party feel. Rooms are not huge but filled with chintzy cushions, sofas to sink into, frills and flowers, an honesty bar, a drawing room with a merry fire in winter, a conservatory for cream teas, and a dining room where Clinton prepares locally-caught fish and meat reared in Kent. He and Lisa swapped jobs in London hotels for the 'good life' in Kent; they have impeccable pedigrees and know what works… whether you're here for a conference, a wedding or a great escape, you'll appreciate their relaxed perfectionism. Bedrooms are the best feature; all are elegant, with pretty furniture, half-testers, sleigh beds and long views – some to the links, some to the sea. Go for a bracing shingleside walk, try your hand at croquet or drive the fairways on the neighbouring green. *Minimum stay two nights at weekends.*

Price	£90–£160. Singles £65–£95.
Rooms	10: 8 doubles, 2 twins.
Meals	Dinner, 4 courses, £39.50. Cream teas from £5.95.
Closed	One week at Christmas.
Directions	M20 junc. 10, A2070 south, then A259 east through New Romney. Right to Littlestone; left at sea & on for 1 mile.

Clinton & Lisa Lovell
Coast Road,
Littlestone,
New Romney,
Kent TN28 8QY

Tel   01797 364747
Fax   01797 367156

The Relish

It's not just the super-comfy interiors that make The Relish such a tempting port of call. There's a sense of generosity here: a drink on the house each night in the sitting room; tea and cakes on tap all day; free internet throughout. This is a grand 1850s merchant's house on the posh side of town with warmly contemporary interiors; wind up the cast-iron staircase to find bedrooms that make you smile. Hypnos beds with padded headboards wear crisp white linen and pretty throws. You get a sense of space, a sofa if there's room, big mirrors and fabulous bathrooms. All are great value for money. Downstairs there are candles on the mantelpieces above an open fire, stripped wooden floors and padded benches in the dining room; in summer, you may decamp onto the terrace for breakfast, a four-acre communal garden stretching out beyond. You're one street back from Folkestone's cliff-top front for huge sea views; steps lead down to smart gardens and the promenade. There are takeaway breakfasts for early Eurostar departures and a local restaurant guide in every room. Brilliant. *Minimum stay two nights at weekends in summer.*

Price	£85–£115. Four-poster £130. Singles from £59.
Rooms	10: 2 twins/doubles, 6 doubles, 1 four-poster, 1 single.
Meals	Restaurants nearby.
Closed	22 December–2 January.
Directions	In centre of town, from Langholm Gardens, head west on Sandgate Road. 1st right into Augusta Gardens/Trinity Gardens. Hotel on right.

Chris & Sarah van Dyke
4 Augusta Gardens, Folkestone,
Kent CT20 2RR

Tel	01303 850952
Fax	01303 850958
Email	reservations@hotelrelish.co.uk
Web	www.hotelrelish.co.uk

Cloth Hall Oast

Sweep up the rhododendron-lined drive to this immaculate Kentish oast house and barn. For 40 years Mrs Morgan lived in the 15th-century manor next door where she tended both guests and garden; now she has turned her perfectionist's eye upon these five acres. There are well-groomed lawns, a carp-filled pond, pergola, summer house, heated pool and flower beds – two of orange and yellow, four all-white. Light shimmers through swathes of glass in the dining room; there are off-white walls and pale beams that soar from floor to rafter. Mrs Morgan is a courteous hostess and an excellent cook; discuss in the morning what you'd like for dinner – duck with cherries, sole Véronique – later you dine at an antique table gleaming with crystal and candelabra. There are three bedrooms for guests: a four-poster on the ground floor, a triple and a queen-size double on the first. Colours are soft, fabrics are frilled but nothing is busy or overdone; you are spoiled with good bathrooms and fine mattresses, crisp linen and flowered chintz. And there's a sitting room for guests, made snug by a log fire on winter nights.

Price	£130.
Rooms	3: 1 four-poster, 1 triple, 1 double.
Meals	Dinner, 4 courses, £26.
Closed	Christmas.
Directions	Leave village with windmill on left, taking Golford Road east for Tenterden. After a mile, right, before cemetery. Signed right.

Mrs Katherine Morgan
Cranbrook,
Kent TN17 3NR
Tel   01580 712220
Fax   01580 712220
Email   clothhalloast@aol.com

The Inn at Whitewell

You'll be hard-pressed to find anywhere better. The inn sits just above the river Hodder with views across parkland to rising fells in the distance. Merchants used to stop at this old deerkeeper's lodge and fill up with wine, food and song before heading north through notorious bandit country; superb hospitality is still assured but the most that will hold you up today is a stubborn sheep. Back at the inn the bar is welcoming and the fire roars; grab a paper and a pint and watch the world from here. Bedrooms are large, warm and cosy, some with fabulous Victorian showers, others with deep cast-iron baths and Benesson fabrics; all have art and Bose music systems, some have peat fires; the biggest look onto the river. Families and dogs are welcome here and the food is a treat; Whitewell fish pie is their most famous dish and the restaurant – with fabulous views – serves à la carte treats like fillet of beef for two. There are also seven miles of private fishing, even their own well-priced Vintner's. Mildly eccentric, great fun.

Price	£96–£137. Singles £70–£98. Suite £120–£162.
Rooms	23: 9 twins/doubles, 13 four-posters, 1 suite.
Meals	Bar meals from £5.50. Dinner, à la carte, from £25.
Closed	Never.
Directions	M6 junc. 31a, B6243 east through Longridge, then follow signs to Whitewell for 9 miles.

Charles Bowman
Whitewell, Clitheroe,
Lancashire BB7 3AT

Tel	01200 448222
Fax	01200 448298
Email	reception@innatwhitewell.com
Web	www.innatwhitewell.com

Hipping Hall

You get a bit of time travel at Hipping Hall: 15th-century bricks and mortar, 21st-century lipstick and pearls. It's all the result of a total refurbishment, and funked-up classical interiors elate. Zoffany wallpaper in a swanky sitting room, red leather armchairs in an airy bar, and varnished floorboards in the old hall — overlooked by a minstrels' gallery, its ceilings open to the rafters. The flagged conservatory is home to an ancient well and opens onto a courtyard where tables and chairs are scattered in summer. Upstairs, fabulous bedrooms in various shades of white contrast with the vibrant colours of the ground floor. Fine ivory carpets, white leather headboards, muslin canopies and padded window seats. Bathrooms are the best and come in slate or creamy limestone, some with power showers, others with deep baths too, all with fluffy white towels and bathrobes. As for the food, expect something special, perhaps English asparagus with a garlic purée, fillet of veal with glazed sweetbreads, then caramelised pears with a prune and armagnac ice cream. *Minimum stay two nights at weekends.*

Price	£145-£280. Singles from £105. Half-board from £97.50 p.p.
Rooms	9: 7 doubles, 2 twins/doubles.
Meals	Lunch, 3 courses, £25. Dinner, 3 courses, £42.50.
Closed	1st two weeks in January.
Directions	M6 junc. 36, then A65 east. House on left, 2.5 miles after Kirkby Lonsdale.

Andrew Wildsmith
Cowan Bridge, Kirkby Lonsdale,
Lancashire LA6 2JJ

Tel	01524 271187
Fax	01524 272452
Email	info@hippinghall.com
Web	www.hippinghall.com

Entry 127 Map 6

Allington Manor

Minutes from the old A1 but as quiet as a mouse, the village has a pub, a post office and the Viking Way; the walking is stunning. The Dutch-influenced Jacobean manor house is elegant yet solid, and filled with suits of armour, ancient weaponry and old oak furniture. Walk straight into the large square hall with flagstone floor (this part of the house goes back to 1630) and Garth, Kate or Sam will bring you tea or a drink in an elegant sitting room, complete with twinkling fire on cold days. There isn't a trace of fuss or pomposity so you'll quickly feel at home. Proper home cooking (local beef or lamb) is served in a long dining room with ancient brick walls and lovely stone mullioned windows overlooking the garden. Bedrooms are large with soothing colours (blues, greens, creams), one with an enormous wooden bâteau bed, another with a four-poster; two have free-standing roll top baths to pamper yourself in. Curtains and fabrics are thickly lined and generous – not that there's any noise to mask. Walk, cycle, visit Lincoln or Nottingham, see Belvoir Castle or Burleigh House – all are near.

Price	£95–£140. Singles from £85.
Rooms	3: 2 doubles, 1 four-poster.
Meals	Dinner with wine, £22.50–£27.50.
Closed	Never.
Directions	From Nottingham, A52 to Sedgebrook; left into Allington. House on right, just before pub & post office.

Garth Vincent
Allington, Grantham,
Lincolnshire NG32 2DH

Tel	01400 282574
Fax	01400 282658
Email	enquiries@allingtonmanor.co.uk
Web	www.allingtonmanor.co.uk

base2stay

Stylish rooms and attractive prices make this is a brilliant base for those in town for a night or longer. Part hotel, part serviced apartments, the idea here is to keep things simple and pass on the savings to guests. You won't find a bar or a restaurant, you will find a tiny kitchen cleverly concealed behind cupboard doors in each room. You get fridges, kettles, sinks and microwaves, so chill drinks, make your own breakfast or zap up an evening meal. Super rooms come in a cool contemporary style and offer a lot for the money: halogen lighting, crisp white linen, air conditioning – and flat-screen TVs through which you can surf the internet at no cost (there are points for laptops too). Watch movies on demand, play games, raid the hotel's music library for 1,500 tracks. Bathrooms are equally good and come with limestone tiles, big white towels and power showers. There's a directory of local restaurants that deliver to the door, 24-hour reception, good security, a daily maid service. Some rooms interconnect, and a base breakfast box can be delivered to your door. Bars, clubs and restaurants are close.

Price	£99–£119. Triples £149. Suites £189. Singles £89.
Rooms	67: 32 twins/doubles, 13 triples, 18 singles, 4 suites, all with kitchenettes.
Meals	Base breakfast £4.50.
Closed	Never.
Directions	Tube: Earl's Court (3-minute walk). Bus: 74, 328, C1, C3. Parking £30 a day, off-street.

Nassar Khalil
25 Courtfield Gardens,
Earl's Court, London SW5 0PG

Tel	0845 262 8000
Fax	0845 262 8001
Email	info@base2stay.com
Web	www.base2stay.com

Temple Lodge

Temple Lodge, once home to the painter Sir Frank Brangwyn, is sandwiched between a courtyard and a lushly landscaped garden. The peace here is remarkable, making it a very restful place – simple yet human and warmly comfortable. Michael and a small devoted team run it with quiet energy. You breakfast overlooking the garden, there are newspapers to browse, no TVs, and bedrooms to make you smile. Expect crisp linen, garden views and prints of famous artists (each room is named after a painter). They are surprisingly stylish – clean, uncluttered with a hint of country chic – and represent exceptional value for money. None has its own bathroom; if you don't mind that, you'll be delighted. The Thames passes by at the end of the road (you can follow it down to Kew); the Riverside Studios – for theatre and film – are close. The Gate Vegetarian Restaurant is nearer still, ten paces across the courtyard; it is a well-known eatery and was Brangwyn's studio, hence the enormous artist's window. The house is a non-denominational Christian centre with two services a week, which you may take or leave as you choose.

Price	£50–£65. Singles £40.
Rooms	9: 1 double, 3 twins, 5 singles all sharing 3 baths & 1 shower.
Meals	Continental breakfast included. Restaurants nearby.
Closed	Never.
Directions	Tube: Hammersmith (3-minute walk). Bus: 9, 10, 27, 295.

Michael Beaumont
51 Queen Caroline Street,
Hammersmith,
London W6 9QL

Tel	020 8748 8388
Fax	020 8748 8322
Email	templelodgeclub@btconnect.com

The Cranley Hotel

In a charming quiet London street of brightly painted Georgian houses, the Cranley has a neat front garden with wooden tables and chairs, clipped bay trees and wide steps up to the front door. The hall leads straight into a calm drawing room with deep Wedgewood blue walls, original fireplaces, good antiques, coir carpets and the odd lively rug. Bedrooms, some with private terraces, are extremely comfortable: pale carpets, lilac walls, embroidered headboards over huge beds, plain cream curtains with bedspreads to match, pretty windows and cream-tiled snazzy bathrooms. Robes and slippers, state-of-the-art technology, air conditioning, prettily laid tables for breakfast if you don't want it in bed... A cream tea with warm scones and clotted cream in the afternoon comes with the package, along with champagne and canapés at 7pm before you go off to an excellent local restaurant booked by the friendly staff. South Kensington and the Kings Road are both close.

Price	£175–£320. Singles £140–£250. Suites £380–£450..
Rooms	39: 19 doubles, 6 twins, 8 four-posters, 4 singles, 2 suites.
Meals	Continental breakfast £12.50; full English £17.50. Restaurants nearby.
Closed	Rarely.
Directions	Tube: Gloucester Road (4-minute walk). Bus: 49, 74, C1. Parking: £30 a day, off-street.

	Lory Caprioli
	10 Bina Gardens,
	South Kensington, London SW5 0LA
Tel	020 7373 0123
Fax	020 7373 9497
Email	info@thecranley.com
Web	www.steinhotels.com/thecranley

Entry 131 Map 3

Knightsbridge Green Hotel

This hotel has a battalion of faithful guests who return for the central position, the reasonable prices, the unfussy rooms and the ever-present Paul. He aims to greet everyone personally during their stay, and if you meet him by the lift, he'll chauffeur you up to your room. This is a family-owned hotel, you can expect a warm welcome. Spotlessly clean bedrooms tend to be fairly standard but they are surprisingly big, and while the design may be simple it is also pleasing. There are marble bathrooms, off-white walls, canvas curtains, air-conditioning and flat-screen TVs. The hotel doesn't have a bar, but it is licensed and drinks are brought to your room, as is breakfast: croissants, freshly squeezed orange juice, and bacon and sausages from Harrods if you pay the extra. Rooms at the back have been vibrantly decorated to make up for the lack of light in the stairwell and a couple are nicely old-fashioned with warm floral fabrics and big beds (ever-popular with long-standing guests). All things Knightsbridge are on your doorstep, and the tube is a hop and a skip across the road. *Children under five free.*

Price	£150–£175. Singles £115–£130. Suites £175–£205.
Rooms	28: 4 twins, 5 doubles, 7 singles, 12 suites.
Meals	Breakfast £5.50–£12.
Closed	Never.
Directions	Train: Victoria (to Gatwick); Paddington (to Heathrow). Tube: Knightsbridge (2-minute walk). Bus: 9, 10, 14, 19, 22, 52, 137. Parking: £30 a day, off-street.

Paul Fizia
159 Knightsbridge,
London SW1X 7PD

Tel	020 7584 6274
Fax	020 7225 1635
Email	reservations@thekghotel.com
Web	www.thekghotel.co.uk

Searcy's Roof Garden Bedrooms

A one-off, the sort of place you could only find in England. From the street you enter directly a 1927 freight elevator (it's had a facelift), then ascend three floors – by-passing Searcy's, the 160-year-old catering company whose headquarters these are. Step out of the lift and into comfy bedrooms decorated in country-house style – Laura Ashley wallpaper, canopied beds, fresh flowers, a smattering of antiques. Bathrooms can be eccentric – two rooms have baths in the actual bedroom – but most are tucked away snugly and all come with waffled robes, big white towels and Molton Brown treats. Breakfast is brought to you with a complimentary newspaper and is occasionally accompanied by the sound of the Household Cavalry passing below. In summer, you can move outside and scoff croissants on a very pretty roof garden surrounded by pots of colour. Air-conditioning and wireless internet run throughout, dry cleaning can be arranged, and if you want to eat in, local restaurants will deliver. Excellent value close to Harrods, and Hyde Park a short stoll.

Price	£160. Singles £110. Suite £200.
Rooms	10: 7 twins/doubles, 2 singles, 1 family suite.
Meals	Continental breakfast included. 24–hour room service (light meals). Restaurants nearby.
Closed	Christmas & New Year.
Directions	Train: Victoria (to Gatwick). Tube: Knightsbridge (5-minute walk). Bus: 9, 10, 14, 19, 22, 52, 74, 137. Parking: £35 a day, off-street.

Demitrius Neofitidis
30 Pavilion Road, Knightsbridge,
London SW1X 0HJ

Tel	020 7584 4921
Fax	020 7823 8694
Email	rgr@searcys.co.uk
Web	www.30pavilionroad.co.uk

The Goring

The Goring is a London institution, an epitome of Englishness, with a dining room for Dover sole or breast of pheasant and a bar for oysters and champagne. Ninety-six years a hotel with a Goring ever at the helm, it is the oldest family-run hotel in London (built in 1910) and the first hotel in the world to have central heating and a bathroom in every room. It is both grand and charming, proud of its traditions – there's still a cocktail party for guests on Sunday evenings – and, thanks to its warm, professional staff, is a happy ship indeed. Enter a world of marble floors, yellow walls and chandeliers by the dozen. Liveried doormen at reception dress like (friendly) Napoleonic generals; one of them, Peter, has worked here for 30-odd years. The restaurant has recently been refurbished by David Linley, good-sized bedrooms are smart and traditional with a dash of flair: crisp linen, woollen blankets, plush carpets and fresh flowers; bathrooms are wood-panelled, rooms at the back have gorgeous garden views. Two minutes from Buckingham Palace – yet Beeston Place is peaceful for such a central position.

Price	£260–£505. Singles £210–£325. Suites £345–£620.
Rooms	71: 47 twins/doubles, 17 singles, 7 suites.
Meals	Breakfast £18.50. Lunch £29.75. Dinner £40.
Closed	Never.
Directions	Train: Victoria (to Heathrow). Tube: Victoria (2-minute walk). Bus: 2, 8, 16, 36, 38, 52, 73, 82. Parking £30 a day, off-street.

Jeremy Goring
Beeston Place, Victoria,
London SW1W 0JW

Tel	020 7396 9000
Fax	020 7834 4393
Email	reception@goringhotel.co.uk
Web	www.goringhotel.co.uk

No. 5 Maddox Street

This is the epitome of London cool, a zen-sleek, highly discreet, central London wonderland. The style is effortless. Terrazzo stone stairs sweep you up past polished plaster walls sealed with beeswax. In reception, tropical fish laze behind a wall of glass; in other rooms, you can lounge on leather cushions in front of a fire. Every suite is an apartment; two have planted terraces, several have decked balconies and the one in the loft has a leather staircase. Be seduced by pressed-bamboo floors, waffled bathrobes, oil-burners throughout. There are glass tables, chenille sofas, creamy leather headboards, lacquered walls. Beds are dressed in crisp Egyptian cotton and faux-fur blankets, limestone bathrooms delight. Every conceivable electronic gadget: CD and DVD players, fax machines, private lines... think of it, they've got it. And there are four different types of breakfast (including 'Vitality' for hangovers), great room service from local restaurants, private kitchens stuffed with goodies (from ice cream to champagne) and chefs who come in to cook for you. Bond Street and Soho are on the doorstep.

Price	£260–£370. £475 for 4. £640 for 6.
Rooms	12 suites: 9 for 2, 2 for 4, 1 for 6, all with living rooms & kitchens.
Meals	Breakfast £10–£20. Room service.
Closed	Never.
Directions	Train: Paddington (to Heathrow). Tube: Oxford Circus (4-minute walk). Bus: 3, 6, 8, 12, 15, 23, 88, 159. Parking: £30 a day, off-street.

Tracy Lowy
Mayfair,
London W1S 2QD

Tel	020 7647 0200
Fax	020 7647 0300
Email	no5maddoxst@living-rooms.co.uk
Web	www.no5maddoxst.com

Entry 135 Map 3

22 York Street

The Callis family live in an 1820s, Georgian-style townhouse in W1 – not your average London residence and one that defies all attempts to pigeonhole it. There may be 12 bedrooms but you can still expect the feel of home. Michael keeps things friendly and easy-going, which might explain the salsa dancing lessons that once broke out at breakfast – a meal of great conviviality taken around a curved wooden table in a big, bright kitchen. Here, a weeping ficus tree stands next to the piano, which, of course, you are welcome to play. There's always something to catch your eye, be it the red-lipped oil painting outside the dining room or the old boots on the landing. Wooden floors run throughout. The house has a huge sitting room (original high ceilings, shuttered windows) with sofas, books and backgammon. Bedrooms, spotless and comfy, have Provençal eiderdowns, good beds, country rugs, perhaps a piano or a chaise-longue. There's a computer for guests to use, WiFi throughout. Madame Tussaud's, Regent's Park and Lord's are close. A very friendly place.

Price	£120. Family rooms £162. Singles from £89.
Rooms	12 twins, doubles, family & single rooms (1 with separate bathroom).
Meals	Pubs/restaurants nearby.
Closed	Never.
Directions	Train: Paddington (to Heathrow). Tube: Baker Street (2-minute walk). Bus: 2, 13, 30, 74, 82, 113, 139, 274. Parking: £25 a day, off-street.

Michael & Liz Callis
Marylebone,
London W1U 6PX

Tel	020 7224 2990
Fax	020 7224 1990
Email	mc@22yorkstreet.co.uk
Web	www.22yorkstreet.co.uk

The Royal Park Hotel

Paddington is just round the corner, while the fabulous Italian fountains in Hyde Park are a three-minute stroll. These fine old houses are dignified and handsome; in this case, three houses rolled into one in a grand gesture of solidarity – but so discreetly that you would hardly know there was a hotel here at all. It is easy to imagine the carriages trundling up to the door in Victorian times. Inside, interiors shine. If you arrive at tea time you can dig into scones and jams in one of the two small drawing rooms. Champagne and canapés follow later 'on the house' – a lovely touch that encourages guests to chat. The bedrooms are impeccable, generous with their beds, handmade mattresses, crisp sheets, woollen blankets, plump pillows and elegant bathrooms – and with almost every conceivable minor luxury (robes, flat-screen TVs, air conditioning). Hundreds of restaurants wait on your doorstep, but stroll across the park in the summer for dinner at the Cadogan Hotel, part of this family. Kind staff look after you well and make sure you get what you want.

Price	£115–£270. Singles £115–£170. Suite £265–£300.
Rooms	48: 28 doubles, 5 twins, 2 four-posters, 2 singles, 11 suites.
Meals	Continental breakfast £12.50; full English £17.50. Restaurants nearby.
Closed	Rarely.
Directions	Train: Paddington (to Heathrow). Tube: Lancaster Gate; Paddington (both 4-minute walk). Bus: 7, 12, 15, 23, 27, 36, 94. Parking: £30 a day, off-street.

Gareth Rowlands
3 Westbourne Terrace, Lancaster Gate,
Hyde Park, London W2 3UL

Tel	020 7479 6600
Fax	020 7479 6601
Email	info@theroyalpark.com
Web	www.steinhotels.com/theroyalpark.com

Miller's

This is Miller's, as in the antique guides, and the collectibles on show in the first-floor drawing room make it one of the loveliest in this book. Continental breakfast is taken around a 1920s walnut table, while at night, cocktails are served on the house, a fire crackles in the carved-wood fireplace and a couple of hundred candles flicker around you. It is an aesthetic overdose, exquisitely ornate, every wall stuffed with gilt-framed pictures. An eclectic collection of regulars include movie moguls, fashion photographers, rock stars, even a professional gambler. An opera singer once gave guests singing lessons at breakfast. Wander at will and find an altar of Tibetan deities (well, their statues), a 1750s old master's chair, busts and sculptures, globes, chandeliers, plinths, rugs, and a three-legged chair stuffed on top of a Regency wardrobe. Things get moved around all the time, so expect the scene to change. Muralled walls in the hall were inspired by the Pope's palace at Avignon. Bedrooms upstairs are equally embellished; some bathrooms are minute. Wild extravagance in cool Notting Hill.

Price	£175–£270.
Rooms	8: 6 doubles, 2 suites.
Meals	Continental breakfast included. Dinner, 3 courses, about £30.
Closed	Never.
Directions	Train: Paddington (to Heathrow). Tube: Notting Hill Gate, Bayswater. Bus: 7, 23, 28, 31, 70. Parking: £25 a day, off-street.

Martin Miller
111a Westbourne Grove,
London W2 4UW

Tel   020 7243 1024
Fax   020 7243 1064
Email   enquiries@millersuk.com
Web   www.millersuk.com

Portobello Gold

A quirky gallery/pub, one of Alastair's favourites: Portobello Gold thrives on an easy-going, funky conviviality. You are swept in on a tide of local bonhomie; only the determinedly lonely could be lonely here. Drink great beers, roast away in front of an open fire, eat in the excellent restaurant where a glass roof opens in summer and canaries cackle in a jungle of foliage. There's art on the walls, live music on Sunday evenings, tables on the pavement from which to watch Portobello's fashionistas stroll by. Bedrooms tend to be small, like cabins on a boat, and those at the front can't escape the noise of a lively road below, but if you're after a cheap room in a friendly place on one of the hippest streets in London, you'll be happy; just don't expect the Ritz. The roof terrace apartment comes with putting green and barbecue, the new suite has an open fire and a world first: a foldaway four-poster. The cyber café is free to hotel guests, there are Trappist ales, Belgian beers, fancy wines available by the glass. All-day Sunday lunches are great fun, but make sure you pay: Bill Clinton didn't.

Price	£60-£90. Suite £120. Apartment £150-£170.
Rooms	8: 4 doubles, 2 twins/doubles, 1 suite, 1 apartment for 6.
Meals	Continental breakfast included; full English £7.50. Bar meals from £6. Dinner £20-£25.
Closed	Never.
Directions	Train: Paddington (to Heathrow). Tube: Notting Hill (5-min walk). Bus: 12, 27, 28, 31, 52, 328. Parking meters outside.

Michael Bell & Linda Johnson-Bell
95-97 Portobello Road,
Notting Hill, London W11 2QB

Tel	020 7460 4910
Fax	020 7229 2278
Email	reservations@portobellogold.com
Web	www.portobellogold.com

Europa House

Half a mile south the Grand Union Canal sweeps through Little Venice, but you may wish to spurn it for these idyllic communal gardens: three acres of weeping willows, well-kept lawns and absolute peace. The apartments are equally divine: big and airy, extremely comfy, nicely private (John Malkovich stayed here when filming *The Libertine*), all with sitting rooms, fully-equipped kitchens and marble bathrooms. The style is crisply uncluttered – glass tables, big sofas, spacious halls, trim carpets – and there's a refreshingly open-plan feel. Creamy walls soak up the light; comfortable beds wear Egyptian cotton. Two apartments have terraces, all come with hi-fis, DVD players, wireless internet connection and video entrance phones. You could cook for yourself (there are stores close by), but Clifton Road has an easy-going village feel and is stuffed with delis, cafés and irresistible shops... stroll down for breakfast at Vicki's, coffee at the Clifton Road Nursery, lunch at Raoul's. Maid service daily (Monday-Friday) and Regent's Park is close.

Price	£170 for 2. £255–£310 for 4.
Rooms	12 apartments: 1 for 2, 11 for 4.
Meals	Self-catering.
Closed	Never.
Directions	Train: Paddington (to Heathrow). Tube: Warwick Road; Maida Vale (both 5-minute walk). Bus: 6, 16, 46, 98. Parking: £15 a day, off-street.

Linda Campbell
79A Randolph Avenue,
Maida Vale, London W9 1DW

Tel	020 7724 5924
Fax	020 7724 2937
Email	linda@westminsterapartments.co.uk
Web	www.westminsterapartments.co.uk

Strattons

Nowhere is perfect, but Strattons comes close. It's one of the country's most eco-friendly hotels and if you arrive by public transport, you get a 10% discount on B&B. Silky bantams strut on the lawn, funky classical interiors thrill. Les and Vanessa met at art school and every square inch of their Queen Anne villa is crammed with mosaics and murals, marble busts, cow-hide rugs on stripped wood floors, art packed tight on the wall. It is an informal bohemian country-house bolthole of French inspiration in a small market town. Bedrooms are exquisite: a carved four-poster, a tented bathroom, Indian brocade and stained glass. There's trompe l'œil panelling, bespoke wallpaper and sofas by a log fire. Wonderful food in the candlelit restaurant (turn right by the chaise-longue) is all organic, perhaps nettle and barley broth, slow-cooked leg of Papworth lamb, rhubarb and ginger crème brûlée. Les talks you through the cheese board with great panache, and breakfast (toasted stilton, goat's cheese omelette) is equally divine. Don't miss the Brecks for cycle tracks through Thetford forest. *Minimum stay two nights at weekends.*

Price	£150–£175. Singles from £120. Suites from £200.
Rooms	10: 1 twin/double, 4 doubles, 5 suites.
Meals	Dinner, 4 courses, £40.
Closed	Christmas.
Directions	Ash Close runs off north end of market place between W H Brown estate agents & fish & chip restaurant.

Vanessa & Les Scott
4 Ash Close, Swaffham,
Norfolk PE37 7NH

Tel	01760 723845
Fax	01760 720458
Email	enquiries@strattonshotel.com
Web	www.strattonshotel.com

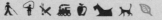

Fritton House Hotel

A small, chic, country-house hotel on the Somerleyton estate. Walks start from the back door, where paths lead out through sublime parkland and run down to Fritton lake. You can walk round it, row on it or take to the skies above it in a hot-air balloon. The building is 16th-century and was once a smuggler's inn; these days, warmly groovy interiors excite. Come for stripped wood floors, Cole & Son wallpapers, Farrow & Ball paints, sand-blasted beams. There's a smart drawing room at the front with super sofas, old shutters, country rugs and fresh flowers, then an airy bar and restaurant with leather armchairs, exposed brick walls and doors onto a gravelled terrace for views of the estate. Seriously indulging bedrooms flood with light and come with timber-framed walls, padded headboards and mahogany dressers. Beds are dressed in crisp white linen and warmed with Welsh wool blankets, while funky bathrooms have colourful resin floors, deep baths and power showers. Sheep graze in the fields around you, brasserie food keeps you happy and visits to Somerleyton can be arranged. Brilliant. *Minimum stay two nights at weekends in high season.*

Price	£130–£170. Singles from £90.
Rooms	9: 5 doubles, 2 twins/doubles all en suite; 1 double, 1 twin/double sharing bath (same-party bookings only).
Meals	Lunch from £8. Dinner, 3 courses, about £27.
Closed	Never.
Directions	From Beccles A143 north for Great Yarmouth. In Fritton, right, signed Fritton Lake. Hotel on right before lake.

Sarah Winterton
Church Lane, Fritton,
Norfolk NR31 9HA

Tel	01493 484008
Fax	01493 488355
Email	frittonhouse@somerleyton.co.uk
Web	www.frittonhouse.co.uk

The Norfolk Mead Hotel

The setting is enchanting, you can paddle your canoe from the bottom of the garden to the Broads, and there are day boats to be hired minutes from the hotel. But make time for these eight acres – lawns, trees, walled garden, pool, fish-stocked lake and a dinghy for messing about on the river. The sugar planter's house was built in 1740 – big, gracious, beautifully proportioned. Come for the food and the easy-going comforts of a country-house hotel. A coronet bedhead, a Victorian bath with brass fittings, a striped attic snug, and individual touches: ribboned sheaves of Norfolk lavender, a basket of primroses, a teddy on the pillows. There's a fine entrance hall with sofas and log fire, a bar that opens to the garden, and menus from a creative young chef who loves his kitchen. Food is light, delicate and much admired – partridge from Norfolk, mussels from Morston, whisky and orange jelly with hazelnut tuiles, perfect cheese biscuits (homemade). Jill's daughter Nicky can massage or manicure you, and the barn owl may hoot you to sleep. *Minimum stay two nights at weekends in high season.*

Price	£85–£160. Singles £70–£95. Suites £180–£190. Half-board from £72 p.p.
Rooms	15: 7 doubles, 3 twins, 1 garden suite, 2 cottage suites (each 1 double, 1 twin).
Meals	Sunday lunch £16.95. Dinner £32.50.
Closed	Rarely.
Directions	From Norwich, B1150 to Coltishall, over bridge; after 600 yds, bear right at petrol station, 1st right before church; down drive, signed.

Jill & Don Fleming
Coltishall, Norwich,
Norfolk NR12 7DN

Tel	01603 737531
Fax	01603 737521
Email	info@norfolkmead.co.uk
Web	www.norfolkmead.co.uk

Entry 143 Map 7

Saracens Head

A true country inn with nourishing food, real ale, good wines, an enchanting old courtyard walled garden, Norfolk's bleakly lovely coast – this is why people come here. But the food is the deepest seduction. Robert and his team cook up "some of Norfolk's most delicious wild and tame treats". Tuck into Morston mussels with cider and cream, pigeon, Cromer crab, venison. Vegetarians are pampered too. Then Robert works his own magic on old favourites such as bread and butter pudding... The bar is as convivial as a bar could be, a welcome antidote to garish pub bars with their fruit machines – Robert will have none of them. There's a parlour room for residents, decidedly civilised: terracotta walls with friezes, candles in bottles, a black leather banquette, open log fires. Retire to lovely bedrooms with bold colours, sisal floors, linen curtains, pretty touches; wake to a fabulous breakfast. The whole mood is of quirky, committed individuality – slightly arty, slightly unpredictable and in the middle of nowhere. *Minimum stay two nights & half-board only at weekends.*

Price	£90. Singles £50. Half-board from £75 p.p.
Rooms	6: 5 doubles, 1 twin.
Meals	Bar meals from £4.95. Dinner, 2 courses, about £17.
Closed	Christmas Day.
Directions	From Norwich, A140 past Aylsham, then left, for Erpingham. Don't bear right for Aldborough, go straight through Calthorpe. Over x-roads. On right after about 0.5 miles.

Robert & Rachel Dawson-Smith
Wolterton, Erpingham,
Norfolk NR11 7LX

Tel	01263 768909
Fax	01263 768993
Email	saracenshead@wolterton.freeserve.co.uk
Web	www.saracenshead-norfolk.co.uk

Byfords

The bustling market town of Holt is filled with unusual and interesting shops. In the middle of it all sits Byfords, its oldest building, made of brick and flint. Pass the tables and chairs on the pavement and walk in to the delicatessen, its wooden shelves brimming with wines, oils, jams, chutneys and coffees. The place hums with shoppers, here for the local meat and cheeses, and the coffee and homemade cakes in the busy café. Iain and Clair have gone for the wow factor in the bedrooms: enormous Vi-sprung mattresses on oak bed frames, sumptuous linen and plump silky cushions, soft leather chairs on polished wood floors. Modern music systems and Bang & Olufsen TVs abound, views of higgledy-piggledy roof tops are an unexpected surprise, and bathrooms are luxurious with underfloor heating, fluffy towels and drenching showers. Downstairs windows and doors are flung open for outdoor dining when it's warm, and there's a green oak conservatory with open-plan kitchen, so you can watch your supper being cooked. Evenings are peaceful, with candles and log fires on winter nights. *Minimum stay two nights at weekends.*

Price	From £130. Singles from £90.
Rooms	9 + 1: 7 doubles, 2 twins.
	1 self-catering apartment for 5.
Meals	Dinner, 3 courses, from £21.
Closed	Christmas Day.
Directions	A148 to Cromer. Holt is approx. a 20-minute drive past Fakenham. Car parking available for residents.

	Iain Wilson
	1-3 Shirehall Plain, Holt,
	Norfolk NR25 6BG
Tel	01263 711400
Email	queries@byfords.org.uk
Web	www.byfords.org.uk

The Globe Inn

Set back a few hundred yards from the bustling harbour at Wells, the Globe sits on leafy Buttlands Green. The 19th-century coaching inn has been given a thorough makeover by Tom and Polly Coke, who transformed the Victoria on their family estate at Holkham: expect the best. It's a big hit with visitors and locals alike, and the bar – fire, coastal photographs, wooden floor – emanates a happy buzz. The restaurant, in New England style, already has a good reputation for food that's unstuffy, fresh, modern; lots comes from the estate. Only the season's finest will do: spring lamb with fresh asparagus, roasted seabass, game pie. On sunny days you can take your plates and your pints (Adnams and Woodfordes) out into the red-brick courtyard, bordered on one side by a vast, as yet, unused, ballroom. Bedrooms are a treat – as fresh and untraditional as can be, with oak floors, blinds, sumptuous velvet cushions and terrific bathrooms with big baths and monsoon showers. Children and dogs love it too, what with child-size pies, crabbing on the quay and walks on the hugest beach ever. *Minimum stay two nights at weekends.*

Price	£65-£130.
Rooms	7: 5 doubles, 2 twins.
Meals	Lunch & dinner, 2 courses, from £14.
Closed	One week in February.
Directions	North from Fakenham on B1105. Hotel on green in centre of village.

	Tom Coke
	The Buttlands, Wells-next-the-Sea,
	Norfolk NR23 1EU
Tel	01328 710206
Fax	01328 713249
Email	globe@holkham.co.uk
Web	www.globeatwells.co.uk

The Victoria at Holkham

A little English whimsy on Norfolk's magical coast. Outside you find a brick-and-flint pub on the Holkham estate (birthplace of the Bowler hat); inside you discover a country-house inn of colonial inspiration. Tom (Viscount) Coke and his wife Polly have renovated from top to toe, so come for stone flags, stripped wood, a buzzing bar and candles everywhere. Flop into deep sofas in front of the fire, slip through Rajasthani doors for supper in the orangery, or head into the garden for a pint on the terrace. Bedrooms upstairs (pricey at weekends) vary in size, but all are grand and gracious with warm colours, silky curtains, country rugs, antique furniture. The four-poster is so high there's a stool to help you up, while those at the front have views over the marshes to a ridge of coastal pine. If you want pure peace escape to fabulous self-catering follies on the estate (The Triumphant Arch is magnificent). An avenue of trees leads down to Holkham's super beach, so hire bikes, grab a picnic, listen to the geese fly overhead. And don't miss the Big Hall in summer. *Minimum stay two nights at weekends.*

Price	£120-£160. Suite £145-£225. Singles from £100. Children in parents' room £15. Lodges £120-£220.
Rooms	10 + 4: 9 doubles, 1 attic suite. 4 self-catering lodges for 2-6.
Meals	Lunch & dinner £15-£40. Bar meals available all day.
Closed	Never.
Directions	On A149, 2 miles west of Wells-next-the-Sea.

Phil Lance
Park Road, Wells-next-the-Sea,
Norfolk NR23 1RG

Tel	01328 711008
Fax	01328 711009
Email	victoria@holkham.co.uk
Web	www.victoriaatholkham.co.uk

The Hoste Arms

Nelson was once a local. Now it's farmers, fishermen and film stars who jostle at the bar and roast away on winter evenings in front of a roaring fire. In its 300-year history the Hoste has been a court house, a livestock market, a gallery and a brothel. These days it's more a pleasure dome than an inn and even on a grey February morning it was buzzing with life, the locals in for coffee, the residents polishing off leisurely breakfasts, diligent staff attending a wine tasting. The place has a genius of its own with warm bold colours, armchairs to sink into, panelled walls, its own art gallery. Fabulous food can be eaten anywhere and anytime, so dig into honey-glazed ham hock, fillet of English beef or seared sea bass with fennel. In summer, life spills out onto tables at the front or you can dine on the terrace in the garden at the back. Rooms are all different: a tartan four-poster, a swagged half-tester, leather sleigh beds in the Zulu wing and Fired Earth bathrooms. Burnham Market is gorgeous, the north Norfolk coast is on your doorstep (bring your shrimping net). And don't miss the ladies' loo!

Price	£122-£216. Singles from £90. Suites £158-£273. Half-board from £73 p.p.
Rooms	36: 12 twins/doubles, 4 four-posters, 5 singles, 7 suites. Zulu wing: 5 doubles, 3 suites.
Meals	Lunch from £10. Dinner from £25.
Closed	Never
Directions	A148 east from King's Lynn for Fakenham. Left after 2 miles onto B1153, then right at Great Bircham; onto B1155 for Burnham Market.

Emma Tagg
The Green, Burnham Market,
Norfolk PE31 8HD

Tel	01328 738777
Fax	01328 730103
Email	reception@hostearms.co.uk
Web	www.hostearms.co.uk

The White Horse

The setting is magical. Fabulous views reach across the marshes and the water with its moored boats, and dinghies sailing on the evening high tide. The coastal path starts right outside this neat inn with its benches, parasols and troughs of plants and flowers: the perfect spot for a pint after a stroll. Inside, the fishy theme continues but in a modern, crisp way: seascape colours, natural materials, pictures of boats, bowls of pebbles and shells, big windows to the views. Bedrooms are beautiful. Those upstairs capture the ever-changing light; those on the ground floor have wide doors which open onto flower-filled terraces and are decorated in duck-egg blues, with tongue and groove and a New England feel. From here you can spot oyster catchers, ringed plovers, several species of tern and, in winter, geese; don't forget your binoculars. Dine by candlelight on mussels and oysters from yards away, homemade bread and ice creams, all of it as local and seasonal as possible. Watch the sun slide over the marshes as you unwind, slowly. *Minimum stay two nights at weekends.*

Price	£100-£140.
Rooms	15: 9 doubles, 4 twins, 2 family.
Meals	Lunch & dinner, 2 courses, from £16.
Closed	Never.
Directions	Midway between Hunstanton & Wells-next-the-Sea on A149 coast road.

Cliff Nye
Brancaster Staithe,
Norfolk PE31 8BY

Tel	01485 210262
Fax	01485 210930
Email	reception@whitehorsebrancaster.co.uk
Web	www.whitehorsebrancaster.co.uk

Entry 149 Map 7

Titchwell Manor

A warmly contemporary hotel, with vast tracts of sandy beach at the end of a one-mile lane. In between is Titchwell's famous RSPB sanctuary; guided tours include the May dawn chorus – stupendous stuff. The hotel, a brick and flint Victorian manor, has a cool and airy colonial feel, with stripped wooden floors and the odd tumbling fern in a gorgeous conservatory dining room. The hotel stands on the road; views from bedrooms at the front drift across fields, then out to sea. Beach towels and picnics can be arranged, so wander down to Brancaster Bay for lazy days, then return for fabulously fresh food in the restaurant: mussels, oysters and lobster straight from the sea, venison from the Holkham estate. Bedrooms are light and airy, nicely uncluttered, with warm colours, crisp linen and padded headboards. Delicious courtyard rooms open onto a parterre herb garden of lavender and rosemary and come with tiled floors, neutral colours, flat screen TVs and super bathrooms; some at the back have French windows onto small terraces. There's a walled garden for afternoon tea and golf all along the coast.

Price	£108–£170. Singles from £74. Half-board from £75 p.p.
Rooms	25: 7 doubles, 2 twins. Stables: 4 doubles. Herb Garden: 10 doubles, 2 twins/doubles.
Meals	Lunch from £5. Sunday lunch £17. Picnics £10. Dinner, à la carte, about £30.
Closed	Never.
Directions	North from King's Lynn on A149 to Titchwell. Hotel in village on right.

Margaret Snaith
Titchwell, Brancaster,
Norfolk PE31 8BB

Tel	01485 210221
Fax	01485 210104
Email	margaret@titchwellmanor.com
Web	www.titchwellmanor.com

Gin Trap Inn

An actor and a lawyer run this old English Inn. Steve and Cindy left London for the quiet life and haven't stopped since, adding a conservatory dining room at the back and giving the garden a haircut. The Gin Trap dates to 1667, while the horse chestnut tree that shades the front took root in the 19th century; a conker championship is in the offing. A smart whitewashed exterior gives way to a beamed locals' bar with a crackling fire and the original dining room in Farrow & Ball hues. Upstairs, you find three delightful bedrooms in smart country style. Two have big bathrooms with claw-foot baths and separate showers, all come with timber frames, cushioned window seats, Jane Churchill fabrics and the odd chandelier; walkers will find great comfort here. Come down for delicious food: Norfolk mussels, local sausages, then poached winter fruits. Ringstead – a pretty village lost in the country – is two miles inland from the coastal road, thus peaceful at night. You're on the Peddars Way, Sandringham is close and fabulous sandy beaches beckon.

Price	£70–£120. Singles from £60.
Rooms	3 doubles.
Meals	Lunch from £7.
	A la carte dinner from £20.
Closed	Rarely.
Directions	North from King's Lynn on A149. Ringstead signed right in Heacham. Pub on right in village.

Steve Knowles & Cindy Cook
High Street, Ringstead,
Hunstanton,
Norfolk PE36 5JU

Tel	01485 525264
Email	thegintrap@hotmail.co.uk
Web	www.gintrapinn.co.uk

Entry 151 Map 7

The Kings Head Hotel

A Victorian inn – once part of the Sandringham estate – with a red roof and trimmed lawns. The sort that you might imagine would be filled with chintz. Instead, find a huge hall with a cream ceramic floor, low spotlights, suede sofas and, at the end, a dramatic wall with squares of bevelled mirror above a black table with black and gold lamps. The restaurant is pure Notting Hill with square white plates and stainless steel; the food is excellent – locally-sourced as much as possible – and includes plenty of Cromer crab. Grab a comfortable chair in the wooden-floored drawing room with cream rugs and a roaring fire, or relax in your bedroom. It will be swish and spotless with a huge bed, a flat-screen TV, a port decanter, fresh milk and homemade biscuits. Bathrooms are filled with goodies from the Natural Soap Company in Wells. An acre of lawned garden has a play area for kids and plenty of places for sitting, so eat out here if the weather is fine. Staff are efficient and naturally smiley, so you'll be well looked after.

Price	£125–£220. Singles from £75.
Rooms	12 doubles.
Meals	Lunch £5.95–£12.95. A la carte dinner from £24.50.
Closed	Never.
Directions	From King's Lynn, A148 to Fakenham. Turn left on B1153 after Hillington village. Drive through Flitcham. As you come into Bircham, the hotel is on left hand side.

Mark Orton
Great Bircham,
Norfolk PE31 6RJ

Tel	01485 578265
Fax	01485 578635
Email	welcome@the-kings-head-bircham.co.uk
Web	www.the-kings-head-bircham.co.uk

No. 1 Sallyport

A boutique B&B that stands a stone's throw from Berwick's Tudor ramparts. Tiny lanes and cobbled alleyways sweep up to this 17th-century listed townhouse; step inside and you find seriously funky interiors. Bedrooms are wild – a fire and huge plasma screen in one, cherubs in a bay window in another. Wander at will and find leather sleigh beds, beautifully upholstered armchairs, shimmering Osborne & Little wallpaper, shiny hardwood floors. All rooms come with DVD players and a selection of films, Bose sound systems (bring some CDs), fridges in which to chill your wine (the house isn't licensed, so bring your own). Super-cool bathrooms, most with deluge showers, come with Fired Earth tiles and waffle bathrobes. Dinner can be arranged. Elizabeth used to have her own restaurant and will whisk up a feast, perhaps Dublin Bay prawns, leg of lamb casserole, warm orange tart; communal breakfast served in a cool country dining room are equally seductive. As for medieval Berwick, it was built by an Italian architect from Lucca and is far prettier than you might imagine. *Minimum stay two nights at weekends.*

Price	£95. Suites £130-£150.
Rooms	6: 2 doubles, 4 suites.
Meals	Packed lunch £7.50. Supper £12-£15. Dinner £35, by arrangement. BYO.
Closed	Never.
Directions	Leave A1 for A1167. Right at T-junc and over bridge into Berwick. Right into Marygate, right into West St, left into Bridge St and house on right.

Elizabeth Middlemiss
Off Bridge Street, Berwick-upon-Tweed,
Northumberland TD15 1EZ

Tel	01289 308827
Fax	01289 308827
Email	info@sallyport.co.uk
Web	www.sallyport.co.uk

Eshott Hall

Slip into graceful inertia for a weekend, or longer; take the slog out of a drive up to Scotland or ramble and yomp to your heart's content through (some say) the finest countryside in Britain with its dreamy castles and white beaches. Whatever the excuse, you will be indulged in this listed Palladian house. Bedrooms flourish fine linen, thick fabrics, restful colours; warm bathrooms have showers, large baths and grand views over the estate and its medieval woodland. You are only 20 minutes from Newcastle with its variety of shops, restaurants, galleries and theatres, but you are surrounded by wildlife (bats, deer, badgers and red squirrels). Ho and Margaret are passionate conservationists: ceramic floors, working shutters, a rare staircase and a stained-glass window designed by William Morris are just a few of the stunning architectural features. The garden is delightful with rare old trees, a Victorian fernery, a covered pergola and oodles of woodland trails. Enjoy local and seasonal food and vegetables from the walled garden by candlelight in the formal dining room or in the Lost Wing.

The estate's walled garden provides organic fruit and vegetables, hens range freely and for every guest that stays, a tree is planted in the Friend's Wood, a sustainable supply for harvest in 30-50 years. Each acre holds 500 trees, a mixed bag of hardwoods, conifers and birch to provide a habitat for wildlife, especially the red squirrel. Back at the hall, dairy produce is from a neighbouring farm, Cheviot beef and lamb come from local farmers, cereals are traditionally milled at Heatherslaw. There are organic Northumbrian beers as well as jams and preserves from the Tarset valley. As for the water, it comes from beneath your feet; Eshott stands above its own aquifer.

Price	£130. Singles £80.
Rooms	5: 4 doubles, 2 twins/doubles.
Meals	Dinner, 3 courses, £35. By arrangement.
Closed	22 December-5 January.
Directions	East off A1, 7 miles north of Morpeth, 9 miles south of Alnwick, at Eshott signpost. Hall gates approx. 1 mile down lane.

Ho & Margaret Sanderson
Morpeth,
Northumberland NE65 9EN

Tel	01670 787777
Fax	01670 787999
Email	thehall@eshott.co.uk
Web	www.eshotthall.co.uk

SPECIAL
GREEN ENTRY
see page 17

Entry 154 Map 9

The Pheasant Inn

A really super little inn, the kind you hope to chance upon. The Kershaws run it with great passion and an instinctive understanding of its traditions. The stone walls hold 100-year-old photos of the local community; from colliery to smithy, a vital record of its past. The bars are wonderful: brass beer taps glow, anything wooden — ceiling, beams, tables — has been polished to perfection and the clock above the fire keeps perfect time. The attention to detail is a delight, the house ales expertly kept: Timothy Taylor's and Theakston's Black Sheep. Robin cooks with relish, again nothing too fancy, but more than enough to keep a smile on your face — cider-baked gammon, grilled sea bass with herb butter, wicked puddings, Northumbrian cheeses; as for Sunday lunch, *The Observer* voted it the best in the North. Bedrooms in the old hay barn are as you'd expect: simple and cosy, good value for money. You are in the glorious Northumberland National Park — no traffic jams, no rush. Hire bikes and cycle round the lake, canoe or sail on it, or saddle up and take to the hills. *Minimum stay two nights at weekends.*

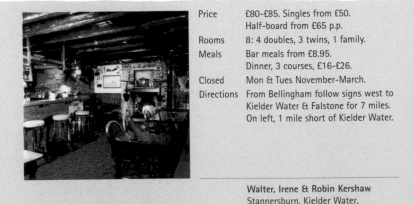

Price	£80-£85. Singles from £50. Half-board from £65 p.p.
Rooms	8: 4 doubles, 3 twins, 1 family.
Meals	Bar meals from £8.95. Dinner, 3 courses, £16-£26.
Closed	Mon & Tues November-March.
Directions	From Bellingham follow signs west to Kielder Water & Falstone for 7 miles. On left, 1 mile short of Kielder Water.

Walter, Irene & Robin Kershaw
Stannersburn, Kielder Water,
Northumberland NE48 1DD

Tel	01434 240382
Fax	01434 240382
Email	enquiries@thepheasantinn.com
Web	www.thepheasantinn.com

Lace Market Hotel

Follow the cobbled streets to the heart of the old town and there's the Lace Market Hotel, perfectly carved out of three Georgian houses next to St Mary's church. On Sunday mornings you can lie in bed and listen to heavenly voices soar. Swish, contemporary interiors are crisp and warm – not minimalist, just stylish. Bedrooms come in different sizes, all have American oak furniture, crisp white linen, clean lines and smoked glass. In several you can soak in the bath and look out on the old court house opposite, while suites come with chrome banisters, wraparound windows and raised platforms for big beds. Head downstairs for cocktails at a marble bar, then wander through to a mirrored restaurant and dine on the best of British – or pop in next door to the hotel's funky alehouse, where you can sit in comfy wing-backed armchairs under a red-brick vaulted roof and dine on bistro food. Work off any excess free of charge at local health club down the road, a stunning conversion of a Victorian railway station. Trendy bars, restaurants, shops and clubs are on your doorstep – come to have fun.

Price	£119–£139. Singles from £90. Suites £185–£239.
Rooms	42: 33 doubles, 6 singles, 3 suites.
Meals	Continental breakfast £9.95; full English £14.95. Lunch (Tues–Fri) from £11.95. Dinner, 3 courses, around £27 (not Sun).
Closed	Rarely.
Directions	From city centre follow brown signs for Lace Market, Galleries of Justice & St Marys Church. NCP behind hotel: £7 per 24 hours.

John Quero
29-31 High Pavement, Nottingham,
Nottinghamshire NG1 1HE

Tel	0115 8523232
Fax	0115 8523223
Email	stay@lacemarkethotel.co.uk
Web	www.lacemarkethotel.co.uk

Entry 156 Map 6

Langar Hall

Langar Hall is one of the most engaging and delightful places in this book – reason enough to come to Nottinghamshire. Imogen's exquisite style and natural joie de vivre make this a mecca for those in search of a warm, country-house atmosphere. The house sits at the top of a hardly noticeable hill in glorious parkland, bang next door to the church. Imo's family came here over 150 years ago. Much of what fills the house arrived then and it's easy to feel intoxicated by beautiful things: statues and busts, a pillared dining room, ancient tomes in overflowing bookshelves, a good collection of oil paintings. Bedrooms are wonderful, some resplendent with antiques, others with fabrics draped from beams or trompe l'œil panelling. Heavenly food, simply prepared for healthy eating, makes this almost a restaurant with rooms – you'll need to book if you want to enjoy Langar lamb, fish from Brixham, game from Belvoir Castle and garden-grown vegetables. In the grounds: medieval fishponds, canals, a den-like adventure play area and, once a year, Shakespeare on the lawn.

Price	£95–£185. Suite £210. Singles £80–£115.
Rooms	12: 7 doubles, 2 twins, 1 four-poster, 1 suite, 1 chalet for 2.
Meals	Lunch from £13.50. A la carte dinner about £30.
Closed	Never.
Directions	From Nottingham, A52 towards Grantham. Right, signed Cropwell Bishop, then straight on for 5 miles. House next to church on edge of village, signed.

Imogen Skirving
Langar,
Nottinghamshire NG13 9HG

Tel	01949 860559
Fax	01949 861045
Email	info@langarhall.co.uk
Web	www.langarhall.com

Falkland Arms

In a perfect Cotswold village, the perfect English pub. Five hundred years on and the fire still roars in the stone-flagged bar under a low-slung timbered ceiling that drips with jugs, mugs and tankards. Here, the hop is treated with reverence; ales are changed weekly and old pump clips hang from the bar. Tradition runs deep; they stock endless tins of snuff with great names like Irish High Toast and Crumbs of Comfort. In summer Morris Men jingle in the lane outside and life spills out onto the terrace at the front and into the lovely big garden behind. This lively pub is utterly down-to-earth and in very good hands. Dig into pork pies and plates of cheese in front of the fire or hop next door to the tiny beamed dining room for Paul's home-cooked delights. Bedrooms are cosy, some verging on snug; the attic room is wonderfully private. Brass beds and four-posters, maybe a bit of old oak and an uneven floor; you'll sleep well. The house is blissfully short on modern trappings, nowhere more so than in the bar, where mobile phones meet with swift and decisive action. Very special, book early for weekends.

Price	£80–£110.
Rooms	5 doubles.
Meals	Lunch & dinner: main courses £8–£15. Must book for dinner. Not Sunday evenings.
Closed	Never.
Directions	North from Chipping Norton on A361, then right onto B4022, signed Great Tew. Inn by village green.

Paul Barlow-Heal & Sarah-Jane Courage
Great Tew, Chipping Norton,
Oxfordshire OX7 4DB

Tel	01608 683653
Fax	01608 683656
Email	sjcourage@btconnect.com
Web	www.falklandarms.org.uk

The Kings Head Inn

About as Doctor Dolittle-esque as it gets. Achingly pretty Cotswold stone cottages around a village green with quacking ducks, a pond and a perfect pub with a cobbled courtyard. Archie is young, affable and charming with locals and guests, but Nic is his greatest asset – a milliner, she has done up the bedrooms on a shoestring and they look fabulous. All are different, most have a stunning view, some family furniture mixed in with 'bits' she's picked up, painted wood, great colours and lush fabrics. The bar is lively – not with music but with talk – so choose rooms over the courtyard if you prefer a quiet evening. Breakfast and supper are taken in the pretty flagstoned dining room (exposed stone walls, Farrow & Ball paints, pale wood tables), while you can lunch by the fire in the bar on devilled kidneys, sausage and mash, or perhaps fish pie; there are homemade puds and serious cheeses, too. Lovely unpompous touches like jugs of cow parsley in the loo. There's loads to do, antiques in Stow, golf at Burford, walking and riding in gorgeous country, even a music festival in June.

Price	£70–£125. Singles from £55.
Rooms	12: 10 doubles, 2 twins.
Meals	Lunch & dinner: main courses £9.95–£17.95. Bar meals from £4.
Closed	Christmas Day & Boxing Day.
Directions	East out of Stow-on-the-Wold on A436, then right onto B4450 for Bledington. Pub in village on green.

Archie & Nic Orr-Ewing
The Green, Bledington,
Oxfordshire OX7 6XQ

Tel	01608 658365
Fax	01608 658902
Email	kingshead@orr-ewing.com
Web	www.kingsheadinn.net

Burford House

Burford House is a delight, intensely personal, full of elegant good taste, relaxing, and small; small enough for Simon and Jane to influence every corner, which they do with ease and good cheer. Classical music and the scent of fresh flowers drift through beautiful rooms, all of which have been stylishly upgraded: oak beams, leaded windows, good fabrics, antiques, simple colours, log fires, immaculate beds, roll top baths and a little garden for afternoon teas. And there's an honesty bar, with homemade sloe gin and cranberry vodka to be sipped from cut-glass tumblers. Hand-written menus promise ravishing breakfasts and tempting lunches, and they will recommend the best places for dinner. Both are happy in the kitchen: Simon cooks and Jane bakes, and Cotswold suppliers provide honey, jams, smoked salmon and farmhouse cheeses. Jumble the cat is 'paws on', too. Unwind, then unwind a little more. Enchanting river walks start in either direction through classic English countryside. Guests return time after time. A perfect little find in a perfect Cotswold town. *Minimum stay two nights at weekends.*

Price	£125–£155. Singles from £85.
Rooms	8: 3 doubles, 2 twins, 3 four-posters.
Meals	Light lunch & afternoon tea (not Sundays). Pubs/restaurants in Burford.
Closed	Rarely.
Directions	In centre of Burford. Free on-street parking, free public car park nearby.

	Jane & Simon Henty
	99 High Street, Burford,
	Oxfordshire OX18 4QA
Tel	01993 823151
Fax	01993 823240
Email	stay@burfordhouse.co.uk
Web	www.burfordhouse.co.uk

Entry 160 Map 3

Old Parsonage Hotel

A country house in the city, with a lively bar for excellent meals, a rooftop terrace for afternoon tea and a hidden garden where you can sit in the shade and listen to the bells of St Giles. Step through an ancient front door to find logs smouldering in the original stone fire place, the papers spread out beneath an old carved window and a rich collection of classical art emblazoning the walls. Warm stylish bedrooms are scattered all over the place, some at the front (where Oscar Wilde entertained lavishly when he was sent down), others at the back in a sympathetic extension where some suites have French windows onto tiny balconies and a couple of the less-expensive rooms open onto private terraces. Expect Vi-sprung mattresses, flat-screen TVs, crisp white linen, spotless bathrooms and friendly staff on hand to advise. Oxford starts beyond the wall and the hotel owns a couple of bikes that you are free to spin off on. They also have a punt on the Cherwell and will pack you a picnic, so glide effortlessly past spire and meadow, then tie up for lunch.

Price	£160-£200. Suites £225.
Rooms	30: 25 twins/doubles, 4 suites, 1 single.
Meals	Breakfast £12-£14. Lunch & dinner £5-£30.
Closed	Never.
Directions	From A40 ring road, south at Banbury Road r'bout to Summertown city centre. On right next to St Giles Church.

Marie Jackson
1 Banbury Road, Oxford,
Oxfordshire OX2 6NN

Tel	01865 310210
Fax	01865 311262
Email	info@oldparsonage-hotel.co.uk
Web	www.oldparsonage-hotel.co.uk

Old Bank Hotel

You're in the heart of old Oxford. Stroll south past Corpus Christi to Christ Church meadows and the Thames, or leave the hotel to the north and find All Souls, the Radcliffe Camera and the Bodleian Library. Back at the Old Bank, a wonderful world of warm contemporary elegance and an important collection of modern art and photography adorning the walls – even in bedrooms. Downstairs, the old tiller's hall is now a vibrant bar/brasserie with fine arched windows giving views onto the high street; come for cocktails before a convivial meal. Bedrooms upstairs are exemplary, with big comfy beds, piles of cushions, Denon CD players, flat-screen TVs. Bigger rooms have sofas, you get robes in super bathrooms and there's free broadband access throughout. Serene service means curtains are pleated, beds are turned down, the daily papers delivered to your door. There's room service, too, and umbrellas in every cupboard. Breakfast is served in the tiller's hall or on the deck in the courtyard in summer. Free off-street parking is priceless. Brilliant.

Price	£175–£210. Suite £325. Singles from £160.
Rooms	42: 10 twins/doubles, 31 doubles, 1 suite.
Meals	Breakfast £10.95–£12.95. Lunch & dinner £5–£30.
Closed	Never.
Directions	Cross Magdalen Bridge for city centre. Straight through 1st set of lights, then left into Merton St. Follow road right; 1st right into Magpie Lane. Car park 2nd right.

Marie Jackson
92-94 High Street, Oxford,
Oxfordshire OX1 4BN

Tel	01865 799599
Fax	01865 799598
Email	info@oldbank-hotel.co.uk
Web	www.oldbank-hotel.co.uk

Entry 162 Map 3

The Trout at Tadpole Bridge

A 17th-century Cotswold inn on the banks of the Thames; pick up a pint, drift into the garden and watch life float by. Gareth and Helen bought the Trout after a two-year search and have cast their fairy dust into every corner: expect super bedrooms, oodles of style, delicious local food. The downstairs is open plan and timber-framed, with stone floors, gilt mirrors, wood-burners and logs piled high in alcoves. Bedrooms at the back are away from the crowd; three open onto a small courtyard where wild roses ramble on creamy stone – but you may prefer to stay put in your room and indulge in unabashed luxury. You get the best of everything: funky fabrics, trim carpets, monsoon showers (one room has a claw-foot bath), DVD players, flat-screen TVs, a library of films. Sleigh beds, brass beds, beautifully upholstered armchairs... one room even has a roof terrace. You can watch boats pass from the breakfast table, feast on local sausages, tuck into homemade marmalade courtesy of Helen's mum. Food is as local as possible, there are maps for walkers to keep you thin. *Minimum stay two nights at weekends May-October.*

Price	£100. Suite £130. Singles from £70.
Rooms	6: 3 twins/doubles, 2 doubles, 1 suite.
Meals	Lunch & dinner £5–£30. Not Sunday nights November–April.
Closed	Rarely.
Directions	A420 southwest from Oxford for Swindon. After 13 miles, right for Tadpole Bridge. Pub on right by bridge.

Gareth & Helen Pugh
Buckland Marsh, Faringdon,
Oxfordshire SN7 8RF

Tel	01367 870382
Fax	01367 870515
Email	info@troutinn.co.uk
Web	www.troutinn.co.uk

The Boar's Head

A dapper estate village with a church, a pub and a post office, the pub being the home of the village cricket club. It's a friendly place with a battalion of locals who come for open fires, the daily papers, local ales and gorgeous food. Sunday lunch rolls on to six and the bar is lively most evenings, making it the hub of a small community. Gilt mirrors and old oils hang on the walls. There are big oak tables in the restaurant and doors onto a terrace for alfresco summer suppers. Rooms upstairs are unmistakably smart. The small double has a beamed ceiling, the big double comes with a claw-foot bath, the suite has a sofa for kids and views over the village. All have good beds, crisp linen and piles of cushions. Passion bursts from the kitchen, the food is popular as a result. Everything is homemade: bread, pasta, pastries, ice cream, so try hot onion and gruyère tart, Cornish mussels with a spinach gratin, stuffed pheasant and mustard mash, bread and butter pudding with Bailey's ice cream. It's all cooked by big-hearted Bruce, who still finds time to chat. *Check-in before 3pm, after 6pm, or by arrangement.*

Price	£85–£105. Suite £130. Singles from £75.
Rooms	3: 2 doubles, 1 suite.
Meals	Lunch: main courses £8–£19. A la carte dinner from £20.
Closed	Rarely.
Directions	A417 west from Didcot for Wantage. Through West Hendred and Ardington signed left. In village, left by bus stop and pub on left.

Bruce & Kay Buchan
Church Street, Ardington, Wantage,
Oxfordshire OX12 8QA
Tel   01235 833254
Email   info@boarsheadardington.co.uk
Web   www.boarsheadardington.co.uk

The Miller of Mansfield

Ice-age melt water formed the Goring Gap; 14,000 years later 'cool' is back in town. The Miller, once a sedate red-brick coaching inn, has had a makeover and the results are decidedly groovy. You'll find pink suede beds, Cole & Son wallpaper, leather armchairs in the bar and silver-leaf mirrors above open fires. Beams have been sand blasted, 400-year-old oak panelling brought up from Devon to dress the bar. Expect black suede bar stools, fairy-light chandeliers and candles flickering on the mantelpiece. Bedrooms pack a punch. The chrome four-poster has a leather bedhead, there are cow-hide rugs on white wood floors. You get plasma screens, bath robes and fluffy towels, while flower-power colours come in pink, orange and electric green. Bathrooms are extravagant, some with monsoon showers, others with free-standing stone baths; one has a Japanese bath for two (two have no door from the bedroom). You get seriously good food and wine in the restaurant, so walk by the Thames, take to the hills, then return to the Miller for a night of carousing. Bells peel at the Norman church. One for the young at heart.

Price	£105–£150. Suites from £150.
Rooms	10: 7 doubles, 1 twin, 2 suites.
Meals	Continental breakfast included; full English £9.50. Tapas and bar meals available all day. Lunch from £10. Dinner from £25.
Closed	Never.
Directions	North from Reading on A329. In Streatley right onto B4526. Over bridge; hotel on left.

Sara Bates
High Street, Goring on Thames,
Oxfordshire RG8 9AW

Tel	01491 872829
Fax	01491 873100
Email	reservations@millerofmansfield.com
Web	www.millerofmansfield.com

The Cherry Tree Inn

A cherry orchard flourished here 400 years ago and farm workers lived in these brick and flint cottages. Five trees survive on the sprawling lawn at the front, so come in spring for the blossom. Beds of lavender lead up to the front door, inside you find ancient stone flagging and low beamed ceilings. It's a real treat, with board games in a cupboard, fairylights in the fireplace and a different colour on the walls in each room. Food is the big draw and on a Sunday in February a fanatical crowd gathered. Huge bowls of mussels flew from the kitchen, then plates of rare roast beef, finally a tarte tatin with a calvados sauce that brought sighs of ecstasy from a lucky diner. Rooms in the next-door barn are super value for money, stylish and private, with walls of colour, creamy carpets, silky red throws and leather headboards. Two have high beamed ceilings, bathrooms with slate floors are just the ticket, and each room has its own thermostat. A breakfast club for locals runs on the first Saturday of each month, so you may have company. Expect kippers, scrambled eggs, the full works.

Price	£95.
Rooms	4 doubles.
Meals	Lunch from £7.50.
	A la carte dinner from £22.50.
Closed	Christmas & New Year.
Directions	A4070 north from Reading. After four miles, right, through Checklade, to Stoke Row. Pub in village.

Richard Coates & Paul Gilchrist
Stoke Row,
Henley-on-Thames,
Oxfordshire RG9 5QA

Tel	01491 680430
Email	info@thecherrytreeinn.com
Web	www.thecherrytreeinn.com

Phyllis Court Club Hotel

Phyllis Court is a class apart — classically English, with the sort of protocol you'd expect from a private members' club. Founded almost a century ago to create somewhere swish for bright young things from the city to zoom up to in their new motor cars, it still attracts the great and the good. It isn't hard to see why. Apart from the grandstand and its own Thames frontage with moorings — it's bang opposite the finishing line of the Royal Regatta — the house itself is grandly self-effacing: tweed, tennis and *The Telegraph* blend with a sense of fun. Members number 3,000 today, and run the place with great pride — and grace. There *are* 'rules' but Muirfield it isn't! The club is named after the old English word for a red rose, 'fyllis'. Once moated, Phyllis Court was rebuilt in the 17th century, then again in the 18th and 19th. Bedrooms are easy on the eye and full of spoiling touches; the long drive sweeps past lawn and croquet courts. There are river walks, and Henley buzzes with day-trippers just as it always has. *Teas & meals for residents only. Minimum stay two nights at weekends.*

Price	£138–£169. Singles £95–£133.
Rooms	17: 9 doubles, 8 twins/doubles.
Meals	Dinner, 3 courses, à la carte, around £27.50.
Closed	Never.
Directions	From Henley-on-Thames, A4155 towards Marlow. Club on right.

Shirley Cunningham
Marlow Road, Henley-on-Thames,
Oxfordshire RG9 2HT

Tel	01491 570500
Fax	01491 570528
Email	enquiries@phylliscourt.co.uk
Web	www.phylliscourt.co.uk

The Olive Branch

A Michelin-starred pub in a sleepy Rutland village, where bridle paths lead out across peaceful fields. The inn dates to the 17th century and is built of Clipsham stone... as are the Houses of Parliament. Inside, a warm, informal rustic chic hits the spot perfectly; come for open fires, old beams, exposed stone walls and choir stalls in the bar. Chalk boards on tables in the restaurant reveal the names of the evening's diners, while the English food – cauliflower soup, roast rib of beef, caramelised lemon tart – elates. As do the hampers of terrine, cheese and homemade pies that you can whisk away for picnics in the country. Bedrooms in Beech House across the lane are impeccable. Three have terraces, one has a free-standing bath, all come with crisp linen, pretty beds, Robert's radios, real coffee. Super breakfasts – smoothies, boiled eggs and soldiers, the full cooked works – are served in a smartly renovated barn, with flames leaping in the wood-burner. The front garden fills in summer, the sloe gin comes from local berries, and Newark is close for the biggest antiques market in Europe. Superb.

Price	£90–£130. Suites £140–£180. Singles from £75.	
Rooms	6: 1 twin/double, 2 doubles, 3 suites.	
Meals	Lunch from £13.95. Dinner, 3 courses, about £30.	
Closed	25 & 26 December; 1 January.	
Directions	A1 north past Stamford. Clipsham exit signed left after four miles. In village.	

Ben Jones & Sean Hope
Main Street, Clipsham,
Rutland LE15 7SH

Tel	01780 410355
Fax	01780 410000
Email	info@theolivebranchpub.com
Web	www.theolivebranchpub.com

Hambleton Hall

A sublime country house, one of the loveliest in England. The position here is matchless. The house stands on a tiny peninsular that juts into Rutland Water. You can sail on it or cycle round it, then come back to the undisputed wonders of Hambleton: sofas by the fire in the panelled hall, a pillared bar in red for cocktails and a Michelin star in the dining room. French windows in the sitting room (beautiful art, fresh flowers, the daily papers) open onto idyllic gardens. Expect clipped lawns and gravel paths, a formal parterre garden that bursts with summer colour and a walled swimming pool with huge views over grazing parkland down to the water. Bedrooms are the very best. Hand-stitched Italian linen, mirrored armoires, mullioned windows, marble bathrooms – and Stefa's eye for fabrics, some of which coat the walls, is faultless; the Croquet Pavilion, a suite with two bedrooms, has its own terrace. Polish the day off with a serious dinner, perhaps scallop ravioli, breast of Goosnargh duck, then poached pear with caramel ice cream. Wonderful. *Minimum stay two nights at weekends.*

Price	£200-£365. Singles from £170. Pavilion £500-£600.
Rooms	17: 15 twins/doubles, 1 four-poster. Pavilion: 1 suite (1 four-poster, 1 twin/double) for 4.
Meals	Continental breakfast included; full English £14.50. Lunch from £21.50. Dinner £40-£70.
Closed	Never.
Directions	From A1, A606 west towards Oakham for about 8 miles, then left, signed Hambleton. In village, bear left and hotel signed right.

Tim & Stefa Hart
Hambleton, Oakham ,
Rutland LE15 8TH

Tel	01572 756991
Fax	01572 724721
Email	hotel@hambletonhall.com
Web	www.hambletonhall.com

Pen-y-Dyffryn Country Hotel

An old rectory on the side of a blissful hill with long views stretching out across the valley. The church is below, and in Wales (nobody knows when the border was moved). This is a small, welcoming country house with a fire in the sitting room, a terrace for afternoon tea and a good collection of pictures on the walls. Best off all is David Morris's delicious cooking, so head to the dining room for food that's as local as possible, with game from the valley; try spiced parsnip and apple soup, rack of Welsh lamb in a thyme butter sauce, dark chocolate terrine with a cointreau sauce. There are fine organic cheeses, too. Bedrooms are warmly stylish without being grand, some with great views, others with a fine canopy bed; modern bathrooms – one has a two-seater spa bath – come with thick fluffy towels. Four new rooms are more private and have their own patios. There's plenty of space in the house making it ideal for a gathering, with lots of comfortable chairs and sofas to hide in with a good book. Excellent walking from the door and the smoked haddock at breakfast is divine. *Minimum stay two nights at weekends.*

Price	£108–£158. Singles £84.
Rooms	12: 8 doubles, 4 twins.
Meals	Dinner from £33.
Closed	Rarely.
Directions	From A5, head to Oswestry. Leave town on B4580, signed Llansilin. Hotel 3 miles on left just before Rhydycroesau.

Miles & Audrey Hunter
Rhydycroesau, Oswestry,
Shropshire SY10 7JD

Tel	01691 653700
Fax	01978 211004
Email	stay@peny.co.uk
Web	www.peny.co.uk

Entry 170 Map 5

The Inn at Grinshill

A ridge of pine soars high above the village; bring the boots and take to Shropshire's wild, wonderful hills. Down at the inn, nothing but good things; this is a wonderfully welcoming bolthole, a top-to-toe renovation which now shines. Wander at will and you find an 18th-century panelled family room with rugs and games, a 19th-century bar with quarry-tiled floors and a crackling fire, and a 21st-century dining room, serene in cream, flooded with light courtesy of glazed coach-house arches. Bedrooms upstairs are just as good, with good beds, piles of pillows, crisp white linen and wispy mohair blankets or shiny quilted eiderdowns. And TVs hidden behind mirrors, DVD players and indulging bathrooms. Back downstairs, ambrosial delights pour from the kitchen – the breast of duck served with an orange and lemon marmalade was faultless. A grand piano gets played on Friday nights and life spills out into the garden in summer. Church bells peel, roses ramble, there's cricket in the village at the weekend and the Shropshire Way passes by outside. Don't miss the magical follies at Hawkstone Park.

Price	£100. Singles from £50.
Rooms	6: 3 doubles, 2 twins, 1 single.
Meals	Lunch from £9.95; Sunday lunch £14.50. A la carte dinner about £25. Not Sunday evening or bank holiday evenings.
Closed	Never.
Directions	A49 north from Shrewsbury. Grinshill signed left after 5 miles.

Kevin & Victoria Brazier
High Street, Grinshill, Shrewsbury,
Shropshire SY4 3BL
Tel   01939 220410
Fax   01939 220327
Email   info@theinnatgrinshill.co.uk
Web   www.theinnatgrinshill.co.uk

Mr Underhill's at Dinham Weir

A taste of Provence in sleepy Ludlow. You're bang on the water with the river Teme passing serenely in front and Ludlow castle high on the hill behind. Step in off the lane and you find yourself cocooned in a colourful courtyard; you may eat here in summer surrounded by lavender and roses while the river pours over the weir and the odd duck squawks. Glassed arched walls in the airy restaurant bring in the view, so come for a heavenly, seven-course, Michelin-starred tasting menu, highlights of which may include pavé of halibut with lemon grass and ginger broth, slow-roasted forest venison with red wine and thyme, black cherry sponge with cinnamon ice cream, and a plate of delicious cheeses. Everything is made in house, including the croissants at breakfast. Rooms come in whites and creams with crisp linen, flat-screen TVs, bath robes and handmade mattresses. Those in the main house are not huge, but overlook river and courtyard, two suites across the lane have proper sitting rooms, and the Shed (some shed!) is a timber-framed palace bang on the water. Wonderful.

Price	£140-£190. Singles from £120. Suites £240.
Rooms	9: 4 doubles, 2 twins/doubles, 3 suites.
Meals	Dinner, 7-course tasting menu, £45-£51. Not Monday or Tuesday.
Closed	Occasionally.
Directions	Head to castle in Ludlow centre, take Dinham Road to left of castle; down hill, right at bottom before crossing river. On left, signed.

Chris & Judy Bradley
Dinham Bridge, Ludlow, Shropshire SY8 1EH
Tel   01584 874431
Web   www.mr-underhills.co.uk

Miller's at Glencot House

An intoxicating country house in a sublime position with lawns that run down to the river Axe and a cricket pitch on the far bank. In summer you can pick up a deckchair, wander down to the water and watch the village team toil in the sun while you dig into afternoon tea. Glencot is a perfect place, a bohemian paradise tucked away in Somerset's leafy lanes. It's all part of Martin Miller's benevolent empire – antique guides, distilled gin, London bolthole, academy of arts, now country retreat. And while England's green and pleasant land encircles this Jacobean mansion, its interiors reveal a thrilling flamboyance that cuts at the establishment grain and shows the designers how to decorate a real country house. Everywhere you go a hundred beautiful things loom into view: busts, bronzes, oils by the truckload, a baby grand in the music room, a pair of peacocks in the drawing room, chandeliers tumbling from ceilings. Bedrooms are immaculate, wildly ornate, rich in colour, with walls of art, draped four-posters, gilt mirrors in tidy bathrooms. Irreverent, exhilarating, magical. One of the best.

Price	£165–£185. Four-posters £240–£265.
Rooms	15: 5 four-posters, 7 doubles, 3 twins/doubles.
Meals	Lunch from £12.95. Sunday lunch £15.95. Dinner, 3 courses, £29.50.
Closed	Rarely.
Directions	From Wells, follow signs to Wookey Hole. Sharp left at finger post, 100m after pink cottage. House on right in Glencot Lane.

Justin Huber
Glencot Lane, Wells,
Somerset BA5 1BH

Tel	01749 677160
Fax	01749 670219
Email	relax@glencothouse.co.uk
Web	www.glencothouse.co.uk

Combe House Hotel

Amble down through the woods from the heights of the lush Quantocks (as fine a walking area as Exmoor), stroll through the village and up again to the hotel – its arms open to a scene of bucolic bliss. You are here because the setting is magical, the gardens enchanting, the food excellent (fruit and veg grown in their own organic garden, local meat and fish) and the mood exactly what you need in the Quantocks. The sign by the entrance sets the tone: here is an informal, easy-going, open-minded welcome to all, muddy-booted walkers included. The interior is surprisingly smart, with yellow carpet and a yellow theme in the big dining room; there is a modern bar with black leather armchairs and a little anteroom with a good sofa. The overall effect is one of cosy efficiency. Refurbished bedrooms are nicely colourful and come with thick fabrics, piles of pillows and spotless bathrooms. A good library, a heated indoor swimming pool, a sauna and tennis mean there's plenty to do without going out and enough chairs and tables scattered about the lawn to encourage privacy or conviviality.

Price	£115–£130. Singles from £65. Half-board from £75 p.p.
Rooms	15: 11 doubles, 4 singles.
Meals	Dinner, 3 courses, from £28.50.
Closed	Never.
Directions	From Bridgwater, A39 to Minehead. At Holford, left in front of Plough Inn and follow lane through village. Bear left at fork signed Holford Combe; drive near to end of road on right.

Andrew Ryan
Butterfly Combe, Holford, Bridgwater,
Somerset TA5 1RZ

Tel	01278 741382
Fax	01278 741322
Email	enquiries@combehouse.co.uk
Web	www.combehouse.co.uk

Bindon Country House Hotel

Bindon is lovely, a big old pile that hides on the edge of woodland where wild flowers flourish. Once derelict, it now shines, and if you want you can take the whole place and have it to yourselves – open fires, tiled entrance hall, stained-glass windows, wall tapestries, plaster moulded ceilings, galleried staircase and glass-domed roof to boot. Step into the snug panelled bar, past the wrought-iron candlesticks, for coffee served with piping hot milk and delicious homemade biscuits. In summer doors are flung open and you can sit by a magnificent stone balustrade that looks over rose gardens down to an old dovecote. Bright bedrooms come in different sizes: two oval rooms at the front of the house are *huge*, all dusky pink furniture, patterned wallpaper, high brass beds and Victorian baths. The rest are a good size, very comfortable; a couple are warm and cosy up in the eaves. High teas for children, gorgeous food, a small heated pool and a tennis court. In short, a treat, so come to get married or simply to retreat for a day or two. *Minimum stay two nights at weekends.*

Price	£145-£225. Singles £115. Half-board from £95 p.p. (min. 2 nights). Exclusive use £1,250 self-catering (min. 2 nights).
Rooms	12: 10 twins/doubles, 2 four-posters.
Meals	Lunch £12.95. Dinner, 5 courses, £35.
Closed	Rarely.
Directions	From Wellington, B3187 for 1.5 miles; left at sharp S-bend for Langford Budville; right for Wiveliscombe; 1st right; on right.

Lynn & Mark Jaffa
Langford Budville, Wellington,
Somerset TA21 0RU

Tel	01823 400070
Fax	01823 400071
Email	stay@bindon.com
Web	www.bindon.com

Farmer's Inn

You don't often trek into deepest Somerset and wash up at a deeply groovy inn, but that's what you get at the Farmer's, so brave the narrow country lanes and head to the top of the hill for colour and comfort in equal measure. All the country treats are on hand. Outside, cows in the fields, cockerels crowing and long clean views; inside, friendly natives, open fires and a timber-framed bar. It's all the result of a total renovation, and one airy room now rolls into another giving a sense of space and light. Imagine terracotta-tiled floors and beamed ceilings, yellow-painted tongue-and-groove panelling, old pine dining tables dressed with pots of rosemary and logs piled high in the alcoves. Bedrooms are the best, some big, some huge. They come with off-white walls, seagrass mats on shiny wooden floors, cast-iron beds, power showers or claw-foot baths. One has a daybed, others have sofas, one has a private courtyard. Super food flies from the kitchen – grilled sardines, rib-eye steak, chocolate and mint mousse – and you can eat on the terrace in summer. Great walking, too: bring the boots.

Price	£90-£120.
Rooms	5: 4 doubles, 1 twin.
Meals	Bar meals from £4.50.
	A la carte dinner from £25.
Closed	Rarely.
Directions	M5 junc. 25, then south on A358. Right at Nag's Head pub, up hill for two miles, following signs towards RSPCA. On left.

Debbie Lush
Slough Green, Higher West Hatch,
Taunton, Somerset TA3 5RS

Tel	01823 480480
Fax	01823 481177
Email	letsgostay@farmersinnwesthatch.co.uk
Web	www.farmersinnwesthatch.co.uk

Bellplot House Hotel & Thomas's Restaurant

There are chic inns, there are smart hotels and there's Betty's. This may not be the trendiest place in the book, but what you find comes straight from the heart. With honest prices, quirky interiors and delicious food Bellplot delivers what few others do: a personal world. It's a family affair – Betty greets, her husband Denis pulls the pints, their son Thomas cooks in the kitchen. Step into stripped floors, yellow walls, a pool table in the bar and a dining room in country-house green. This is where you come for dinners with a difference, perhaps green pea soup, Lancashire hot pot, freshly baked lemon meringue pie. This unashamedly old-school menu (every supplier is listed on the back) prompted a visiting New Yorker to declare the food the best he'd tasted in Britain. Bedrooms are sprinkled about. They tend to be large and are furnished in a homely style: warm and spotless, lots of colour, crisp white linen, compact bathrooms. Some have sofas, all come with TVs and WiFi. You're on the high street, but it's quiet at night. Montacute House and Forde Abbey are both close.

Price	£79.50. Family £89.50. Singles £69.50.
Rooms	7: 5 doubles, 1 family, 1 single.
Meals	Breakfast £5–£9. Picnic lunch £12. Dinner, 3 courses, £20–£25. Not Sunday.
Closed	Rarely.
Directions	In centre of Chard, 500 yds from the Guildhall. Car park available.

Betty Jones
High Street, Chard,
Somerset TA20 1QB

Tel	01460 62600
Fax	01460 62600
Email	info@bellplothouse.co.uk
Web	www.bellplothouse.co.uk

Lord Poulett Arms

In a ravishing village, an idyllic village inn, French at heart and quietly groovy. Part pub, part country house, with walls painted in reds and greens and old rugs covering flagged floors, the Lord Poulett gives a glimpse of a 21st-century dream local, where classical design fuses with earthy rusticity. A fire burns on both sides of the chimney in the dining room; on one side you can sink into leather armchairs, on the other you can eat under beams at antique oak tables while candles flicker. Take refuge with the daily papers on the sofa in the locals' bar or head past a pile of logs at the back door and discover an informal French garden of box and bay trees, with a piste for boules and a creeper-shaded terrace. Bedrooms upstairs come in funky country-house style, with fancy flock wallpaper, perhaps crushed velvet curtains, a small chandelier or a carved-wood bed. Two rooms have slipper baths behind screens in the room; two have claw-foot baths in bathrooms one step across the landing; Roberts radios add to the fun. Delicious food includes summer barbecues, Sunday roasts and the full works at breakfast.

Price	£88. Singles £59.
Rooms	4: 2 doubles both en suite; 2 doubles, each with separate bath.
Meals	Lunch & dinner: main courses £9-£15.
Closed	Never.
Directions	A303, then A356 south for Crewkerne. Right for West Chinnock. Through village and first left for Hinton St George. Pub on right in village.

Steve & Michelle Hill
High Street, Hinton St George,
Crewekerne, Somerset TA17 8SE

Tel	01460 73149
Email	steveandmichelle@lordpoulettarms.com
Web	www.lordpoulettarms.com

Little Barwick House

A dreamy restaurant with rooms lost in the hills three miles south of Yeovil. Tim and Emma rolled west ten years ago and have gathered a legion of fans who come to feast on their ambrosial food. Their stage is this small Georgian country house which stands in three acres of peace. A curtain of trees shields it from the outside world, horses graze in the paddock below and afternoon tea is served in the garden in summer, so sip your Earl Grey accompanied by birdsong. Inside, graceful interiors flood with light courtesy of fine windows that run along the front. There's an open fire in the cosy bar, eclectic reading in the pretty sitting room, and stripped floors in the high-ceilinged dining room. Upstairs, super bedrooms hit the spot with warm colours, crisp linen, silk curtains and a country-house feel. But dinner is the main event, heaven in three courses. Everything is homemade and cooked by Tim and Emma, an equal partnership in the kitchen. Try confit of pork belly roasted with honey, saddle of roe deer with a mushroom risotto, apple strudel with calvados ice cream. A real treat. *Minimum stay two nights at weekends.*

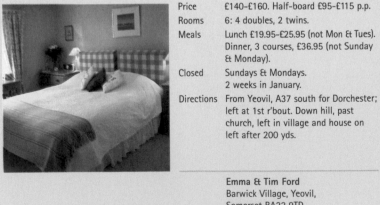

Price	£140–£160. Half-board £95–£115 p.p.
Rooms	6: 4 doubles, 2 twins.
Meals	Lunch £19.95–£25.95 (not Mon & Tues). Dinner, 3 courses, £36.95 (not Sunday & Monday).
Closed	Sundays & Mondays. 2 weeks in January.
Directions	From Yeovil, A37 south for Dorchester; left at 1st r'bout. Down hill, past church, left in village and house on left after 200 yds.

Emma & Tim Ford
Barwick Village, Yeovil,
Somerset BA22 9TD

Tel	01935 423902
Fax	01935 420908
Email	reservations@barwick7.fsnet.co.uk
Web	www.littlebarwickhouse.co.uk

Devonshire Arms Hotel

A lively English village with a well-kept green; the old school house stands to the south, the church to the east and the post office to the west. The inn (due north) is 400 years old and was once a hunting lodge for the Dukes of Devonshire; a rather smart pillared porch survives at the front. These days open-plan interiors are warmly contemporary with high ceilings, shiny blond floorboards and fresh flowers everywhere. Hop onto brown leather stools at the bar and order a pint of Crop Circle, or sink into sofas in front of the fire and crack open a bottle of wine. In summer, life spills onto the terrace at the front, the courtyard at the back and the lawned garden beyond. Super bedrooms run along at the front; all are a good size, but those at each end are huge. You get low-slung wooden beds, seagrass matting, crisp white linen and freeview TV. One has a purple claw-foot bath, some have compact showers. Delicious food is on tap in the restaurant – chargrilled scallops, slow-cooked lamb, passion fruit crème brûlée – so take to the nearby Somerset levels and walk off your indulgence in style.

Price	£75–£130. Singles from £60.
Rooms	9: 8 doubles, 1 twin.
Meals	Lunch from £5. Dinner from £10.
Closed	Rarely.
Directions	A303, then north on B3165, through Martock, to Long Sutton. Pub on green in village.

Philip & Sheila Mepham
Long Sutton, Langport,
Somerset TA10 9LP

Tel	01458 241271
Fax	01458 241037
Email	mail@thedevonshirearms.com
Web	www.thedevonshirearms.com

The Queen's Arms

Stride across rolling fields, feast on Corton Denham lamb, retire to a perfect room. Buried down several Dorset and Somerset-border lanes, this 18th-century stone pub has an elegant exterior – more country gentleman's house than pub. Inside, Rupert and Victoria (ex-Londoners with experience in the business) have created a calm, relaxing space. The bar, with its rug-strewn flagstones and bare boards, pew benches, deep sofas and crackling fire, has not lost its country feel. In the dining room – big mirrors on terracotta walls, new china on old tables – happy eaters dine on robust British dishes distinguished by fresh ingredients from local suppliers. Try smoked haddock and spinach tart with a glass or two of Jim Barry's Aussie shiraz, follow with pan-fried calf's liver, black spot bacon, mash and gravy; find room for a comforting crumble. The bedrooms and bathrooms are beautifully designed in gorgeous colours; a duck-egg blue wall here, dear little red and cream checked curtains there. All have lovely views and the bathrooms are immaculate. There's a garden too, small but sunny.

Fresh food locally sourced has cut food miles substantially and brought fabulous seasonal country fare into the dining room. Apple juice and cider come from Bridge Farm in the next door village, Montgomery Cheddar is from South Cadbury two miles north, vegetables are grown by Rowswell's in Illminster, one of Somerset's most lauded food producers. Fish comes fresh from the Bridport catch, Andrew Barclays of Wincanton provide Dorset meat, and lamb is reared in the village (staff help out at lambing). The inn itself has two Gloucester Old Spots and a battalion of roaming mixed-breed hens, whose flavoursome eggs are served at breakfast.

Price	£75–£120.
Rooms	5: 4 doubles, 1 twin.
Meals	Lunch from £4.20. Dinner from £19.50.
Closed	Rarely.
Directions	From A303 take Chapel Crosse turning, through South Cadbury village. Next left & follow signs to Corton Denham. Pub at end of village, on right.

Rupert & Victoria Reeves
Corton Denham,
Somerset DT9 4LR

Tel   01963 220317
Email   relax@thequeensarms.com
Web   www.thequeensarms.com

SPECIAL
GREEN ENTRY
see page 17

The Westleton Crown

This is one of England's oldest coaching inns, with 800 years of continuous service under its belt. It stands in a village two miles inland from the sea at Dunwich, with Westleton Heath running east towards Minsmere Bird Sanctuary. Inside, you find the best of old and new. A recent refurbishment has introduced Farrow & Ball colours, leather sofas and a tongue-and-groove bar, and they mix harmoniously with panelled walls, stripped floors and ancient beams. Weave around and find nooks and crannies in which to hide, flames flickering in an open fire, a huge map on the wall for walkers. You can eat wherever you want, and a conservatory/breakfast room opens onto a terraced garden for summer barbecues. Fish comes straight off the boats at Lowestoft, local butchers provide local meat. Lovely bedrooms are scattered about and come in cool lime white with comfy beds, Egyptian cotton, flat-screen TVs. Super bathrooms are fitted out in Fired Earth, and some have claw-foot baths. Aldeburgh and Southwold are close by. *Minimum stay two nights at weekends.*

Price	£110–£160. Singles from £85.
Rooms	25: 20 doubles, 2 twins, 2 family, 1 single.
Meals	Lunch & dinner £5–£30.
Closed	24 & 25 December.
Directions	A12 north from Ipswich. Right at Yoxford onto B1122, then left for Westleton on B1125. On right in village.

Matt Goodwin
The Street, Westleton, Southwold,
Suffolk IP17 3AD

Tel	01728 648777
Fax	01728 648239
Email	info@westletoncrown.co.uk
Web	www.westletoncrown.co.uk

Wentworth Hotel

Come for a little time travel; this stretch of the Suffolk coast will sweep you back to sleepy England at its loveliest: fishing boats on shingle beaches, an estuary for super walks and a music festival in summer. The Wentworth matches the mood perfectly; it's warmly old-fashioned, quietly grand, full of its own traditions. Michael's family have been here since 1920, when scores of fishermen worked the shore; the few that remain haul their boats up onto the beach across from the hotel terrace. Inside you find a warm seaside elegance, nothing too racy; instead, sunshine colours, fresh flowers, flickering coal fires, oils on the walls and shelves of books. Also: delightful sitting rooms, a bar for all seasons, and part of the hotel resembles a grand ocean liner. The restaurant looks out to sea, comes in Georgian red and spills onto the sunken lawn in summer for views of passing boats. Bedrooms (many with sea views) are plush: Zoffany wallpaper, reds and golds, French armoires, comfortable beds. Joyce Grenfell used to stay for the Aldeburgh Festival and has a room named after her. *Minimum stay two nights at weekends.*

Price	£108-£220. Singles from £63. Half-board £57-£120 p.p.
Rooms	35: 24 twins/doubles, 4 singles. Darfield House: 7 doubles.
Meals	Lunch from £7.50. Dinner from £15.
Closed	Never.
Directions	A12 north from Ipswich, then A1094 for Aldeburgh. Past church, down hill, left at x-roads; on right.

Michael Pritt
Wentworth Road, Aldeburgh,
Suffolk IP15 5BD

Tel	01728 452312
Fax	01728 454343
Email	stay@wentworth-aldeburgh.co.uk
Web	www.wentworth-aldeburgh.com

The Crown and Castle

The road runs out at sleepy Orford, so saddle up and follow cycle tracks or bridle paths into the forest. You can also hop on a boat and chug over to Orfordness, the biggest vegetated shingle spit in the world. In WWII it housed a military research base where Barnes Wallace (bouncing bomb) and Robert Watson-Watt (radar) toiled all day, returning at night to the splendour of the Crown, a Victorian redbrick inn that stands close to a 12th-century castle. Today the feel is light and airy, very comfortable, with stripped wood floors, open fires and eclectic art. A mouthwatering menu (half a pint of Orford prawns, Cornish crab, roasted Suffolk pheasant) caused indecision, but the warm duck salad with spiced pear was exceptional. Rooms in the main house come in pastels, those at the back have long watery views. Garden rooms (dull on the outside, lovely within) are big and airy, with padded headboards, seagrass matting, spotless bathrooms and doors onto a communal garden. All have crisp white linen, TVs and videos. Wellington boots wait at the back door, so pull on a pair and discover Suffolk.

Price	£90–£145. Singles from £72. Half-board from £75 p.p.
Rooms	18: 16 doubles, 2 twins.
Meals	Lunch from £9.50. A la carte dinner from £24.50.
Closed	Never.
Directions	A12 north from Ipswich to A1152 east of Woodbridge, then B1084 into Orford. Hotel on market square.

David & Ruth Watson
Orford,
Suffolk IP12 2LJ

Tel	01394 450205
Email	info@crownandcastle.co.uk
Web	www.crownandcastle.co.uk

Chequers

It's not just the fine butcher's shop, nor even the famous underwear shop, that makes a trip to Wickham Market a must – now there is Chequers too. Once an old pub, it had been boarded up for years before Katie and Mark got their clever hands on it. The three 'rooms' all have their own access and places to sit; the problem will be in choosing which one. The Garden Room has cottage windows, open beams and seagrass flooring and the Coach House an oriental twist and an iron bed with a fur throw; the Hay Loft is a love nest with mood lighting and a leather bed. All have state-of-the-art bathrooms, huge beds with clouds of white linen and extras like full room service. Sit in your own little gravelled garden and order champagne, beer or wine (you can BYO too, for corkage); breakfast (full local and organic blow-out or something lighter) is delivered and there's really no reason to leave. Except you're in striking distance of Southwold and Aldeburgh and only minutes from Snape Maltings Concert Hall. Sheer indulgence. *Minimum stay two nights at weekends.*

Price	£80–£145. Singles from £65.
Rooms	3 doubles.
Meals	Pubs nearby.
Closed	Rarely.
Directions	Take A12 turn-off to Wickham Market, north of Ipswich, past Woodbridge. Through Market Square, down lane opposite Spring Lane.

Katie & Mark Casey
220 High Street, Wickham Market,
Woodbridge, Suffolk IP13 0RF

Tel	01728 746284
Fax	01728 746284
Email	katie@kckc.co.uk
Web	www.chequerssuffolk.co.uk

The Old Rectory

An old country rectory with contemporary interiors; what would the rector think? You get stripped floors in the dining room, a 21st-century orange chaise-longue by the honesty bar and windows dressed in fabulous fabrics. Michael and Sally swapped Hong Kong for Suffolk and the odd souvenir came with them: wood carvings from the Orient and framed Burmese chanting bibles. In winter, a fire smoulders at breakfast; in summer, you feast in a huge stone-flagged conservatory where doors open onto two acres of orchard and lawns. A warm country-house informality flows within, so help yourself to a drink, sink into a sofa or spin onto the terrace in search of sun and birdsong. Smart bedrooms are warmly decorated; one is up in the eaves, one overlooks the church, another has a claw-foot bath. Delicious food includes organic sausages and homemade jams at breakfast, perhaps parsnip soup and roast rack of Suffolk lamb at dinner, then almond and lemon tart. Sutton Hoo is close as is Snape Maltings (performing opera singers occasionally stay and warm up for work in the bedrooms). A happy house. *Minimum stay two nights at weekends.*

Price	£85–£120. Singles from £75.
Rooms	7: 3 doubles, 2 twins, 2 four-posters.
Meals	Dinner, 3 courses, £28. Not Saturday or Sunday.
Closed	Occasionally.
Directions	North from Ipswich on A12 for 15 miles, then right onto B1078. In village, over railway line; house on right just before church.

Michael & Sally Ball
Campsea Ashe,
Woodbridge,
Suffolk IP13 0PU

Tel 01728 746524
Email mail@theoldrectorysuffolk.com
Web www.theoldrectorysuffolk.com

The White Hart Inn

The White Hart is exquisite on all counts, but the way things are done here is second to none. The inn, beamed and timber-framed, dates from the 15th century, and comes with open fires, stripped boards and flagged floors, but the hallmark here is a rural English elegance, with airy rooms, attentive service and very friendly staff. Locals love it and flock in to feast on "scrumptious food", to quote an enraptured guest – perhaps green pea soup, fillet of beef, then crème brûlée – and to sup from an interesting collection of wines. Bedrooms, which vary in size, have a warm country style: yellow walls and checked fabrics, crisp linen and thick blankets, sofas or armchairs and wonderful art; some have wildly sloping floors, two have vaulted ceilings, one has original murals that may be the work of Constable's brother (he painted them to pay for a meal, or so the story goes). Breakfast on duck eggs, freshly-baked croissants, Suffolk bacon, even fried bread. The village is gorgeous. Don't miss St James' church, the 14th-century tower or the old post office next door.

Price	£86–£129. Singles £66–£109.
Rooms	6: 5 doubles, 1 twin.
Meals	Lunch from £12.90. Dinner around £27.
Closed	2 weeks in January.
Directions	Nayland signed right 6 miles north of Colchester on the A134 (no access from A12). In village centre.

	Michel Hédoin
	High Street, Nayland, Colchester, Suffolk CO6 4JF
Tel	01206 263382
Fax	01206 263638
Email	nayhart@aol.com
Web	www.whitehart-nayland.co.uk

The Great House

Lavenham is a Suffolk gem, a medieval town made prosperous by 14th-century wool merchants, hence the timber-framed houses that jut out over narrow streets. The Great House stands across the market place from the Guildhall, its 18th-century façade giving way to a 15th-century interior of timber frames, varnished wood floors, beamed ceilings and a carved bressumar beam that straddles the inglenook and which dates to 1550. The poet Stephen Spender once lived here and the house became a meeting places for artists, but these days it's the irresistible allure of French cooking that draws the crowd. You might get fois gras, local lamb, crème brûlée, but whatever you do, don't miss the cheese board: it's a work of art. Super-comfy bedrooms at the top of a creaky wooden staircase have antique dressers, fresh flowers, bowls of fruit, a decanter of sherry and sparkly marble bathrooms. One room has a Jacobean four-poster: an island in a sea of rugs; another, in the roof, has huge beamed timbers. Four rooms have their own sitting area and those at the front overlook the square. *Minimum stay two nights at weekends.*

Price	£96–£165. Singles from £70. Half-board from £82.50 p.p.
Rooms	5: 1 double, 4 suites.
Meals	Continental breakfast £8.50; full English £12.50. Lunch from £14.95. Dinner from £25.95. Not Sunday nights & Mondays.
Closed	First 3 weeks in January.
Directions	A1141 to Lavenham. At High Street, 1st right after The Swan or up Lady Street into Market Place.

Régis & Martine Crépy
Market Place, Lavenham,
Suffolk CO10 9QZ

Tel	01787 247431
Fax	01787 248007
Email	info@greathouse.co.uk
Web	www.greathouse.co.uk

The Bildeston Crown

There are flagstones in the locals' bar, warm reds on the walls and sweet-smelling logs smouldering in open fires. The inn dates from 1529, the interior design from 2005. Not that the feel is overly contemporary; ancient beams have been reclaimed from under a thick coat of black paint and varnished wood floors shine like honey. There are gilded mirrors and oils on the walls, candles in the fireplace, happy locals at the bar. An airy open-plan feel runs throughout, with lots of space in the dining room and smart leather chairs tucked under hand-made oak tables. You'll also find flowers in the courtyard, old radiators and high-backed settles in the front bar and local Suffolk beers to quench your thirst. Bedrooms come in different sizes, but all are stuffed with luxury. Imagine regal reds and golds, faux fur blankets, silk curtains, perhaps a bust in a gorgeous bathroom. A hi-tech music system holds 1,000 albums (listen as you soak); and there are flat-screen TVs. Hire bikes from the shop next door and dive into the country, or come for the beer festival in the last week of May.

Price	£110–£150. Singles £70–£90. Suite £180.
Rooms	12: 8 doubles, 3 twins, 1 single, 1 suite.
Meals	Bar meals from £5. A la carte dinner from £25; 8-course tasting menu £50.
Closed	Never.
Directions	A12 junc. 31, then B1070 to Hadleigh. A1141 north, then B1115 into village. Pub on right.

Hayley Robertson
Bildeston,
Suffolk IP7 7ED

Tel	01449 740510
Fax	01449 741843
Email	info@thebildestoncrown.co.uk
Web	www.thecrownbildeston.com

Ounce House

Bury St Edmunds, an ancient English town, is a dream; if you've never been, don't delay. The Romans were here, the barons hatched plans for Magna Carta within the now-crumbled walls of its ancient monastery and its Norman abbey attracted pilgrims by the cartload. The town was made rich by the wool trade in the 1700s and highlights include the cathedral (its exquisite new tower looks hundreds of years old) and the magnificent Abbey Gardens (perfect for summer picnics). Just around the corner, Ounce House, a handsome 1870 red-brick townhouse, overflows with creature comforts, so slump into leather armchairs in front of a carved fireplace and gaze at walls of art. You'll also find a snug library, a lawned garden and homely bedrooms packed with books, mahogany furniture and fresh flowers. Princely breakfasts are served on blue-and-white Spode china at one vast table. This is B&B in a grand-ish home, and Jenny and Simon will pick you up from the station or book a table at a local restaurant. Try The Chalice (traditional English) or Maison Bleu (good seafood). Don't miss the May arts festival.

Price	£90–£120. Singles £70–£85.
Rooms	3: 2 doubles, 1 twin.
Meals	Restaurants 5-minute walk.
Closed	Rarely.
Directions	A14 north, then central junction for Bury, following signs to historic centre. At 1st r'bout, left into Northgate St. On right at top of hill.

Simon & Jenny Pott
Northgate Street, Bury St Edmunds,
Suffolk IP33 1HP

Tel	01284 761779
Fax	01284 768315
Email	pott@globalnet.co.uk
Web	www.ouncehouse.co.uk

Park House Hotel

Come for the boundless peace of an English country garden. This warm Edwardian house sits in 12 green acres, with croquet on the lawn, a grass tennis court, shrubs and roses in well-kept beds, and a six-hole golf course that slips into the country. Dreamy views from the back shoot off to the South Downs, and there's a swimming pool, too, so snooze in the sun while a tractor works the fields beyond. As for the house, it's as good as the garden: warm, peaceful, utterly spoiling. You get an open fire in the sitting room, flickering candles in the dining room and a snug honesty bar with doors onto the terrace. Super bedrooms come in crisp country style: vintage wallpaper, Farrow & Ball colours, mahogany bedside tables, perhaps a chaise-longue in a bay window. The suite has a private terrace and all rooms have lovely touches (good art, fresh flowers, flat-screen TVs). Fancy bathrooms are de rigeur with separate showers and robes. There's an airy conservatory for delicious breakfasts, a terrace for al fresco treats in summer. Walks start from the front door. *Special rates for Goodwood.*

Price	£135–£185. Family £155–£250. Suite/cottage £175–£250.	
Rooms	15 + 1: 8 twins/doubles, 4 doubles, 2 family. 1 suite/self-catering cottage.	
Meals	Lunch from £5.95. Dinner, 3 courses, £31.95.	
Closed	Rarely.	
Directions	South from Midhurst on A286. At sharp left bend, right (straight ahead), signed Bepton. On left after 2 miles.	

	Rebecca Crowe
	Bepton, Midhurst,
	Sussex GU29 0JB
Tel	01730 819000
Fax	01730 819099
Email	reservations@parkhousehotel.com
Web	www.parkhousehotel.com

Entry 191 Map 3

York House Rooms

A great deal of privacy and a huge amount of luxury go hand-in-hand at this rather posh house – a sanctuary after the rigours of Goodwood or Cowdray. A local stone house with an 1800s façade (the B&B wing is in a restored separate building) it also lives next to the South Downs so is a bonus for weary walkers. You have your own front door, a sitting room with a flat-screen TV, glossy magazines, bedrooms with French linen and wool blankets, and bathrooms that blast and cosset. These are tranquil, well thought-out interiors (Felicity designs) that hum with good taste: a simple lily here, a French chair there, goose down pillows on toile de Jouy-ed beds. Fabrics and textiles are expensive and in the most respectable colours: aubergines, mushrooms, deep blues and greys. And there's a tickety-boo walled garden, where you can have organic breakfast and admire raised beds with topiary and box hedging. If flowers are your thing, John Brookes's garden is near – or head to Petworth and do some antique bargain hunting. *Special rates for Goodwood. Minimum stay two nights at weekends.*

Price	£140–£180. Singles £100–£140.
Rooms	2 suites.
Meals	Pubs/restaurants nearby.
Closed	Christmas.
Directions	From London A3 to Hindhead, then A286 to Midhurst. Just before Midhurst left to Easebourne. At T-junc. left, immed. left again into Easebourne St. 150 yds on left.

Felicity & Ian Lock
York House, Easebourne Street,
Easebourne, Midhurst,
Sussex GU29 0AL

Tel	01730 814090
Email	felicity@yorkhouserooms.co.uk
Web	www.yorkhouserooms.co.uk

The Chilgrove White Horse

A restaurant with rooms hiding in the shell of an 18th-century inn that sits at the foot of the South Downs. Lose yourself in gorgeous hills. There are cycle tracks, paths for hikers, circular walks that pass the odd pub. Back at the White Horse you'll find ducks on the pond and a garden in which to watch the sun drop behind the hills. Inside is a sparkling, timber-framed restaurant. There's a small airy bar for pre-dinner drinks, but the emphasis here is firmly on food. Tables are smartly dressed with crisp linen and gleaming glass, logs smoulder on the fire, alcoves bust with hundreds of bottles (the wine list is longer than an elephant's trunk). Food is as local and organic as can be, so dig into goat's cheese tart, rack of lamb, raspberry crème brûlée. Peaceful bedrooms open onto a private garden. Expect light colours, pretty rugs, fresh flowers, power showers and bins to recycle your rubbish; bigger rooms have sofas and fridges. Breakfast hampers are brought to your room, so eat in the garden when the sun shines. Chichester is close, as is the Witterings for sand dunes and sea.

Price	£95–£160. Singles £65–£95.
Rooms	9 twins/doubles.
Meals	Lunch £7–£25. A la carte dinner about £35. Not Sunday night or Monday.
Closed	Rarely.
Directions	South from Midhurst on A286. Through West Dean, then right onto B2141. On right after 2 miles.

Charles & Carin Burton
Chilgrove, Chichester,
Sussex PO18 9HX

Tel	01243 535219
Fax	01243 535301
Email	info@whitehorsechilgrove.co.uk
Web	www.whitehorsechilgrove.co.uk

West Stoke House

A long drive through gorgeous countryside brings you to a pale stone, perfectly proportioned house with huge high-ceilinged rooms and large light windows; a Georgian pile with all the trimmings. But the feel is more restaurant with rooms than hotel, and you eat well here; there's a French twist to the fresh local fish and meat, tables are neatly laid with fresh flowers and large windows pull in the light. To the gorgeous French antiques and stunning oak floors are added abstract impressionistic paintings by local artists, modern lighting and pale, contemporary colours. If all is serene and comfortable downstairs, upstairs is no less so, with clever use of textures and colours from papal purple to palest rose pink, pristine linen, cashmere bed throws and flat-screen TVs. Bathrooms are bang up to date with a minimalist look – free-standing baths and excellent lighting. Explore three acres of gardens with a croquet lawn and large cedar woods; there are old benches and wicker seats to lounge in and sculpture to admire. Chichester and its good theatre are a short drive. *Minimum stay two nights at weekends.*

Price	£150-£175. Singles from £95.
Rooms	7 twins/doubles, 1 suite.
Meals	Lunch £22.50. Dinner £39.
Closed	Christmas Day & Boxing Day.
Directions	A3 south to Milford, A286 to Lavant. Turn right in Lavant for West Stoke.

Rowland Leach
West Stoke, Chichester,
Sussex PO18 9BN

Tel	01243 575226
Fax	01243 574655
Email	info@weststokehouse.co.uk
Web	www.weststokehouse.co.uk

The Royal Oak Inn

There's a cheery wine-bar feel to the Royal Oak; locals and young professionals come with their children and it's all as rural as can be. Inside, a modern-rustic look with traditional touches prevails: stripped floors, exposed brickwork, dark leather sofas, open fires, racing pictures on the walls – the inn was once part of the Goodwood estate. The dining area is big, light and airy, with a conservatory from which you can spill out onto a terrace that's warmed by outdoor lamps on summer nights. Five chefs conjure up delicious salmon and chorizo fishcakes, honey and clove roasted ham, fillet steak. Bedrooms have a contemporary feel. Some are in converted buildings, the rest are at the back of the pub, up the stairs; ask for one with a view. All have CD players, plasma screens, a DVD library and top toiletries – the best of modern – along with excellent lighting, brown leather chairs and big comfy beds. Staff are attentive, breakfasts are good and fresh, a secret garden looks over the South Downs, and you're well-placed for Chichester Theatre and Goodwood. *Minimum stay two nights at weekends.*

Price	£90–£130. Singles £65–£75.
Rooms	6 + 2: 4 doubles, 1 twin, 1 cottage for 2. 2 self-catering cottages: 1 for 3, 1 for 4.
Meals	Lunch & dinner, à la carte, £12.50–£25.
Closed	Christmas Day & Boxing Day.
Directions	From Chichester A286 for Midhurst. First right at first mini roundabout into E. Lavant. Down hill, pass village green, over bridge, pub 200 yds on left. Car park opposite.

Nick & Lisa Sutherland
Pook Lane, East Lavant, Chichester,
Sussex PO18 0AX

Tel	01243 527434
Fax	01243 775062
Email	enquiries@royaloaklavant.co.uk
Web	www.thesussexpub.co.uk

Entry 195 Map 3

The Ship Hotel

Admiral Sir George Murray served with Nelson and led the fleet at the Battle of Copenhagen; this grand Georgian townhouse was once his home. The hotel opened in 1939 and Eisenhower came for dinner before D-Day (the menu and guest list is framed on the first-floor landing). More recently, it was rescued from neglect, and a fine furbishment has given Chichester the hotel it deserves. The feel inside is airy and open-plan, while the hall, with its Adams' staircase leading up past arches and pillars to a painted ceiling rose, adds a touch of long-lost glamour; at Christmas an enormous tree soars. Downstairs, contemporary interiors shine. Stripped floors in the bar lead past comfy sofas and chattering locals to the brasserie, where fine arched windows look across to Priory Park. Come for croissants at breakfast, dressed crab at lunch, rib-eye steaks at dinner. Super-comfy bedrooms, all refurbished, have silky curtains, trim carpets, Egyptian cotton, padded headboards. Also: digital radios, flat-screen TVs, excellent bathrooms. Sand dunes wait at the Witterings. Brilliant. *Minimum stay two nights at weekends.*

Price	£115-£140. Singles from £89. Family £145. Suites £160.
Rooms	36: 27 twins/doubles, 5 singles, 2 family, 2 suites.
Meals	Lunch & dinner £5-£25.
Closed	Never.
Directions	A286 south from Midhurst into city. At one-way ring road, straight over (not left); left into North Street. Hotel on left.

Liz Darvill
North Street, Chichester,
Sussex PO10 1NH

Tel	01243 778000
Fax	01243 788000
Email	enquiries@chichester.theplacehotels.co.uk
Web	www.shiphotelchichester.co.uk

Arundel House

Arundel is a dream, old England at the foot of a Norman castle. Below, the Arun runs off to sea; above, a cathedral soars towards heaven. Arundel House – a listed Georgian merchant's house close to the quay – stands on the tiny high street, opposite the Tudor post office, around the corner from the market place, where castle turrets rise above rippling red roofs. Inside, warm contemporary interiors have light wood floors, clean white walls and raspberry dining chairs to match the house speciality: kir royale mixed with crème de framboise. Spotless bedrooms have the lot: wooden beds, crisp white linen, smart red throws, plasma screen TVs, swanky bathrooms. Head down for cocktails and canapés, then feast on Luke's delicious food, maybe crab and smoked haddock fishcakes, pink lamb with a rosemary jus, caramelised banana parfait with a bitter chocolate sorbet. Breakfast (fresh OJ, the full works) is equally sinful and will set you up for the day. Come by train, bring your boots, follow the river, take to the hills. There's an August arts festival and the castle opens April to November.

Price	£80–£160.
Rooms	5 doubles.
Meals	Lunch (Tuesday–Saturday) & dinner (not Sundays) £16–£30.
Closed	Rarely.
Directions	A27 to Arundel, then one-way system into town. Through market square (castle on left) and opp. post office. Parking vouchers for car park at reception.

Billy Lewis-Bowker & Luke Hackman
11 High Street, Arundel,
Sussex BN18 9AD

Tel	01903 882136
Fax	01903 881179
Web	www.arundelhouseonline.com

The Griffin Inn

A proper inn, one of the best, a community local that draws a well-heeled and devoted crowd. The occasional touch of scruffiness makes it almost perfect; fancy designers need not apply. The Pullan family run it with huge passion. You get cosy open fires, 400-year-old beams, oak panelling, settles, red carpets, prints on the walls… this inn has aged beautifully. There's a lively bar, a small club room for racing on Saturdays and two cricket teams play in summer. Bedrooms are tremendous value for money and full of uncluttered country-inn elegance: uneven floors, lovely old furniture, soft coloured walls, free-standing Victorian baths, huge shower heads, crisp linen, fluffy bathrobes, handmade soaps. Rooms in the coach house are quieter, those in next-door Griffin House quieter still. Smart seasonal menus include fresh fish from Rye and Fletching lamb. On Sundays in summer they lay on a spit-roast barbecue in the garden, with ten-mile views stretching across Pooh Bear's Ashdown Forest to Sheffield Park. Not to be missed. *Minimum stay two nights bank holiday weekends.*

Price	£80–£140. Singles £60–£80 (Sun-Thur).
Rooms	13: 6 doubles, 7 four-posters.
Meals	Bar lunch & dinner £10–£20. Restaurant £22–£30.
Closed	Christmas Day.
Directions	From East Grinstead, A22 south, right at Nutley for Fletching. On for 2 miles into village.

Bridget, Nigel & James Pullan
Fletching, Uckfield,
Sussex TN22 3SS

Tel	01825 722890
Fax	01825 722810
Email	info@thegriffininn.co.uk
Web	www.thegriffininn.co.uk

Newick Park Hotel

A classic Georgian house in 255 acres overlooking the South Downs with a lake, fishing, tennis, swimming, old-fashioned service and the cry of peacocks. Inside, ornate picture frames, chandeliers, heavy curtains and a large, light, creamy sitting room with sofas, books and a roaring fire. Food is English with a French influence, game is from the estate, some vegetables and soft fruits are grown in the walled garden (the gardener works closely with the chef) and there's home-buzzed honey, too. Bedrooms vary in size and most are traditional and chintzy; some have little window seats and sofas, all have supremely comfortable beds, fresh flowers, stunning views and some fine antiques. Recently renovated rooms outside the house have a more contemporary feel. Come to relax and to be pampered – and don't miss the Victorian dell garden with its rare collection of very old royal ferns, camellias, azaleas and rhododendrons, with masses of bulbs in spring and a lake walk. Or pop into Brighton (only 20 minutes away) for antique hunting and funky shops. *Minimum stay two nights at weekends during Glyndebourne.*

Price	£165–£285. Singles from £125.
Rooms	16 twins/doubles.
Meals	Lunch from £16.50. Dinner around £38.
Closed	31 December–5 January.
Directions	From Newick Village turn off the green and follow signs to Newick Park for 1 mile until T-junction. Turn left; after 300 yds, entrance on right.

Michael & Virginia Childs
Newick,
Sussex BN8 4SB

Tel	01825 723633
Fax	01825 723969
Email	bookings@newickpark.co.uk
Web	www.newickpark.co.uk

Wingrove House

A lovely house at the end of Alfriston High Street with delightful terraces that give the feel of Provence. A vine runs along an old stone wall, colour bursts from well-kept beds, olive trees shimmer. If the sun shines you can breakfast here with the daily papers, so dig into scrambled eggs and croissants and wash it all down with freshly squeezed juice. This is the last house in a pretty red-brick village; the South Downs Way leads out through wood and field to the cliffs of Beachy Head. If that sounds too energetic, climb up to a lovely first-floor veranda and watch lazily as walkers stride off. Downstairs you find stripped floors, pine benches and a wood-burner in the bar. In the restaurant, elegant airy interiors give way to the lower terrace where you can eat on warm nights, perhaps pan-fried sweetbreads with toasted brioche, braised blade of beef with mash and green beans, vanilla parfait with a champagne soup. Airy bedrooms are named after wine houses, all found on the wine list. You get good beds, crisp linen, flat-screen TVs and wicker chairs; two open onto the veranda.

Price	£95–£165. Singles from £70.
Rooms	5: 4 doubles, 1 twin.
Meals	Lunch from £15.
	Dinner, 3 courses, about £28.
Closed	Rarely.
Directions	M23, A23, then A27 east from Brighton. Past Berwick, then south at r'about for Alfriston. In village on left.

David & Carry Allcorn
Alfriston,
Sussex BN26 5TD

Tel	01323 870276
Fax	01323 870630
Email	info@wingrovehousehotel.com
Web	www.wingrovehousehotel.com

Stone House

One of the bedrooms has a bathroom with enough room for a sofa and two chairs, but does that make it a suite? Jane thought not. The bedroom is also big, has a beautiful four-poster, floods with light and, like all the rooms, has sumptuous furniture and seemingly ancient fabrics. All this is typical of the generosity you find here. Stone House has been in the Dunn family for a mere 500 years and Peter and Jane have kept the feel of home. Downstairs, amid the splendour of the drawing room, there's still space for lots of old family photos; across the hall in the library, logs piled high wait to be tossed on the fire. Weave down a corridor to ancient oak panelling in the dining room for Jane's unbeatable cooking; she's a Master Chef who runs cookery courses that sell out in seconds. She's also a gardener, with a sensational half-acre walled kitchen garden that bursts with fresh produce – they're 99% self-sufficient in summer. There are 1,000 acres to explore and indulgent picnic hampers for Glyndebourne, including chairs and tables, can be arranged. Perfect. *Minimum stay two nights at weekends May-September.*

Price	£125–£245. Singles £80–£115.
Rooms	6: 3 twins/doubles, 2 four-posters, 1 suite.
Meals	Lunch £24.95, by arrangement. Dinner £24.95.
Closed	Christmas & New Year.
Directions	From Heathfield, B2096; 4th turning on right, signed Rushlake Green. 2 miles down hill & up into village. 1st left by village green to x-roads; house on far left, signed.

Peter & Jane Dunn
Rushlake Green, Heathfield,
Sussex TN21 9QJ

Tel	01435 830553
Fax	01435 830726
Web	www.stonehousesussex.co.uk

Zanzibar Hotel

A sparkling Regency townhouse on the seafront at Hastings, where groovy bedrooms travel the world. Africa, Antarctica, South America… those at the front are exceptional and look straight out to sea. Downstairs, high ceilings and white walls soak up sea light. A total renovation has restored antique radiators, ceiling roses and chandeliers, while ethnic wood carvings, Indian wall hangings and mounted fossils add decoration. An honesty bar in the conservatory leads out to a terraced garden, champagne breakfasts are brought up to you – possibly because it's too hard to coax guests from their rooms. One suite has its free-standing bath behind a voile curtain and a chandelier twinkling above; another has a tiny sauna in its bathroom. Bedrooms at the back are smaller (though never small). One has a sitting room/bathroom and a bed on the mezzanine with a very low ceiling, another has a Japanese bath. All have fine linen, designer touches and the usual high-tech trappings. Don't miss Hastings: the promenade, cliff walks, fishermen's huts, 1066 and all that. *Minimum stay two nights at weekends.*

Price	£99–£175.
Rooms	8 doubles.
Meals	Tapas from £3. Restaurants nearby.
Closed	Never.
Directions	West from Hastings on coast road (A259). Pass pier, then speed camera; hotel on right before zebra crossing.

Max O'Rourke
9 Eversfield Place,
St Leonards-on-Sea,
Sussex TN37 6BY

Tel	01424 460109
Email	info@zanzibarhotel.co.uk
Web	www.zanzibarhotel.co.uk

Entry 202 Map 4

Jeake's House

Rye, one of the Cinque Ports, is a perfect town for whiling away an afternoon; follow the tidal river, wander past old fishing boats, potter around Church Square, visit a gallery. Jeake's House, on a steep, cobbled street in the heart of it all, has a colourful past as wool store, school and home of American poet Conrad Potter Aiken. Carpeted corridors weave along to cosy bedrooms which come with beams and timber frames. They're generously furnished, excellent value. Some have stunning old chandeliers, others four-posters, one has a telly concealed in the woodburner. A mind-your-head stairway leads up to a generous attic room for views over roof tops and chimneys. The galleried dining room – once an old Baptist chapel, now painted deep red – is full of busts, books, clocks, mirrors and fabric flowers: a fine setting for a full English breakfast. A cosy honesty bar with armchairs, books and papers is a convivial spot for a nightcap, the hearth is lit in winter and musicians will swoon at the working square piano. Jenny, efficient and friendly, has created a lovely atmosphere. *Children over eight welcome.*

Price	£88-£120. Singles £79.
Rooms	11: 7 twins/doubles, 3 four-poster suites, all en suite; 1 double with separate bath.
Meals	Restaurants in Rye.
Closed	Never.
Directions	From centre of Rye on A268, left off High St onto West St, then 1st right into Mermaid St. House on left. Private car park, £3 a day for guests.

Jenny Hadfield
Mermaid Street, Rye,
Sussex TN31 7ET

Tel	01797 222828
Fax	01797 222623
Email	stay@jeakeshouse.com
Web	www.jeakeshouse.com

The George in Rye

Ancient Rye has a big history. It's a reclaimed island, a wealthy cinque port which once held its own army yet regularly fell into French hands. Henry James lived here, too, and the oldest working church clock in England chimes in a gracious square at the top of the hill. As for the George, it stands serenely on the cobbled high street. It was built in 1575 from reclaimed ships' timbers and its exposed beams and joists remain on display to this day. A contemporary revamp in classical style trumpets airy interiors, stripped floors, panelled walls and open fires – Jane Austen in the 21st century. There's a huge leather sofa in the bar by the fire, screen prints of the Beatles on the walls in reception, voile curtains and parquet floors in the restaurant. Divine bedrooms come in all shapes and sizes, but fabulous fabrics, Frette linen, flat-screen TVs and Vi-spring mattresses are standard, as are Aveda soaps by the bath and cashmere covers on hot water bottles. Superb food in the restaurant – seared scallops, Romney Marsh lamb, Seville orange ice cream – can be washed down by local English wines. Exceptional.

Price	£125–£175. Suites £225. Singles from £95.
Rooms	24: 15 doubles, 4 twins/doubles, 5 suites.
Meals	Lunch & dinner £5–£35.
Closed	Never.
Directions	Follow signs up hill into town centre. Through arch; pub on left. Parking at foot of hill.

Alex & Katie Clarke
98 High Street, Rye,
Sussex TN31 7JT
Tel   01797 222114
Fax   01797 224065
Email   stay@thegeorgeinrye.com
Web   www.thegeorgeinrye.com

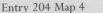

The Bell

An old pub on a tiny green in a pretty village. Step inside to find a post office at one end, bar and restaurant at the other. Locals pop in for bread, travellers come for a drop of ale. Ashley oversees daily life with easy-going conviviality, stopping to chat while juggling the phone. Downstairs you find a big airy room, with a panelled wall at one end that gives way to smartly dressed tables, stripped wooden floors and leather sofas in the bar. Vases are filled with fresh flowers, baskets piled with logs, candles flicker on the mantelpiece. Spotless bedrooms wait above. Those at the back are simpler and come in light colours, most with compact shower rooms. Those at the front overlook the village and are more colourful altogether. One has a crushed velvet headboard that fills the wall; you may get mohair blankets, flat-screen TVs, a kitsch mural in the shower. Come down for a good meal served informally, perhaps whitebait and lemon, Moroccan chicken, raspberry Charlotte with chocolate sauce. Stratford is on your doorstep for all things Shakespeare. The NEC is close, as are the M40 and M42.

Price	£75–£115. Singles from £55.
Rooms	9: 8 doubles, 1 twin.
Meals	Continental breakfast included; full English £5. Lunch from £6.95. Dinner, 3 courses, about £25. Not Sunday eve.
Closed	Rarely.
Directions	M42, junc. 3, then A435 south for Reddich. Tanworth signed left. In village on green.

Ashley Bent
The Green, Tamworth-in-Arden,
Henley-in-Arden, Warwickshire B94 5AL

Tel	01564 742212
Email	reservations@thebellattanworthinarden.co.uk
Web	www.thebellattanworthinarden.co.uk

Mallory Court

A super-smart country house which dates to 1910 but looks ancient. It stands in ten acres of formal English gardens with trim lawns, planted beds, a tennis court and sun loungers flanking the pool. Inside, a panelled restaurant, open fires, cavernous sofas, the loveliest staff, a clipped elegance at every turn. Bedrooms in the main house come in grand traditional style. Most are huge, all have big beds dressed in Egyptian cotton, some have bay windows giving views over the grounds or original Art Deco marble bathrooms. One has a muralled ceiling, another has golden wallpaper, all have bowls of fruit, flat-screen TVs and white bath robes. Simpler rooms in the Knight's Suite have an uncluttered, more contemporary style. A Michelin star in the dining room pulls in the locals and offers rich and irresistible treats, perhaps bisque of shellfish with crab tortellini and pernod cream, fillet of beef with wild mushrooms and a madeira sauce, and roasted pear with sorbet and a caramel sauce. In summer, you can eat on the terrace by a glorious fig tree with huge views off to distant country.

Price	£185–£255. Suites £325–£365. Singles from £115. Knight's Suite rooms: £145.
Rooms	30: 6 doubles, 2 twins/doubles, 1 single, 10 suites. Knight's Suite: 11 twins/doubles.
Meals	Lunch from £23.50. Dinner, 3 courses, £39.50–£55. Meals also in brasserie.
Closed	Never.
Directions	M40 junc. 13, then B4087 thro' Bishop's Tachbrook. Right at traffic lights onto A425; on right.

Mark E. Chambers
Harbury Lane , Bishop's Tachbrook,
Leamington Spa, Warwickshire CV33 9QB
Tel   01926 330214
Fax   01926 451714
Email   reception@mallory.co.uk
Web   www.mallory.co.uk

The Howard Arms

The Howard buzzes with good-humoured babble as well-kept beer flows from the flagstoned bar. Logs crackle contentedly in a vast open fire; a blackboard menu scales the wall above; a dining room at the far end has unexpected elegance, with great swathes of bold colour and some noble paintings. Gorgeous bedrooms are set discreetly apart from the joyful throng, mixing period style and modern luxury beautifully: the double oozes olde worlde charm, the twin is more folksy (American art, patchwork quilts) and the half-tester is almost a suite, full of antiques. All are individual, all huge by pub standards. The village is a surprise, too, literally tucked under a lone hill, with an unusual church surrounded by orchards and an extended village green. Round off an idyllic walk amid buzzing bees and fragrant wild flowers with a meal at the inn, perhaps seared scallops with a sweet chilli sauce and crème fraîche, then beef, ale and mustard pie, finally spiced pear and apple flapjack crumble. Stratford and the theatre are close. *Minimum stay two nights at weekends.*

Price	£120–138. Singles from £87.50.
Rooms	3: 2 doubles, 1 twin.
Meals	Lunch & dinner £10.50–£26.50.
Closed	Christmas Day.
Directions	From Stratford, south on A3400 for 4 miles, right to Wimpstone & Ilmington. Pub in village centre.

Martin Devereux
Lower Green, Ilmington,
Stratford-upon-Avon, Warwickshire CV36 4LT

Tel	01608 682226
Fax	01608 682226
Email	info@howardarms.com
Web	www.howardarms.com

Fulready Manor

Fulready is majestic, a castle in the fields. It took 12 years to build from 2,000 pieces of hand-cut stone and is designed to last 500 years. It stands in 120 acres of quiet green country, with soothing views at the back over lamb-dotted fields to rippling hills. There's a lake, too, with a rowing boat for excursions to the island. All this you gaze upon dreamily from a glorious drawing room (muralled walls, huge sofas, roaring fire) where mullioned windows from floor to ceiling frame perfect views. Upstairs, bedrooms are just as you'd expect: sublimely decorated. (It helps if your daughter is an interior designer.) Expect Sanderson wallpapers, thick fabrics, mahogany furniture, perhaps an old oak four-poster. One room has tromp l'oeil artwork in the bathroom, another has a sitting room in an en suite turret. Best of all are Michael and Mauveen who pamper you rotten in true B&B fashion with grilled grapefruits and home-laid eggs among myriad breakfast treats. Stratford and Warwick are close and one of Warwickshire's best dining pubs is nearby for tasty dinners.

Price	£110–£150.
Rooms	3: 1 double, 2 four-posters.
Meals	Restaurants within 5 miles.
Closed	Christmas & New Year.
Directions	M40 junc. 11, then A422 west. Left in Pillerton Priors (B4451). Fulready first driveway on left after 0.25 miles.

Michael & Mauveen Spencer
Ettington, Stratford-upon-Avon,
Warwickshire CV37 7PE

Tel	01789 740152
Fax	01789 740247
Email	stay@fulreadymanor.co.uk
Web	www.fulreadymanor.co.uk

The George

The George dates to 1765 and was named after George III, whose daughter, Queen Victoria, once stayed. It stands on Shipston's tiny high street, a handsome pile of red bricks. Inside, a complete renovation has brought colour and style in equal measure. Airy interiors are easy on the eye – a magnet to locals, who pour in for good food and a lively bar that serves local ales and champagne by the glass. The feel is informal, the service is friendly. You get sand-blasted beams, stripped floors, cool colours on the wall. There's a sitting room/library for residents with leather armchairs in front of an open fire, a private dining room with a jet-black chandelier, a decked terrace for a pint in summer. Colourful bedrooms come with crisp white linen, silky curtains, iPod docks and flat-screen TVs. Some are big, some are smaller, two have fine bay windows, all have super bathrooms (walk-in showers or claw-foot baths). Good food in the restaurant may offer Evesham asparagus, homemade fishcakes, raspberry crème brûlée. You're on the northern flank of the Cotswolds, Warwick Castle is close. *Minimum stay two nights at weekends.*

Price	£90–£160. Singles from £67.50.
Rooms	16 doubles.
Meals	Bar meals from £5.
	Dinner, 3 courses, about £25.
Closed	Christmas Day.
Directions	M40 junc. 11, then west on B4035
	to Shipton.

Rachel Hawkins
High Street,
Shipston-on-Stour,
Warwickshire CV36 4AJ

Tel	01608 661453
Email	info@thefabulousgeorgehotel.com
Web	www.thefabulousgeorgehotel.com

The Pear Tree Inn

A cool rustic chic flows effortlessly through the Pear Tree; miss it at your peril. This is a dreamy blend of French inspiration and English whimsy, a sweep of warm airy interiors that make you feel that you've washed up in dining-pub heaven. Step in under the beams, glide across the flagged floors, dive into an armchair and roast away in front of the fire. Keep going and you come to high-ceiling'd dining rooms, where stripped floors are dressed in smart old rugs, with wooden scythes, shovels and ladders hanging from the walls. French windows flood the place with light and open up in summer for alfresco suppers (there's a boules piste out there, too). Exquisite bedrooms (up in the eaves or out in the old barn) come in Farrow & Ball lime white and have suede headboards, wonderfully upholstered armchairs, Bang & Olufsen TVs and funky rugs for colour; bathrooms too, with robes and creamy tiles, are spoiling. As for the food, don't miss that either — particularly the warm pear and almond tart with rosemary ice cream. Locals flock in, so no surprise to discover that Martin and Debbie have opened a farm shop nearby.

Price	£105. Family £140. Singles £75.
Rooms	8: 6 doubles, 2 family.
Meals	Lunch from £13.50. A la carte dinner from £25.
Closed	Christmas & New Year.
Directions	West from Melksham on A365, then right onto B3353 for Whitley. Through village, then left, signed Purlpit. Pub on right after 400 yards.

Martin & Debbie Still
Top Lane, Whitley,
Melksham, Wiltshire SN12 8QX

Tel	01225 709131
Fax	01225 702276
Email	enquiries@thepeartreeinn.com
Web	www.thepeartreeinn.com

The Swan

This graceful town of honey-coloured stone slips down hill to the river Avon, where a 600-year-old bridge spans the water with sublime style. You can pick up riverside paths and follow them eight miles up to Bath, ride your bike, stop at pubs, then hop on a train and come back for supper. The Swan goes back to the 15th century and stands on the high street. Inside, an easy elegance and relaxed informality go hand in hand. Open-plan interiors fill with light, you get stripped boards, flagged floors, high ceilings and country rugs. There's a small terrace for drinks in the sun, a front bar with an open fire and an airy restaurant that fills with locals, so come for great English food – perhaps Devon crab with toast and lemon, fish pie with cheddar mash, lime cheesecake with fresh raspberries. Uncluttered bedrooms are a treat, supremely comfortable with crisp white linen, padded headboards, delicious fabrics and flat-screen TVs. Those at the back on the upper floors overlook the river. All have bold colours on the walls and super little tongue-and-groove bathrooms. *Minimum stay two nights at weekends.*

Price	£95–£140. Singles from £85.
Rooms	12: 8 doubles, 2 twins/doubles, 2 singles.
Meals	Lunch from 4.50. Sunday lunch from £12. Dinner, 3 courses, about £25.
Closed	Never.
Directions	M4 junc. 18, then A46 south for Bath. A4 east, then A363 south to Bradford. On right in village, car park behind.

Mark Heather
1 Church Street,
Bradford-on-Avon, Wiltshire BA15 1LN

Tel	01225 868686
Fax	01225 868681
Email	theswan-hotel@btconnect.com
Web	www.theswan-hotel.com

The Bath Arms

A 17th-century coaching inn on the Longleat estate in a gorgeous village lost in the country; geese swim in the river, cows laze in the fields and lush woodland wraps around you. At the front, the 12 apostles – a dozen pollarded lime trees – shade a gravelled garden, while at the back, two large stone terraces, separated by beds of lavender, soak up the sun (you can eat out here in good weather). Inside are the best of old and new: flagstones and boarded floors mix with a stainless steel bar and Farrow & Ball paints. The feel is smart and airy, with a skittle alley that doubles as a sitting room (they show movies here too) and shimmering Cole & Son wallpaper in the dining room. Stop for caramelised onion tart, bavette steak with Lyonnaise potatoes, then Pimms granita. Bedrooms are a real treat, some in the main house, others in a converted barn. Expect lots of colour, big wallpapers, beds dressed in Eygptian cotton, DVD and CD players; bathrooms come in black slate, some with free-standing baths, others with deluge showers. Longleat is at the bottom of the hill – the walk down is majestic. *Minimum stay two nights at weekends.*

Price	£80–£145. Singles from £60.
Rooms	14: 10 doubles, 2 twins, 2 singles.
Meals	Lunch & dinner £5–£30.
Closed	Never.
Directions	A303, then A350 north to Longbridge Deverill. Left for Maiden Bradley, then right for Horningsham. Through village, on right.

Christoph Brooke
Longleat Estate, Horningsham,
Warminster, Wiltshire BA12 7LY

Tel	01985 844308
Fax	01985 845187
Email	enquiries@batharms.co.uk
Web	www.batharms.co.uk

Spread Eagle Inn

While Stourhead Gardens "echo with references to the heroes and gods of ancient Rome", this proper inn with rooms makes more than a passing nod to Bacchus. Mellow and old-fashioned it may appear but peep inside and you see slate or coir floors, Farrow & Ball colours and understated jugs of garden flowers on old pine tables. In the bar a woodburning stove is merry and the seats are comfy; you can eat here or in the restaurant that doubles as a sitting room. Red walls, large modern paintings and old prints create a mood that is cosy and warm. The higgledy-piggledy stairs are great if you're nimble and the bedrooms peaceful – expect muted colours, white linen, original fireplaces and delightful views. Bathrooms are not state-of-the-art but perfectly plain – and spotless. Food is English and locally supplied: Wiltshire ham with sweet mustard, west country fish soup, griddled organic salmon salad with anchovy mayonnaise. The village is charming – and you can pretend that this stupendous example of a landscape garden with its lake and follies is yours when the hoards have gone home.

Price	£110. Singles £80.
Rooms	5: 2 doubles, 3 twins/doubles.
Meals	Lunch from £6.95. Dinner from £10.50.
Closed	Christmas Day.
Directions	Turn off B3092 signed Stourhead Gardens. Spread Eagle is below main car park on left at entrance to garden. Private car park for Inn.

Tom Bridgeman
Stourton, Warminster,
Wiltshire BA12 6QE

Tel	01747 840587
Email	enquiries@spreadeagleinn.com
Web	www.spreadeagleinn.com

The Lamb at Hindon

The Lamb has been serving ale on Hindon's high street for 800 years, give or take a decade. It is a yard of England's finest cloth, a place where shooting parties come for lunch, where farmers meet to chew the cud. They come for huge oak settles, heavy old beams, deep red walls and roaring fires. A clipped Georgian country elegance lingers; you almost expect Mr Darcy to walk in, give a tormented sigh, then turn on his heels and vanish. You get flagstone floors and stripped wooden boards, window seats and gilded mirrors. Old oils entwined in willow hang on the walls, a bookshelf is stuffed with aged tomes of poetry. At night, candles come out, as do some serious whiskies and the odd Cuban cigar, and in the restaurant you can feast on game terrine, Angus rump, then local cheeses. Bedrooms are warm and comfortable, just as they should be, with mahogany furniture, tartan carpets, the odd four-poster, perhaps a sofa. Fishing can be arranged, or you can shoot off to Stonehenge, Stourhead, Salisbury or Bath. Return for a drink on the terrace and watch village life float by.

Price	£99–£135. Singles from £70.
Rooms	14: 13 doubles, 1 twin.
Meals	Lunch & dinner from £7.50.
Closed	Never.
Directions	M3, A303 & signed left at bottom of steep hill two miles east of junction with A350.

Nick James
High Street, Hindon,
Salisbury, Wiltshire SP3 6DP

Tel	01747 820573
Fax	01747 820605
Email	info@lambathindon.co.uk
Web	www.lambathindon.co.uk

Howard's House

Howard's has been a favourite of ours for years — luxurious without boasting, modest in its success, the sort of place where the sun shines, even in January. With one toe in deep country, this attractive 1623 stone house is the last building in a quiet village of soaring church spire and gently rising hills. Step inside the warm flagstoned entrance hall to beautiful mullioned windows of odd shapes and sizes, masses of space, flowers and bold colours everywhere. Mustard and red walls draw you into the sitting room to relax by a huge stone fireplace — you'll find *Tatler*, *The Economist* and *Classic Car* on the table. Strong teal and stone hues lift the crisp, modern dining room; pastel hues dominate faultless bedrooms with floral fabrics, fresh fruit, homemade biscuits, bathrobes and big towels. French windows lead to furnished patios. The quintessentially English garden has clipped hedges, croquet lawns, a fountain, a pond and vegetable and sensory herb patches; some of the produce ends up on your table; the modern British cooking is consistently good. Beautiful Wiltshire starts right outside.

Price	£155–£175. Singles from £100.	
Rooms	9: 6 doubles, 1 twin/double, 1 four-poster, 1 family.	
Meals	Dinner £25.95; à la carte around £42.	
Closed	Christmas.	
Directions	From Salisbury, A30, B3089 west to Teffont. There, left at sharp right-hand bend, following brown hotel sign. Entrance on right after 0.5 miles.	

Noele Thompson
Teffont Evias, Salisbury,
Wiltshire SP3 5RJ

Tel   01722 716392
Fax   01722 716820
Email   enq@howardshousehotel.co.uk
Web   www.howardshousehotel.co.uk

The Compasses Inn

Set between ancient villages on a lane to nowhere and back, the Compasses is the quintessential English inn, so content with its lot it could almost be a figment of your imagination. Modest, ineffably pretty, perfect inside and out, it's been here since 1368, a low thatched refuge for drovers and smugglers. Duck instinctively into the sudden darkness of the bar and experience a wave of nostalgia as your eyes adjust to a long wooden room with flagstones, oak beams from a galleon, crackling logs and cosy booths divided by farmyard salvage: a cartwheel here, some horse tack there and a piano at one end. The pub glows warmly with Alan and Susie's enthusiasm and the daily changing blackboard proclaims fresh and inventive cooking from two chefs who sometimes pop out for a chat with the guests. Bedrooms are at the top of some stone stairs outside the front door (so there's not too far to stagger) and have the same effortless charm; walls are thick, windows are wonky, bathrooms are new and the sweet serenity of Wiltshire lies just down the lane. The wonderful welcome extends to children and dogs.

Price	From £85. Singles £65.
Rooms	4 + 1: 2 doubles, 2 twins/doubles. 1 self-catering cottage for 2.
Meals	Lunch from £5. A la carte dinner, around £20.
Closed	Rarely.
Directions	From Salisbury, A30 west, 3rd right after Fovant, signed Lower Chicksgrove, then 1st left down single track lane to village.

Alan & Susie Stoneham
Lower Chicksgrove, Tisbury,
Wiltshire SP3 6NB

Tel	01722 714318
Fax	01722 714318
Email	thecompasses@aol.com
Web	www.thecompassesinn.com

The Royal Forester Country Inn

The Wyre Forest starts across the road. There are thousands of acres to explore, on foot, on bike, even on horseback; the inn has two stables, so bring your own pony or ride out locally. As for the inn, it looms on the side of the road without attracting much attention, but for those who stop, there's a treat in store. It goes back to 1411, but despite its flagged floors, timber-framed walls and low beamed ceilings, the feel is distinctly contemporary with an open-plan flow. You find stripped floors and sofas in the bar, a bust of Buddha in one of the restaurants and a 1930s photo of the foresters dominating one wall. Super bedrooms upstairs are simply stylish and have extremely attractive prices. You get walls of colour, coir matting, leather beds, crushed velvet throws and flat-screen TVs. And excellent slate bathrooms with coloured glass sinks. Come back down for well-priced bistro-style food, perhaps moules marinières, T-bone steak, and coconut and malibu crème brûlée; there are monthly gourmet nights: three courses, five wines! The River Severn is close. *Minimum stay two nights at weekends.*

Price	£79. Singles £55.
Rooms	7 doubles.
Meals	Lunch from £4.95.
	Dinner, 3 courses, about £25.
Closed	Never.
Directions	West from Kidderminster on A456.
	On left in village.

Sean Mcgahern & Maxine Parker
Callow Hill, Nr Bewdley,
Worcestershire DY14 9XW

Tel	01299 266286
Email	royalforesterinn@btinternet.com
Web	www.royalforesterinn.co.uk

Colwall Park

Jump on a train at Paddington, watch the world pass by; jump off at Colwall and you're 50 paces from the bar. This is the sunny side of the Malvern Hills and paths lead out into blistering country, so walk your socks off, then come back for afternoon tea under the old lime tree on the lawn. The hotel was built in 1905 for the owners of Colwall race course. These days it's the players from Malvern Theatre who come; a rogue's gallery of famous faces hangs on a wall. This is a comfortable airy hotel with good prices to match. You find mullioned windows, trim carpets, open fires and fresh flowers. There's a pretty sitting room with cosy sofas and a bar at the front where you can dig into light meals (omelettes, fish pie, local sausages); if you fancy a slap-up dinner, wander into the panelled restaurant and try twice-baked cheese soufflé, roast loin of local venison, pistachio crème brûlée with hot chocolate ice cream. Spotless bedrooms come in pastel colours with padded headboards, good linen and a sofa in the bigger rooms (two are huge). Historic Ledbury town is close. *Minimum stay two nights at weekends.*

Price	£120–£140. Singles £80. Suites £150.
Rooms	22: 17 twins/doubles, 3 singles, 1 suite, 1 family suite.
Meals	Lunch from £7.95. Dinner, à la carte, about £35.
Closed	Rarely.
Directions	M5 junc. 7 or M50 junc. 2. Colwall halfway between Ledbury & Malvern. Colwall Park in centre of village.

Iain Nesbitt
Colwall, Malvern,
Worcestershire WR13 6QG

Tel	01684 540000
Fax	01684 540847
Email	hotel@colwall.com
Web	www.colwall.com

The Cottage in the Wood

Walk along a path through the woods, dappled with light, and emerge in a clearing in this English jungle. There, the Cottage gazes across the wide, flat Severn Valley to the distant Cotswolds – a heart-stopping view. It is enough just to be here, near the breezy top of the Malvern Hills, but to find such an endearingly friendly country-house hotel in such a delightful position is a treat. The décor is polished, swagged, patterned and lined – distinctly pre-modern – with a choice antique round every corner. Many of the bedrooms are in a new building and have wonderfully luxurious bathrooms. Service is courteous and charming, the sort you only get when a large and talented family is at the helm, and Dominic's cooking is as exemplary as his father's hotel-keeping. Local produce is used in an imaginative way and portions are generous, perhaps wild mushroom mousse with crème fraiche, Herefordshire beef with a red wine jus, vanilla crème brûlée with Champagne sorbet. Relax, drink in the views, sup from an excellent wine list. A civilised retreat.

Price	£99–£179. Singles £79–£109. Half-board (min. 2 nights) £58–£104 p.p.
Rooms	30: 21 doubles, 8 twins/doubles, 1 four-poster.
Meals	Lunch from £4.95. Dinner, 3 course, about £30. Packed lunch £8.50.
Closed	Rarely.
Directions	M5 junc. 7; A449 through Gt Malvern. In Malvern Wells, 3rd right after Railway Pub. Signed.

John & Sue Pattin
Holywell Road, Malvern Wells,
Worcestershire WR14 4LG

Tel	01684 575859
Fax	01684 560662
Email	reception@cottageinthewood.co.uk
Web	www.cottageinthewood.co.uk

Russell's

Set back from the High Street in this chocolate-box-pretty village full of smart shops is an 18th-century former office to a long-gone factory. Walk in to blasted beams, new pale stone floors, sleek lighting and mellow walls, wooden tables set with slate mats, and glass doors at the back that open to a flagstoned terrace. Food is modern, English and extremely good value; try ham hock with homemade piccalilli or grilled Cornish plaice with rosemary and new potatoes. The global wine list is short but intelligently chosen by Barry, an easy, charming and friendly host. Once dinner is over there's a quiet little sitting room with an honesty bar upstairs, or you could sprawl in a very comfortable chair in your super-crisp bedroom (the suite is spectacular). Beds are large and plump with pure wool throws and clouds of pillows, bathrooms are state-of-the-art with shiny chrome accessories, stone floors, thick towels and nurturing bubbles and creams. Whether you plan to explore the shops or stride the Cotswolds, breakfast (whatever you want really) will set you up beautifully. *Minimum stay two nights at weekends.*

Price	£115–£180. Suite £245–£295.
Rooms	7: 3 doubles, 1 twin/double, 2 family, 1 suite.
Meals	Lunch, 2 courses, from £14.95. Dinner, 3 courses, from £16.95.
Closed	Rarely.
Directions	A44 from Oxford & Evesham; B4632 from Cheltenham; in centre of Broadway on High Street.

Barry Hancox
The Green, 20 High Street, Broadway,
Worcestershire WR12 7DT

Tel	01386 853555
Fax	01386 853964
Email	info@russellsofbroadway.com
Web	www.russellsofbroadway.com

Waterford House

In a lively village dominated by Middleham Castle – northern stronghold of Richard III – is this very pretty Georgian house, now a small hotel. Martin and Anne are exceptional hosts, easy and delightful, their house full of beautiful things. Settle into sofas for drinks and canapés in the cosiest drawing room, then amble across to the red dining room for a memorable meal and ambrosial wines. On summer evenings dine alfresco in the small garden with its summer house and trickling stream. Bedrooms, up narrow – in parts steep – stairs, have bags of old-fashioned comfort: wrought-iron beds, William Morris wallpaper, pictures, books, sherry, homemade cakes. The panelled four-poster with blue bedspread and bolsters is a treat. Middleham is a racing village and has 14 stable yards; horses clop by in the morning on their way to the gallops. Breakfast, served on white linen, is a feast of local produce. Linger as long as you like – it's that sort of place – then grab a rod and fish the Ure or pull on your hiking boots and unravel the Dales. Leyburn, for the biggest auction house in the north, is close.

Price	£85-£115. Singles £65-£75.
Rooms	5: 2 doubles, 1 twin/double, 2 four-posters.
Meals	Dinner, 4 courses, £33 (not Sunday).
Closed	Rarely.
Directions	Southbound from A1 at Scotch Corner via Richmond & Leyburn. Northbound from A1 on B6267 via Masham. House in northern corner of square.

Martin Cade & Anne Parkinson Cade
19 Kirkgate, Middleham,
Yorkshire DL8 4PG

Tel	01969 622090
Fax	01969 624020
Email	info@waterfordhousehotel.co.uk
Web	www.waterfordhousehotel.co.uk

Simonstone Hall

The view from the terrace is magnificent, a five-mile drift through Wensleydale to the summit of Dodd Fell, and in summer you can breakfast here under the shade of beech trees. This is the 1773 shooting lodge of the Earls of Wharncliffe. Stag Fell rises behind. Inside you find a quirky mix of old and new: trophies and oils jostle with wicker armchairs and thick blue carpet. Painted panelling soaks up the light in the drawing room and dining room, there are stripped wood floors in the Orangerie and a pitch pine snug that's warmed by its own wood-burner in the bar. Bedrooms come in different shapes and sizes. Those at the front are big and grand and have the view; those at the back are simpler altogether. Expect a country-house feel: mahogany dressers, ornate fireplaces, shelves of books, perhaps mullioned windows, a four-poster bed or a claw-foot bath. You can eat (very well) all over the place, three courses in the dining room, soup or a steak in the Orangerie and bar. All around you is some of the loveliest walking in the land, and don't forget the Champagne picnic.

Price	£110–£180. Singles from £75.
Rooms	17: 9 doubles, 2 twins/doubles, 5 four-posters, 1 suite.
Meals	Lunch from £5. Dinner around £30. Champagne picnic from £25 for two.
Closed	Rarely.
Directions	From Hawes, north for Muker for about 2 miles. Hotel on left, at foot of Buttertubs Pass.

Caroline Bilingham
Hawes,
Yorkshire DL8 3LY

Tel	01969 667255
Fax	01969 667741
Email	e-mail@simonstonehall.demon.co.uk
Web	www.simonstonehall.com

The Austwick Traddock

Friendly, unpretentious and full of traditional comforts, this family-run hotel is a terrific base for walkers – the Three Peaks are at the door. The house is Georgian with Victorian additions and its name originates from the horse sales that once took place in next door's paddock. Open fires smoulder on winter days, deckchairs dot the garden in summer. Country-house bedrooms have bags of charm: antique dressing tables, quilted beds, perhaps a bergère headboard or a claw-foot bath. Those on the second floor have a cosy attic feel, all have fresh flowers, flat-screen TVs, decanters of sherry and Dales views. As for the restaurant, it's the first in the north of England to be certified 100% organic by the Soil Association; dig into delicious seared scallops, wild venison, lemon soufflé with a Yorkshire curd sorbet. There's a cheerful William Morris feel to it all – polished brass in front of the fire, a panelled breakfast room, beds of lavender in the garden – and the village, with two clapper bridges, is a gem. Don't miss the amazing caves at Ingleborough, or Settle for antiques. *Minimum two nights at weekends May-September.*

Price	£140–£180. Singles £80–£100. Half-board from £80 p.p.
Rooms	10: 7 doubles, 1 twin/double, 1 family, 1 single.
Meals	Lunch £15–£20. Dinner, 3 courses, about £30.
Closed	Rarely.
Directions	0.75 miles off the A65, midway between Kirkby Lonsdale & Skipton.

Bruce Reynolds
Austwick, Settle,
Yorkshire LA2 8BY

Tel	01524 251224
Fax	01524 251796
Email	info@austwicktraddock.co.uk
Web	www.austwicktraddock.co.uk

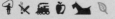

The Tempest Arms

A 16th-century ale house three miles west of Skipton with great prices, friendly staff and an easy style. Inside you find stone walls and open fires, six ales on tap at the bar and a smart beamed restaurant. An airy open-plan feel runs throughout with sofas and armchairs strategically placed in front of a fire that burns on both sides. Delicious traditional food is a big draw — the inn was packed for lunch on a Tuesday in April. You can eat wherever you want, so grab a seat and dig into Yorkshire puddings with a rich onion gravy, cottage pie with a Wensleydale crust, treacle tart with pink grapefruit sorbet. Bedrooms are just as good. Those in the main house are slightly simpler, but most are ten paces beyond in two newly built stone houses and they're rather indulging. You get crisp linen, neutral colours, slate bathrooms and flat-screen TVs. Those at the back have views of the fells, suites are large and worth the money, a couple have decks with hot tubs to soak in. The Dales are on your doorstep, this is a great base for walkers. Skipton, a proper Yorkshire market town, is worth a look.

Price	£80. Suites £95–£110. Singles from £60.
Rooms	21: 9 doubles, 12 suites.
Meals	Lunch & dinner £5–£25.
Closed	Never.
Directions	A56 west from Skipton. Signed left after two miles.

Martin & Veronica Clarkson
Elslack, Skipton, Yorkshire BD23 3AY

Tel	01282 842450
Fax	01282 843331
Email	info@tempestarms.co.uk
Web	www.tempestarms.co.uk

The Weavers Shed Restaurant with Rooms

Sublime simplicity at the top of the hill; the welcome is second to none, the food is some of the best in Yorkshire, and those who make the detour find unbeatable value for money. Wander around outside for a well-kept garden and cobbles in the courtyard, then step inside and discover whitewashed walls, thick stone arches and terracotta-tiled floors. All is bright and breezy – Provence in the Colne Valley! – with menus from around the world framed on the walls. As for the food, Stephen's passion stretches as far as tending a one-acre kitchen garden which supplies most of his needs. You may get duck cooked four ways, calf's liver with a red-onion marmalade, then soufflé of Yorkshire rhubarb with crumble ice cream. Retire to super bedrooms for warm colours, comfy beds, fluffy bath robes – and pop back down in the morning for a fabulous breakfast: flagons of freshly-squeezed orange juice, delicious sausages, homemade marmalades and jams. Take to the glorious Pennines and work off your indulgence or simply climb the hill – *Last of the Summer Wine* is filmed on these streets. Brilliant.

Price	£90–£95. Singles from £70.
Rooms	5: 3 doubles, 1 twin/double, 1 four-poster.
Meals	Lunch from £14.95. Dinner, 3 courses, around £45. Restaurant closed Sun/Mon; no lunch Sat.
Closed	Christmas & New Year.
Directions	From Huddersfield A62 west for 2 miles, then right for Milnsbridge & Golcar. Left at Somerfield; signed on right at top of hill.

Stephen & Tracy Jackson
86–88 Knowl Road, Golcar,
Huddersfield, Yorkshire HD7 4AN

Tel	01484 654284
Fax	01484 650980
Email	info@weaversshed.co.uk
Web	www.weaversshed.co.uk

Entry 225 Map 6

The Angel Inn

The Angel has it all – a perfect English inn. It stands in the middle of a tiny hamlet surrounded by lush grazing land with Rylstone Fell rising behind. You can drop by for a pint of Black Sheep in the half-panelled bar, pop a bottle of champagne on the flower-festooned terrace or seek out the restaurant for a fabulous meal. All the ancient trimmings are here – mullioned windows, beamed ceilings, exposed stone walls, a working Yorkshire range – yet the feel is bright and breezy, especially in the dining rooms, of which there are several to satisfy the legions of fans who come for Bruce Elsworth's delicious concoctions (ham shank and fois gras terrine, wild sea bass with a lobster sauce, chocolate and lavender tart). In case that's not enough, Juliet's son runs a wine cave over the road – above which you find exquisite bedrooms, the lap of luxury. All are different, you may get a French armoire, a brass bed, a claw-foot bath. One is partly muralled, another has an icon in an alcove. Expect the best fabrics, pretty colours, flat-screen TVs. Jazz bands play at summer barbecues. Wonderful.

Price	£130–£155. Suites £155–£180.
Rooms	5: 2 doubles, 3 suites.
Meals	Bar meals from £5.75. Sunday lunch £22.50. A la carte dinner about £25.
Closed	Christmas Day.
Directions	North from Skipton on B6265. Left at Rylstone for Hetton. In village.

Juliet Watkins
Hetton, Skipton,
Yorkshire BD23 6LT

Tel	01756 730263
Fax	01756 730363
Email	info@angelhetton.co.uk
Web	www.angelhetton.co.uk

The Red Lion & Manor House at Burnsall

A very pretty village in the middle of the Dales; fells rise all around, there's cricket on the green in summer and the river Wharfe flows past the hotel garden. Family-run and family-friendly, The Red Lion is an inn for all ages, full of old-world charm. Elizabeth still keeps a matriarchal eye on things but her daughters have taken the helm, their husbands by their sides; Robert farms, providing much for the kitchen, Jim and Olivier cook seriously good food. The net result is a cosy, happy, comfortable inn that hums with contented locals. Expect coal fires, books in the sitting room, a good supply of well-kept ales and pink roses rambling across the mellow stone exterior. Bedrooms above aren't huge but have bags of character: low beamed ceilings, big brass beds, fancy compact bathrooms, fluffy white robes. Rooms next-door in the Manor House come in sleek contemporary style. Eat under pear blossom on the terrace while walkers pass, following the Dales Way along the river. August's Fell Race — eight minutes up, four minutes down — starts from the front door. *Minimum two nights at weekends.*

Price	£125–£145. Singles from £62.50. Manor House: £85–£95.
Rooms	25: Red Lion: 7 doubles, 5 twins/doubles, 1 family, 1 single. Manor House: 11 twins/doubles.
Meals	Brasserie lunch & dinner from £7.50. Dinner in restaurant about £30.
Closed	Never.
Directions	From Harrogate, A59 west to Bolton Bridge; B6160 to Burnsall. Hotel next to bridge.

Elizabeth & Andrew Grayshon
Burnsall, Skipton,
Yorkshire BD23 6BU

Tel	01756 720204
Fax	01756 720292
Email	redlion@daelnet.co.uk
Web	www.redlion.co.uk

The Yorke Arms

An ancient inn on the village green surrounded by nothing but hills and peace. Spin across to the main door and you find a cobbled terrace behind clipped yew hedging, a perfect spot for lunch in summer. Inside, a sublime slice of old England, a country-house dining inn that's been lovingly restored in grand style. You get stone walls, old beams, roaring fires and flagged floors sealed beneath bitumen that are washed and polished every day. The cellars date to the 11th century, the interior design to the 21st. Guests snooze in sofas in the sitting room, a mirrored restaurant floods with light, cricket memorabilia hangs on the wall in the panelled snug. Michelin-starred cooking is a joy: perhaps crispy duck with orange and basil, saddle of venison in a juniper sauce, Grand Marnier and chocolate soufflé. Airy bedrooms are predictably lovely. Expect the best fabrics, gorgeous bathrooms, gilt mirrors, flat-screen TVs, bathrobes and silky curtains. There are home-laid eggs at breakfast and wonderful walking all around.

Price	£180–£240. Singles from £100. Half-board (obligatory on Saturdays) £150–£190 p.p.
Rooms	14: 3 twins/doubles, 7 doubles, 1 four-poster, 3 singles.
Meals	Lunch, 3 courses, from £21. Dinner, 3 courses, about £45. 6-course tasting menu £50 (not Sunday eves).
Closed	Rarely.
Directions	From Ripley, B6165 to Pateley Bridge. Over bridge at bottom of High St; 1st right into Low Wath Road to Ramsgill (4 miles).

Bill & Frances Atkins
Ramsgill-in-Nidderdale,
Harrogate, Yorkshire HG3 5RL

Tel	01423 755243
Fax	01423 755330
Email	enquiries@yorke-arms.co.uk
Web	www.yorke-arms.co.uk

The Boar's Head Hotel

The Boar's Head sits four-square in this peaceful, pretty Model Estate village. Across the street are Birchwood House and the Courtyard, with a further six rooms. Expect firm, generous beds, floral headboards, an armchair or sofa and rag-rolled bathrooms; those in the Courtyard have the odd beam and pretty pine panelling. The sitting rooms are carpeted and draped: pink and green sofas, button-back armchairs, glass-topped tables, ancestor oils with brass lights over, an evening fire. There are games to play, newspapers, menus to drool over and a parasoled garden where you are served long summer drinks by delightful staff. The restaurant is warm crimson, candlelit at night; you drink from blue glass and the food is rich and generous 'modern English', employing Yorkshire beef, guinea fowl and Nidderdale lamb. Up the pretty staircase, past more ancestors, to comfy bedrooms, with sherry and fresh flowers in the best. Visit the castle gardens and the National Hyacinth Collection as a guest of the hotel; umbrellas and wellies are put out on rainy days.

Price	£125–£150. Singles £105–£125. Half-board from £80 p.p. (min. 2 nights).
Rooms	25: 4 doubles, 21 twins/doubles.
Meals	Dinner, 3 courses, from £30. Bistro lunch & dinner: dishes from £9.95.
Closed	Rarely.
Directions	From Harrogate, A61 north for 3 miles, left at r'bout, signed to Ripley & castle.

Sir Thomas & Lady Emma Ingilby
Ripley Castle Estate, Ripley,
Harrogate, Yorkshire HG3 3AY

Tel	01423 771888
Fax	01423 771509
Email	reservations@boarsheadripley.co.uk
Web	www.boarsheadripley.co.uk

Entry 229 Map 6

Gallon House

A bespoke B&B that clings to the side of an impossibly steep hill with a medieval castle tottering on one side, a grand Victorian railway bridge passing on the other and the serene river sparkling below. Ancient steps lead gently down, you can follow the Nidd into the country or hire a boat and mess about on it. Climb back up to this magical house, where walls of glass bring in the view. There's Lloyd Loom wicker in the small conservatory, an open fire in the panelled sitting room, stripped floors and delicious communal breakfasts in the dining room. Best of all is the sun terrace for one of Yorkshire's best views, with parasols and pots of colour, and deckchairs to take the strain. Bedrooms are warmly stylish, not too big, but spoiling nonetheless, with bathrobes and white towels, crisp linen and soft colours, videos and CD players. Two have the view, two have showers in the actual room. As for dinner, Rick, a chef, is a maestro in the kitchen (Marco Pierre White learnt at his shoulder). So come down for something tasty, perhaps salmon fish cakes, rack of lamb, pear and almond tart. A great little place.

Price	£110. Singles £85.
Rooms	3: 2 doubles, 1 twin.
Meals	Dinner, 3 courses, £27.50, by arrangement.
Closed	Christmas & New Year.
Directions	A1(M) junc. 46, A59 west for 3 miles. Climb hill into Knaresborough. Left into Market Place at Barclays bank; 1st right into Kirkgate; on left.

Sue & Rick Hodgson
47 Kirkgate, Knaresborough,
Yorkshire HG5 8BZ

Tel	01423 862102
Email	gallon-house@ntlworld.com
Web	www.gallon-house.co.uk

The Grange Hotel

Half a mile from the city wall where the ancient Minster stands, a Regency townhouse once occupied by the merchants of York. It is handsome, elegant and sumptuously grand. Jeremy and Vivien rescued the Georgian building from years of municipal neglect and an effortless style runs throughout; imagine stone floors, Doric columns and an urn erupting with orchids in the hall. You get deep comfy sofas in the morning room, a vaulted red-brick ceiling in the cellar bar, and unpretentious modern British food in the the bright and airy brasserie, which gets lively during the Races when punters, journalists and famous trainers meet up. The horse racing link is à propos: York's course is considered one of the most exciting in Britain. More racing touches in the bedrooms, and perfect mattresses on good high beds. The quietest are at the back. Expect bold greens and reds, a silky purple four-poster, writing paper on the desks and rich fabrics. A particular treat for Americans, single women, traditionalists and trenchermen – and race-goers, naturally. *Minimum stay two nights at weekends.*

Price	£150-£215. Singles £115-£185. Suite £265.
Rooms	30: 8 doubles, 16 twins/doubles, 2 four-posters, 3 singles, 1 suite.
Meals	Lunch from £12.50. Dinner, 2 courses, from £20.
Closed	Never.
Directions	In centre of town, on A19, 400 yards north of the Minster.

Amie Postings
1 Clifton, York,
Yorkshire YO30 6AA

Tel　　01904 644744
Fax　　01904 612453
Email　info@grangehotel.co.uk
Web　　www.grangehotel.co.uk

The Abbey Inn

Fifty paces from the door, majestic Byland Abbey stands defiant after 900 years. It was one of the first Gothic buildings to rise in the North. Yet in 1536 Henry VIII ordered the dissolution of the monasteries, a fate the abbey could not survive, and over the years locals stripped its roof and looted its stone; still it shines. As for the inn, it dates to 1845 and once served as a farmhouse for the monks of Ampleforth. It's a perfect place with interiors that mix tradition, eccentricity and elegance delightfully. There are busts in alcoves, stone flagged floors, curtains drawn across old doorways, cherubs on the wall. A fire crackles in the bar, the daily papers hang on poles. Bedrooms upstairs sweep you back to long-lost days. Expect beamed ceilings, panelled windows, fancy beds, a sofa if there's room. One has a view straight down the nave, two have ceilings open to the rafters. Breakfast is cooked to order and brought to your room. Downstairs, doors open onto a terrace that gives way to sprawling lawns. Beyond, Wass woods rise, so bring your walking boots.

Price	£95-£135. Suite £155.
Rooms	3: 2 doubles, 1 suite.
Meals	Lunch & dinner £5-£25.
	Not Sunday evening or Monday lunch.
Closed	Rarely.
Directions	From A1(M) junc. 49, A168 for Thirsk, then A19 for York. Left for Coxwold after 2 miles. There, left for Byland Abbey. Opposite abbey.

Deborah Whitwell & Richard Mason
Byland Abbey, Coxwold,
Yorkshire YO61 4BD

Tel	01347 868204
Fax	01347 868678
Email	abbeyinn@english-hetitage.org.uk
Web	www.bylandabbeyinn.com

The Feversham Arms

Yorkshire may have a slew of grand hotels, but you'll be hard pressed to find a more stylish bolthole than this. Simon steered several hotels in the north to prominence and now he's doing it for himself. His 1855 coaching inn seduces the moment you enter. Rich country-house interiors are classically inspired, yet the feel is fresh and contemporary. Wander at will and find tromp l'oeil wallpaper, huge sofas, wonderful art and fires primed for combustion. There are stone walls in a snug bar, a sail-shaded conservatory/restaurant with claret bottles lined up on the walls, and, best of all, a swimming pool courtyard – St Tropez on the Yorkshire Moors. Poolside suites circle around with private terraces for those lucky enough to be in one, but every room has its own magic and a night here is a treat wherever you sleep. A clipped elegance runs throughout, you get fabulous fabrics, beautiful upholstery, perhaps air-blasted beams or a cavernous bath. Beds are turned down, breakfast is brought to your room if that's what you like. Castle Howard is close. Heaven. *Minimum stay two nights at weekends.*

Price	£140–£170. Suites £235–£295. Singles from £130. Half-board from £100 p.p.
Rooms	24: 12 doubles, 12 suites.
Meals	Lunch from £7.50. Dinner, 3 courses, £35–£40.
Closed	Never.
Directions	West from Thirsk on A170. In Helmsley, left at top of square/car park; hotel on right by church.

Simon Rhatigan
1 High Street, Helmsley,
Yorkshire YO62 5AG

Tel	01439 770766
Fax	01439 770346
Email	info@fevershamarmshotel.com
Web	www.fevershamarmshotel.com

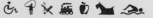

Entry 233 Map 6

The White Swan Inn

Victor swapped the City for the North Yorkshire Moors and this old coaching inn; the place oozes comfort and style. Duck in through the front door to find a snug bar, smart country furniture, fine French wines and eager young staff. Best of all is the dining room; food matters here and you'll find heaven on a plate when you dig into supper. Try seared pigeon breast with pea tart, Levisham mutton with Irish cabbage, poached rhubarb on toasted brioche with rhubarb ice cream. Menus change monthly and 80% of the ingredients are locally sourced, with meat coming from local 'Ginger Pig', who also supply London's River Café. Breakfast is just as good, and inspired one traveller to write a poem, now framed. Bedrooms – some cool and chic, others warmly traditional – come with pleasing colours, elegant fabrics, antique beds, maybe an armchair and a view of the pretty courtyard. Don't miss the beamed club room for roaring fire, board games and an honesty bar. Castle Howard is nearby, the moors are wild and the steam railway a treat. *Pet surcharge, £12.50 per pet.*

Price	£130–£185. Singles from £95. Suites £185–£245.
Rooms	21: 14 doubles, 4 twins/doubles, 3 suites.
Meals	Lunch about £15. Dinner about £25.
Closed	Rarely.
Directions	From North, A170 to Pickering. Entering town, left at traffic lights, then 1st right, Market Place. On left.

Victor & Marion Buchanan
Market Place, Pickering,
Yorkshire YO18 7AA

Tel	01751 472288
Fax	01751 475554
Email	welcome@white-swan.co.uk
Web	www.white-swan.co.uk

Grinkle Lodge

If you appreciate the gradual discovery of unannounced treats (homemade biscuits, good books, bowls of fruit, drinks to hand) then you will love Grinkle Lodge. It is also a temple to Tim and Janette's passion for all things Victorian. Swags and tails abound, hand-painted murals delight, trompe l'oeil entertains and the touch is soft and pretty. Oodles of seductive fabric in the bedrooms, which are deeply comfortable, and bathrooms that sparkle with snowy white towels, robes and plentiful mirrors. A super-warm and restful sitting room, framed by acres of curtain, has a sink-into sofa, a roaring fire and big views over the garden. There's a well-stocked games chest for quiet moments, accompanied by a pre-prandial glass of red wine while ex-restaurateur Tim rustles up roast rack of lamb with wild blackberry and mint sauce. You dine at your own polished antique table in a carpeted dining room where the produce is the best. Expect high quality at every turn, from Grinkle eggs at breakfast and homemade scones at tea. *Minimum stay two nights with half-board at weekends.*

Price	£72–£88.
Rooms	3: 2 doubles, 1 twin.
Meals	Dinner £20. Packed lunch £7.50.
Closed	Rarely.
Directions	From A171 Whitby to Guisborough road travelling north, take right turn to Grinkle and Easington. After 2 miles take right turn. Signed.

Tim & Janette Boskett
Snipe Lane, Grinkle,
Whitby, Yorkshire TS13 4UD

Tel	01287 644701
Email	grinklelodge@yahoo.co.uk
Web	www.grinklelodge.co.uk

Estbek House

A super little find on the Whitby coast. This is a quietly elegant restaurant with rooms ten paces from the beach at Sandsend. It's small, intimate and very welcoming. Tim cooks brilliantly, David pours the drinks and passes on local news. Cliffs rise to the north, the beach runs away to the south, East Beck river passes directly opposite, ducks waddle across the road. There's a terrace at the front for drinks in summer and a small bar on the lower ground; watch Tim at work in his seriously swanky kitchen. Upstairs, two airy dining rooms swim in seaside light and come with stripped floors, painted panelling, old radiators and the odd exposed stone wall, so grab a window seat for watery views and dig into cod fishcakes, duck with slow-roasted figs, Yorkshire rhubarb and stem ginger trifle. Bedrooms above are just the ticket, warmly designed with cast-iron beds, crisp white linen, colourful throws and shuttered windows. Come back down for a delicious breakfast (David's mum makes the marmalade), then walk along cliffs, discover the moors or follow the river upstream to Mulgrave Castle.

Price	£90–£130. Singles from £60.
Rooms	4: 3 doubles, 1 twin.
Meals	Dinner, 3 courses, about £30.
Closed	Occasionally.
Directions	North from Whitby on A174 to Sansend. On left in village by bridge.

David Cross & Tim Lawrence
Eastrow, Sandsend, Whitby,
Yorkshire YO21 3SU

Tel	01947 893424
Fax	01947 893625
Email	info@estbekhouse.co.uk
Web	www.estbekhouse.co.uk

The Endeavour

Named, like so many things along this stretch of coast, after Captain Cook's ship – built at nearby Whitby – this little restaurant with rooms has been successfully squeezed into four storeys of an old cottage in the timeless fishing village of Staithes. Predictably, the menu is stuffed full of fish dishes, all fresh from Whitby's catch – hake, crab, lobster, shark, squid, wild salmon – but carnivores and vegetarians get a look in, too, while puddings are an absolute treat. You eat surrounded by modern art, with windows looking onto a narrow cobbled street that plunges down to the harbour. Bedrooms are comfortable and good value; one looks out to sea, all have big libraries of videos and DVDs, and you'll find a glass of sherry to greet you when you arrive. Breakfast is served from 9.15am, so lie in, then walk to Cook's museum or round the exquisite harbour; waves crash, seagulls screech – little has changed since Cook gazed out to sea. Honest, open, passionate, unpretentious... and no mobile-phone reception. Book ahead. *Private parking spaces reserved for guests.*

Price	£80–£95. Half-board Tues-Fri (min. 2 nights) £125–£140 per room per night.
Rooms	4 doubles.
Meals	Dinner, à la carte, from £35, with wine. Not Sun & Mon except Bank Holidays. Light lunch available in summer.
Closed	Rarely.
Directions	From Whitby, A174 for 8 miles, right for Staithes. Down hill into old village. Parking opposite Staithes art gallery.

Charlotte Willoughby & Brian Kay
1 High Street, Staithes,
Yorkshire TS13 5BH

Tel	01947 840825
Email	endeavour.restaurant@virgin.net
Web	www.endeavour-restaurant.co.uk

Channel Islands

Photo:
www.visitchannelislands.com

La Sablonnerie

If you tell Elizabeth which ferry you're arriving on, she'll send down her horse and carriage to meet you. "Small, sweet world of wave-encompassed wonder," wrote Swinburne of Sark. The tiny community of 500 people lives under a spell, governed feudally and sharing this magic island with horses, sheep, cattle, carpets of wild flowers and birds. There are wild cliff walks, thick woodland, sandy coves, wonderful deep rock pools, aquamarine seas. On the island, no cars, only bikes, horse and carriage and the odd tractor. In the hotel – a 400-year-old farmhouse – no TV, no radio, no trouser press… just a dreamy peace, kindness, starched cotton sheets, woollen blankets and food to die for. Eat in the lovely dining room or in the prettiest of well-tended gardens with gorgeous colourful borders. The Perrées still farm and, as a result, the hotel is almost self-sufficient; you also get home-baked bread and lobsters straight from the sea. Elizabeth is Sercquaise – her mother's family were part of the 1565 colonisation – and she knows her land well. Let her point you to the island's secrets.

Price	£95–£155. Half-board £59.50–£97.50 p.p.
Rooms	24: 5 doubles, 6 twins, 6 family, 1 suite all en suite; 2 doubles, 2 twins, sharing 2 baths.
Meals	Dinner, 5 courses, £30.
Closed	2nd Monday in October–Wednesday before Easter.
Directions	Take ferry to Sark & ask!

Elizabeth Perrée
Little Sark,
Channel Islands GY9 0SD
Tel   01481 832061
Fax   01481 832408

White House Hotel

A coastal path rings idyllic Herm; you'll find high cliffs to the south, sandy beaches to the north and cattle grazing in the hills between. You get fabulous views at every turn – shimmering islands, pristine waters, yachts and ferries zipping about – while the pace of life is wonderfully lazy, so stop at the grocery store, gather a picnic, find a meadow and bask in the sun. There are beach cafés, succulent gardens, an ancient church, even a tavern. Herm's owners are eminently benign; Pennie was born here, Adrian migrated from Guernsey, together they've kept things blissfully simple: no cars, no TVs, just an old-fashioned England that kids love (the self-catering cottages are extremely popular with families). As for the hotel, it's exceptionally comfortable with one toe lingering in an elegant past; come for open fires, delicious four-course dinners, a tennis court with watery views and a pool to keep you cool. Bedrooms are scattered around, some in the village's colour-washed cottages, others with balconies in the hotel. Expect warm colours, padded headboards, and spotless bathrooms.

Pennie's family have been here for nearly 60 years, guardians of a slice of paradise. Cliff walks, beaches and pockets of woodland abound, light pollution is kept to a minimum, music in public places is not allowed. Wander the island and find a small herd of cattle on 100 acres of chemical-free pasture and an extensive programme of tree planting. At the hotel waste is recycled, lighting is low energy, drought-resistant plants fill the garden. Come to escape the hi-tech world, play cricket on the sand, stop for coffee on the beach. And kids are free to be kids, too busy to miss the TV.

Price	Half-board £76–£114 p.p.
Rooms	40: 12 twins/doubles, 5 family rooms. Cottages (some self-catering): 16 twins/doubles, 5 family rooms, 2 singles.
Meals	Half-board only. Lunch from £7. Dinner for non-residents, £24.
Closed	8 October–31 March.
Directions	Via Guernsey. Trident ferries leave from the harbour at St Peter Port 8 times a day in summer (£9 return).

Adrian & Pennie Heyworth
Herm,
Channel Islands GY1 3HR

Tel	01481 722159
Fax	01481 710066
Email	hotel@herm-island.com
Web	www.herm-island.com

SPECIAL
GREEN ENTRY
see page 17

Scotland

Darroch Learg

The country here is glorious – river, forest, mountain, sky – so walk by Loch Muick, climb Lochnagar, fish the Dee or drop down to Braemar and the highland games. Swing back to Darroch Learg to find nothing but good things. This is a smart family-run hotel firmly rooted in a graceful past, an old country house with roaring fires, polished brass, Zoffany wallpaper and ambrosial food in a much-admired restaurant. Ever-present Nigel and Fiona look after guests with great aplomb; many return. Everything is just as it should be: tartan fabrics on the walls in the hall, Canadian pitch pine windows and doors, fabulous views sweeping south across Balmoral forest. Bedrooms upstairs come in different shapes and sizes; all have warmth and comfort in spades. Big grand rooms at the front thrill with padded window seats, wallpapered bathrooms, old oak furniture, perhaps a four-poster. Spotlessly cosy rooms in the eaves are equally lovely, just not quite as big. You get warm colours, pretty furniture, crisp white linen and bathrobes to pad about in. A perfect highland retreat.

Price	£130–£200. Half-board (obligatory May–Sept, & Saturdays all year) £90–£135 p.p.
Rooms	12: 10 twins/doubles, 2 four-posters.
Meals	Sunday lunch £23. Dinner, á la carte, about £40. 7-course tasting menu £45.
Closed	Christmas week & last 3 weeks in January.
Directions	From Perth, A93 north to Ballater. Entering village, hotel 1st building on left above road.

Nigel & Fiona Franks
Braemar Road, Ballater,
Aberdeenshire AB35 5UX

Tel	01339 755443
Fax	01339 755252
Email	enquiries@darrochlearg.co.uk
Web	www.darrochlearg.co.uk

Highland Cottage

A restored cottage high above this pretty, sheltered port in the capital of wild Mull. This is clearly a great place to eat; locals flock here for Croig crab cakes, Ardnamurchan venison or Tobermory smoked salmon parcels. And the puddings don't disappoint; try chocolate nemesis or burnt honey ice cream. Bedrooms aren't enormous but they are comfortable with beautifully ironed sheets and proper blankets, crushed-velvet cushions, silk bedspreads, tartan tiles in the bathrooms, Cadell prints, huge porcelain lamps, a French sleigh bed, even the odd sea view. In the upstairs sitting room there's an honesty bar, CDs wait to be played and pot-boilers (or *Kidnapped* – it's set on the island) wait to be read. If you can rouse yourself, head to Iona, Fingal's Cave, the white sands of Calgary bay. Or just wander around Tobermory, the prettiest town in the Western Isles, with its Highland games, art festivals, yachting regattas, and the daily to and fro of islanders stocking up on supplies. Marvellous. *Children over ten welcome.*

Price	£140–£174. Singles from £125.
Rooms	6: 2 doubles, 2 twins, 2 four-posters.
Meals	Dinner, 4 courses, £40.
Closed	November–February.
Directions	From ferry, A848 to Tobermory. Across bridge at mini-r'bout, immed. right into Breadalbane St. On right opp. fire station.

David & Jo Currie
Breadalbane Street, Tobermory,
Isle of Mull PA75 6PD

Tel	01688 302030
Email	davidandjo@highlandcottage.co.uk
Web	www.highlandcottage.co.uk

The Airds Hotel & Restaurant

Faultless service, ambrosial food and warmly cosy interiors make this one of Scotland's most indulging country-house hotels. Views from the front slide down to Loch Linnhe, sweep over Lismore Island and cross to the towering mountains of Ardnamurchan beyond. A small conservatory, candlelit at night, frames the view perfectly, but in good weather you can skip across the lane to discover a lawned garden of rainbow colours decked out with tables and parasols. Pre-dinner drinks are taken in the sitting rooms – open fires, elegant sofas, fresh flowers, lots of books – after which you're whisked off to the dining room where four delicious courses are served on Limoges china. Whatever can be is homemade, so expect the best, maybe baked goat's cheese with onion confit, cream of cauliflower and mustard soup, seared fillet of brill in a citrus butter sauce, hot chocolate fondant with pistachio ice cream. Retire to smart country-house bedrooms (crisp florals, soft colours, Frette linen, Italian bathrobes) and find your bed turned down, the curtains drawn. There's pink grapefruit and campari sorbet for breakfast, too.

Price	Half-board £125-£200 p.p.
Rooms	11: 4 doubles, 4 twins, 3 suites.
Meals	Half-board only. Lunch £5-£25. Dinner for non-residents, £49.50.
Closed	8-26 January.
Directions	A82 north for Fort William, then A828 south for Oban. Right for Port Appin after 12 miles. On left after 2 miles.

Shaun & Jenny McKivragan
Port Appin, Appin,
Argyll & Bute PA38 4DF

Tel	01631 730236
Fax	01631 730535
Email	airds@airds-hotel.com
Web	www.airds-hotel.com

The Manor House

A 1780 dower house for the Dukes of Argyll — their cottage by the sea — built of local stone, high on the hill, with long views over Oban harbour to the Isle of Mull. A smart and proper place, not one to bow to the fads of fashion: sea views from the lawn, cherry trees in the courtyard garden, a fire roaring in the drawing room, a beautiful tiled floor in the entrance hall and an elegant bay window in the dining room that catches the eye. Compact bedrooms are pretty in blues, reds and greens, with fresh flowers, crisp linen sheets, radios, padded headboards and piles of towels in good bathrooms; those that look seaward have pairs of binoculars to scour the horizon. Sample Loch Fyne kippers for breakfast, sea bass for lunch and, if you've room, duck in redcurrant sauce for supper; try their home-baking, too. Ferries leave for the islands from the bottom of the hill — see them depart from the hotel garden — while at the top, overlooking Oban, watch the day's close from McCaig's Folly; sunsets here are really special. *Children over 12 welcome.*

Price	Half-board £60-£90 p.p.
Rooms	11: 8 doubles, 3 twins.
Meals	Half-board only. Lunch £7-£13. Dinner, 5 courses, £34.
Closed	Christmas.
Directions	In Oban, follow signs to ferry. Hotel on right 0.5 miles after ferry turn-off, signed.

Ann MacEachen
Gallanach Road, Oban,
Argyll & Bute PA34 4LS

Tel   01631 562087
Fax   01631 563053
Email   info@manorhouseoban.com
Web   www.manorhouseoban.com

Lerags House

A spectacular drive down a single track road through lochs and gentle mountains to the lovely house. Built in 1815, the rooms are large and light with high ceilings and sash windows. Cool interiors mix natural colours and light pine surfaces with pale sofas, fresh lilies, straight lines and bold pictures. Charlie and Bella represent an emerging generation of hoteliers: more style, less formality, good prices, great service and Bella's exceptional food. Pan-fried sea bass with rosemary, garlic and lemon-scented puy lentils, chocolate amaretti fudge with vanilla cream... The menu changes daily. Bedrooms are gorgeous: pale earthy colours, big beds with Italian linen. The suite has a view to the loch and its own sitting area, stylish bathrooms are warm and the towels are big. The delightful garden runs down to tidal mud flats; watch the ebb and flow from the dining room while you breakfast on proper porridge. At the end of the road – a brisk stroll of a mile or so – is a beach for uninterrupted walks, or a constitutional dip. Day trips to Mull, Crinan and Glencoe are all easy, all wonderful. *Arrival after 4pm.*

Price	Half-board £82–£95 p.p.
Rooms	6: 4 doubles, 1 twin/double, 1 suite.
Meals	Half-board only. Packed lunch £6.
Closed	Christmas.
Directions	From Oban, south on A816 for 2 miles, then right, signed Lerags for 2.5 miles. House on left, signed.

Charlie & Bella Miller
Lerags, By Oban,
Argyll & Bute PA34 4SE

Tel	01631 563381
Email	stay@leragshouse.com
Web	www.leragshouse.com

Ardanaiseig

You're lost to the world, ten miles down a track that winds past giant rhododendrons before petering out at this baronial mansion. Beyond, Loch Awe rules supreme, 30 miles of deep blue water on which to sail or fish. In one of the loveliest hotel drawing rooms you are ever likely to see (gold leaf panelling, Doric columns rising gleefully) an enormous window frames the view and a single sofa waits for those lucky enough to have it. Elsewhere there are Wellington boots lined up in the hall, roaring fires wherever you go, eccentric art on the dining room wall and a lawned terrace that runs down to the loch. You're in 200 acres of private grounds, in May bluebells riddle the woods. Country-house bedrooms are the real thing (old armoires, feather boa lamp shades, the odd four-poster), but five external rooms are soon to be built in a natural amphitheatre with watery views. To prove the point the boat house (below) has been converted into a funky suite with a wall of glass that opens onto a decked terrace. Dinner is a seven-course feast — as one might expect of this rather flamboyant hotel.

Price	£106–£316. Boathouse £230–£366. Singles from £53. Half-board £84–£214 p.p.
Rooms	17: 8 twins/doubles, 5 doubles, 3 four-posters, 1 boathouse suite.
Meals	Light lunch from £4. Afternoon tea £2–£10. Dinner, 7 courses, £45.
Closed	2 January–8 February.
Directions	A85 to Taynuilt. Left onto B845 for Kilchrenan. Then left at Kilchrenan pub; down track for 4 miles.

Peter Webster
Kilchrenan, By Taynuilt,
Argyll & Bute PA35 1HE

Tel	01866 833333
Fax	01866 833222
Email	info@ardanaiseig.com
Web	www.ardanaiseig.com

Culzean Castle

Americans in search of ancestors would adore it here. Across the viaduct, under the arch, into the Armoury with its 716 flintlock pistols and 400 swords, and up in the lift to the top floor. Culzean (pronounced 'Cullane') is one of Scotland's most popular tourist destinations and was built into solid rock a couple of hundred feet above crashing waves. When the Marquess of Ailsa presented the castle to the Scottish people in 1945, Eisenhower was given the top floor suite – Scotland's thank you for his contribution to the war effort. You stay on the same floor where every room is comfortable and spacious; there are glowing fires, cashmere throws, twinkling chandeliers and thrilling sea views – though the most splendid rooms are on the land side. Bathrooms are grandly traditional, service is courteous and thoughtful and the rest is awe-inspiring: hundreds of portraits, a round drawing room that juts out over the sea, a central oval staircase with 12 Corinthian columns. Tour the castle before the tourists invade at 11am, then take a stirring cliff walk in 560 idyllic acres.

Price	£225-£375. Singles from £140. Whole floor £1,700 per night. Afternoon tea included.
Rooms	6: 4 twins/doubles, 1 four-poster, all en suite; 1 twin/double with separate bath.
Meals	Dinner, 3 courses, £35. By arrangement.
Closed	Rarely.
Directions	From A77 in Maybole, A719 for 4 miles, signed.

Mike Schafer
The National Trust for Scotland,
Maybole, Ayrshire KA19 8LE

Tel	0844 493 2149
Fax	0844 493 2150
Email	culzean@nts.org.uk
Web	www.culzeanexperience.org

Knockinaam Lodge

Lawns run down to the Irish sea, sunsets streak the sky red, roe deer amble down to eat the roses. An exceptional 1869 shooting lodge with unremitting luxuries: a Michelin star in the dining room, 150 malts in the bar and a level of service you might not expect in such far-flung corners of the realm. And history. Churchill once stayed and you can sleep in his big elegant room, where copies of his books wait to be read and where you need steps to climb into an ancient bath. It remains very much a country house: plump cushions on a Queen Anne sofa in an immaculate morning room where the scent of flowers mixes with the smell of burnt wood, invigorating cliff walks, curlews to lull you to sleep, nesting Peregrine falcons, and a rock pool where David keeps lobsters for the pot. In storms, waves crash all around. Trees stand guard high on the hill, their branches buffeted by the wind, bluebells come out by the thousand in spring. Remote, beguiling, utterly spoiling – Knockinaam is worth the detour. John Buchan knew the house and described it in *The Thirty-Nine Steps* as the house to which Hannay fled.

Price	Half-board £95–£200 p.p. Singles from £165.
Rooms	9: 3 doubles, 5 twins/doubles, 1 suite.
Meals	Half-board only. Lunch, by arrangement, £25–£37.50. Dinner, 5 courses, included; non-residents £50.
Closed	Rarely.
Directions	From A77 or A75, signs for Portpatrick. 2 miles west of Lochans, left at smokehouse. Signed for 3 miles.

David & Sian Ibbotson
Portpatrick,
Dumfries & Galloway DG9 9AD

Tel	01776 810471
Fax	01776 810435
Email	reservations@knockinaamlodge.com
Web	www.knockinaamlodge.com

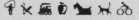

Cavens

A very welcoming country house, with views from the front door that stretch across a quilt of fields to the imperious Solway Firth. The house, a 1753 shooting lodge, stands in six acres of native wood and sweeping lawns. Inside, quietly elegant interiors flood with light making this a very pleasant place to linger. You get busts and oils, seagrass matting, golden sofas and smouldering fires. Cavens is popular among local hoteliers who come to escape for a day or two. They come in part for the food that Angus whisks up single-handedly (perhaps scallops with lime and vermouth, sea bass with roasted fennel, raspberry tartlets, local cheeses). Country-house bedrooms all have garden views. Some are snug, others palatial. You get smart florals, pretty linen, mahogany dressers, bowls of fruit. One has an en suite sunroom, another comes in wild tangerine. Lose yourself in beautiful country: follow the Solway coast, come in November for millions of birds, play golf at spectacular Southerness. Afternoon tea can be eaten in the garden. A treat.

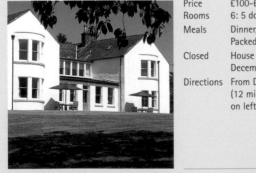

Price	£100–£160. Singles from £80.
Rooms	6: 5 doubles, 1 twin.
Meals	Dinner, 3 courses, £30. Packed lunch available.
Closed	House parties only December-February.
Directions	From Dumfries, A710 to Kirkbean (12 miles). Hotel signed in village, on left.

Jane & Angus Fordyce
Kirkbean,
Dumfries & Galloway DG2 8AA

Tel	01387 880234
Fax	01387 880467
Email	enquiries@cavens.com
Web	www.cavens.com

Greywalls

Gracious, stately and hugely impressive, yet you could curl up on a sofa and feel perfectly at home. Sir Edwin Lutyens built the house in 1901 for a golfer determined to be within a 'mashie niblick' shot of the 18th green; two gate lodges were added for staff, then a nursery wing. Now it's half hotel, half private home – held in equal affection by family and guests. Greywalls is discreet, peaceful, welcoming and unpompous – one guest said staying here was like "breathing silk". Enter a charmed world of log fires, French windows, family portraits, parquet floors. Benches on the lawn look directly onto Muirfiled golf course; Nicklaus stayed in 1966, Watson in 1980, Els in 2002 – all went on to win the Open. There's a panelled library, a cosy bar, chintz in the bedrooms and a dedicated team in the kitchen – the food is sublime. Bedrooms – six in the lodges, more in the house – have everything you could wish for, and there's the Colonel's House for private groups. The walled garden was designed by Gertrude Jekyll: a delightful tapestry of arbours, arches, peonies, lavender and immaculate lawns.

Price	£300. Singles £140.
Rooms	23: 20 twins/doubles, 3 singles.
Meals	Lunch £20-£25 (Friday-Sunday). Dinner £45.
Closed	January & February.
Directions	A198 from A1 & take last road at east end of Gullane village.

Giles Weaver
Muirfield, Gullane,
East Lothian EH31 2EG

Tel	01620 842144
Fax	01620 842241
Email	hotel@greywalls.co.uk
Web	www.greywalls.co.uk

Entry 249 Map 9

The Inn at Lathones

You don't have to be a golfer to fall in love with this inn, but the hallowed fairways of St Andrews are five miles west and after shooting three under par into the wind, your body will thank you for organising a night of luxury to follow. Here you find a whitewashed stone inn that dates to 1603. A super expansion in 2007 has added stylish suites with terraces or balconies overlooking the fields, sparkling bathrooms for an indulging soak, and bedrooms laden with technological excess. Goose down duvets are wrapped in crisp white linen, scatter cushions and local art add colour. Spin across to the inn and find stone walls, timber frames, painted panelling and a wood-burner in the sitting room. Best of all is the food. Nick loves the stuff and has brought in 'trilogy' cooking from France: each course offers three micro-courses built around a central theme – perhaps soups for starters, lamb for main course, a trio of ices for pudding. It's all rather fun and helps you prepare for golf the next day; Scotland's four oldest courses are on your doorstep. *Minimum stay two nights at weekends.*

Price	£180–£245. Suites £295.
Rooms	21: 19 twins/doubles, 2 suites.
Meals	Lunch £14.50–£17.40. Dinner, à la carte, about £40. Packed lunch from £12.
Closed	Christmas & 2 weeks in January.
Directions	From Kirkcaldy, or St Andrews, A915 to Largoward. Inn 1 mile north on roadside.

Nick White
Lathones, St Andrews,
Fife KY9 1JE

Tel	01334 840494
Fax	01334 840694
Email	lathones@theinn.co.uk
Web	www.theinn.co.uk

Rab Ha's

Lively, full of soul, and the price isn't bad either. Down in the trendy Merchant City, Rab Ha's puts on a good show, the cast comprising a collection of bon vivants who gather at night for the odd malt, a drop of beer, a glass of Spanish wine or even a cocktail. Flames fly in a stone fireplace in the candlelit panelled bar, waiters whisk plates to your table in the stylish cellar restaurant. Fabulous food gives lots of choice, anything from traditional favourites like haggis, neaps and tatties to saddle of Rannoch Moor venison; the pre-theatre menu is exceptionally well-priced and they also do a mean Sunday lunch. Bedrooms are modern and spruce with crisp white linen, yellow walls and curvaceous twiggery; excellent bathrooms may come with a claw-foot bath. Don't expect peace and quiet until late; hushed it is not! Continental breakfast can be delivered to your room. Extravagant, energetic Glasgow can be explored by foot: chic shops, groovy galleries and cool clubs are all close. But you may just want to stay put and join in the fun.

Price	£75–£95.
Rooms	4: 3 doubles, 1 twin/double.
Meals	Continental breakfast included. Bar menu, 2 courses, from £11. Lunch & dinner: main courses £12.50–£15.95.
Closed	Christmas Day.
Directions	5-min walk from Queen Street station.

Merwain Graham
83 Hutcheson Street,
Glasgow G1 1SH

Tel	0141 572 0400
Fax	0141 572 0402
Email	e.management@rabhas.com
Web	www.rabhas.com

Isle of Colonsay Hotel

Another fabulous Hebridean island, a perfect place to do nothing at all. Wander at will and find wild flowers in the machair, a golf course tended by sheep and huge sandy beaches across which cows roam. Wildlife is ever present, from a small colony of wild goats to a rich migratory bird population; the odd golden eagle passes overhead, too. At low tide the sands of the south give access to Oronsay. The island's 14th-century priory was one of Scotland's finest and amid impressive ruins its ornate stone cross still stands. As for the hotel, it's a splendid island base and brims with an easy style – airy interiors, stripped floors, fires everywhere, friendly staff. There's a locals' bar for a pint (and a brewery on the island), a pretty sitting room packed with books, a dining room for super food and a decked terrace for drinks in the sun. Recently refurbished bedrooms have local art, warm colours, lovely fabrics and the best beds; those at the front have sea views, all have neat little bathrooms. Fish for brown trout, search for standing stones, lie in the sun and stare at the sky. Wonderful.

Price	£95–£140. Singles from £60.
Rooms	9: 4 doubles, 3 twins, 1 single, 1 family.
Meals	Lunch from £4.50. Packed lunch £7. Dinner, 3 courses, about £25.
Closed	Mid-December-March.
Directions	Colonsay ferry from Oban. Hotel on right, half a mile up road from jetty.

Scott & Becky Omar
Scalasaig,
Isle of Colonsay PA61 7YP

Tel	01951 200316
Fax	01951 200353
Email	reception@thecolonsay.com
Web	www.thecolonsay.com

The Pines

A stone's throw from the town, The Pines – with its woodland grounds that lead to the beautiful river Spey – is an interesting find. Gwen is a gifted cook and Michael chatty and debonair; you'll soon feel at home. Downstairs rooms – a deep red dining room and conservatory with garden views, an attractive sitting room – are bright with patterned carpets, and paintings crowd every wall. Mainly Scottish artists are represented, but this is a good international collection from traditional to modern. The upstairs drawing room has deep sofas; borrow a book from the library and settle here. Expect delicious food: venison from a local estate, gravadlax from Strathaird, eggs free-range, bread homemade. Bedrooms vary in size but all have excellent beds with good linen, and there are spoiling touches with fresh flowers and fruit, an evening turn-down and spotless bathrooms. Stroll through the attractive garden which is bordered on the far side by coniferous woodland; a bat box, squirrel feeders, bird boxes and a bee house will provide the entertainment. Come for peace and quiet and a bit of cossetting.

Price	£100–£125. Singles from £59. Half-board £80–£95 p.p.
Rooms	8: 3 doubles, 4 twins/doubles, 1 single.
Meals	Dinner, 4 courses, £32. Packed lunch available.
Closed	November–February.
Directions	A95 north to Grantown. Right at 1st traffic lights; A939 for Tomintoul, 1st right into Woodside Ave. 500 yds on left.

Michael & Gwen Stewart
Woodside Avenue,
Grantown-on-Spey, Moray PH26 3JR

Tel	01479 872092
Fax	01479 872092
Email	info@thepinesgrantown.co.uk
Web	www.thepinesgrantown.co.uk

Minmore House

In 1822 George IV tasted Glenlivet whisky for the first time. It swiftly became his favourite tipple and was used in all royal toasts thereafter. Minmore was built four years later by George Smith, whose whisky the king so admired, and the house became the family home of one of Scotland's most famous whisky men. These days it's a comfortable country house with a carved bar in a panelled sitting room that pays due homage to the wee dram; there are over a hundred malts to boggle the mind and books to help you choose. Elsewhere: roaring fires, comfy sofas, terraced gardens dripping with colour and 40 free-range hens. Windows at the front frame views of the Ladder hills, but it's Victor's cooking that holds your attention; a four-course dinner may offer hand-dived scallops, minted pea soup, rack of Highland lamb, apple and calvados soufflé. Bedrooms span the scale, some warmly cosy, others lavishly over-the-top. One has a bath with views down the valley, all have crisp linen, trim carpets, fancy bathrobes and a drop of whisky. Highland safaris can be arranged. *Minimum stay two nights at weekends in summer.*

Price	£104-£144. Suites £152-£192. Singles from £67. Half-board from £91 p.p.
Rooms	9: 3 doubles, 4 twins, 2 suites.
Meals	Light lunch £15. Dinner, 4 courses, £39. Full picnic £10.
Closed	26 November-28 December.
Directions	From Aviemore, A95 north to Bridge of Avon; south on B9008 to Glenlivet. At top of hill, 400 yds before distillery.

Victor & Lynne Janssen
Glenlivet,
Banffshire AB37 9DB

Tel	01807 590378
Fax	01807 590472
Email	enquiries@minmorehousehotel.com
Web	www.minmorehousehotel.com

Woodwick House

This Northern outpost of the Sawday realm stands 500 yards up from the sea, with views across the Sound of Gairsay to a small archipelago. The house, once home to the local laird, stands in its own grounds with almost every tree on the island flanking a burn that tumbles over slabs of rock on its way to the sea; in May, bluebells in their millions join the fray. Inside, you find an extraordinary little place, not fancy for a moment, but the spirit here is second to none. Imagine the country house of a friend who doesn't have the money to pack it with smart antiques, so paints the walls, fits fresh carpets and fills it with the feel of home. Colourful bedrooms are simple and spotless, there's a fire in the sitting room, big views from the sunroom, a small dining room for delicious home cooking, a music room for the occasional concert and a TV room stacked with videos in case it rains. James is the star; he loves the Orkneys, has no airs and graces, and your trip to these extraordinary islands will be the richer because of him. History, wildlife and vast skies wait.

Price	£68–£100. Singles £34–£70.
Rooms	7: 3 doubles, 1 twin, all en suite; 1 double, 1 twin, 1 single, with basins, all sharing bathroom.
Meals	Dinner, 3 courses, £25. Packed lunch £7, by arrangement.
Closed	Rarely.
Directions	From Kirkwall, A965 to Finstown; A966 for Evie. Right after 7 miles; next right, past Tingwall ferry turning; left down track to house.

James Bryan
Evie,
Orkney KW17 2PQ

Tel   01856 751330
Fax   01856 751383
Email   mail@woodwickhouse.co.uk
Web   www.woodwickhouse.co.uk

Killiecrankie House Hotel

In the one-time dower house to Blair Castle, you are ideally positioned for all things Highland: the games at Braemar, the festival at Pitlochry, fishing, walking, castles, golf… and whisky, about which Tim, once a big mover and shaker in the wine trade, knows a thing or two. He and Maillie have come north of the border to cook great food, to serve good wines and to provide the sort of comfortable indulgence that caps a hard day's pleasure with rod, club or map. Food is top of the list, with an ever-changing menu of fresh fish and local meat and game, home-grown soft fruits, potatoes, asparagus, leeks and mangetout. Wine buffs will be in heaven: reasonably priced wine by the glass complements each course and the special vegetarian menu could convert an ardent carnivore… for an evening at least. Newly refurbished bedrooms are a good size, cosy, carpeted, warm and light, with views down the Garry Valley. There's a small bar, a snug sitting room with books and games, beautifully maintained grounds and an RSPB sanctuary near the house that's home to buzzards. Bring the binoculars.

Price	Half-board £84–£99 p.p.
Rooms	10: 4 doubles, 4 twins/doubles, 2 singles.
Meals	Half-board only. Lunch from £3.25. Dinner for non-residents, £34.
Closed	January-March.
Directions	A9 north of Pitlochry, then B8079, signed Killiecrankie. Straight ahead for 2 miles. Hotel on right, signed.

Tim & Maillie Waters
Pass of Killiecrankie, By Pitlochry,
Perth & Kinross PH16 5LG

Tel	01796 473220
Fax	01796 472451
Email	enquiries@killiecrankiehotel.co.uk
Web	www.killiecrankiehotel.co.uk

Loch Tummel Inn

A super little inn with huge views from the front that shoot across a shimmering Loch Tummel to a mountain of forest beyond. This is Rob Roy country; legend has it that his hideout, McGreggor's Cave, lies in the forest; pull on your boots and search the far shore while eagle, buzzard and falcon spiral above. For something more adventurous, Robert runs an outdoor sports centre and white-water rafting, mountain biking, kayaking, trekking and riding can all be arranged. Back at the inn a huge window in the first-floor sitting room frames the view, the terrace is shaded by honeysuckle, perfect for lazy lunches; and there's a beer garden across the road for pre-dinner drinks. Inside, tartan carpets run throughout giving a smart country-inn feel. There are 80 malts and a wood-burner in the bar, a pitch pine roof and exposed stone walls in the restaurant; grab the window seats and sit down to a bowl of mussels or an Aberdeen Angus steak. Airy bedrooms have warm colours, pretty fabrics, crisp linen, big beds, spotless bathrooms and DVD players; all but one has loch views.

Price	£65–£120. Singles from £40.
Rooms	6: 2 doubles, 4 twins/doubles.
Meals	Bar meals from £8.
	Dinner, 3 courses, £26.
Closed	Never.
Directions	From Perth, A9 north, turn off after Pitlochry, for Killicrankie. Left onto B8019 for Tummel Bridge & Kinloch Rannoch; inn 8 miles on right.

Robert Gilmour
Strathtummel, By Pitlochry,
Perth & Kinross PH16 5RP

Tel	01882 634272
Fax	01882 634272
Email	info@lochtummelinn.co.uk
Web	www.lochtummelinn.co.uk

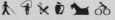

Entry 257 Map 8

The Ardeonaig Hotel

A little bit of heaven on the quiet side of Loch Tay. This is a seriously spoiling hotel, the epitome of 21st-century deep country chic. Whitewashed walls and hanging baskets give way to a courtyard where stone flowerbeds tumble with colour. Best of all is the first-floor library in varnished pine with its enormous window framing imperious views of field, loch and mountain. There are plump sofas, leather armchairs, books and maps, binoculars, too. Elsewhere, a snug bar in tartan, a peat fire in a sparkling sitting room, and views of a tumbling burn through dining room windows. Pete, a South African, had Fish Hoek in London and made a splash cooking up fabulous things, so expect seriously good food, perhaps smoked salmon salad, roast saddle of local hare, purple figs with honey and ginger. Stylish, uncluttered bedrooms are blissfully free of TVs and come in creams and browns, with good art, halogen lighting and cedarwood blinds. Those at the back have exquisite views. Stroll down to the water and find a flotilla of fishing boats; the hotel has rights, so bring your rod. *Minimum stay two nights at weekends.*

Price	£120-£170. Singles from £75. Suites £220-£250. Half-board £90-£150 p.p.
Rooms	20: 11 doubles, 6 twins, 3 suites.
Meals	Bistro meals from £6.50. Dinner £26.50-£40. Tasting menu £49.50.
Closed	Never.
Directions	A9, then A827 to Kenmore via Aberfeldy. In Kenmore take south side road along Loch Tay for 10 miles. On right.

Peter & Sara Gottgens
South Loch Tay Side, By Killin,
Perth & Kinross FK21 8SU

Tel	01567 820400
Fax	01567 820282
Email	info@ardeonaighotel.co.uk
Web	www.ardeonaighotel.co.uk

Monachyle Mhor

Loch Voil washes the shores at the bottom of the hill, mountains surround, skylarks sing on the breezes and cars pass at the rate of one an hour; the twisty road ends two miles up the track. The 1700s farmhouse, warm and unpretentious, is stylish, modern and vibrant within. Rambling Monachyle has glorious colours, lashings of comfort and a lovely, laid-back feel. Best of all: it has food cooked by Tom. The freshest that Scotland has to offer is what sparks his imagination: game, fish, wild berries, artichokes from the organic garden, mushrooms foraged the day before… sensational. This is a family affair and they started here as farmers — still are — then began doing B&B and now that has evolved too. The restaurant is London-swish with Scottish views; the panelled bar with its wood fire deliciously snug. Bedrooms, split between house, barns and coach house, are to die for: huge beds, clean lines, rugs on creaking wooden floors, bathrooms with slate floors, huge showers. Walkers and dogs are welcome, locals fill the place at weekends and there's jazz on the 'lawns' in summer. *Minimum stay two nights at weekends.*

Price	£95–£180. Singles from £85. Suites £155–£235.
Rooms	14: 3 doubles, 2 twins, 9 suites.
Meals	Sunday lunch £31. Dinner £46.
Closed	January.
Directions	M9 junc. 10, onto A84 17 miles north of Callander; left at Kings House Hotel, following signs to Balquhidder. 6 miles along road. Along Loch Voil. Hotel on right up drive, signed.

Tom Lewis
Balquhidder, Lochearnhead,
Perth & Kinross FK19 8PQ

Tel	01877 384622
Fax	01877 384305
Email	info@monachylemhor.com
Web	www.monachylemhor.com

Creagan House

Run with huge skill and passion by Gordon and Cherry, Creagan is decorated not by numbers, nor by fashion, but by enthusiasm, evolving slowly and naturally. The welcome is second to none and the food magnificent – carefully sourced and cooked with great flair by Gordon. Meat and game from Perthshire, seafood straight from the boats (local as much as possible) and served on Skye pottery at long polished oak tables in a baronial dining room. There's a lovely sitting room which doubles up as a bar; you'll find a good wine list and 50 malt whiskies – if you like a dram, you'll be in heaven, and there's a guide to help choose. No airs and graces, just the sort of attention you get in small, owner-run places. Bedrooms at the front face a quiet road and look to meadow, river and mountain – fabulous. All are a decent size for a cottagey house, all are spic and span and the twin is on the ground floor. Canopies on beds, designer wallpaper, solid furniture, flat-screen TVs. You can bag a munro, too; walking sticks at the door will help you up Beinn An T-Sidhein. A perfect wee retreat.

Price	£120–£130. Singles £70–£75.
Rooms	5: 1 four-poster, 3 doubles, 1 twin.
Meals	Dinner £28.
Closed	February.
Directions	From Stirling, A84 north through Callander to Strathyre. Hotel 0.25 miles north of village on right.

Gordon & Cherry Gunn
Strathyre, Callander,
Perth & Kinross FK18 8ND

Tel	01877 384638
Fax	01877 384319
Email	eatandstay@creaganhouse.co.uk
Web	www.creaganhouse.co.uk

An Lochan

This is one of Scotland's most famous inns. It was run for years by a Yorkshireman who decided to treat the Scots to an English inn; remarkably, the locals liked it. These days it's safely back in Scottish hands — with a Scottish name to boot — and a quick wander through delightful rooms confirms that a Scot has trumped the old enemy and made the place better. Simplicity is the virtue. You get slate floors covered in hessian, logs piled high in the fireplace, panelled walls, roaring fires, old beams running above. Tradition and style go hand in hand. Weave into the restaurant and find whitewashed walls and wooden benches smartly upholstered in green tartan; double doors lead through to high ceilings and painted pine in the conservatory. Super food is served informally; expect to eat well, perhaps seafood chowder, haunch of venison, chocolate tart with blood orange jelly. Homely bedrooms tend to be big. You get walls of colour, crisp white linen, black and white bathrooms, the odd stone wall. Gleneagles is ten miles north, tee times can be arranged.

Price	£100. Singles £85. Lodge £150.
Rooms	13: 12 twins/doubles, 1 lodge for 4.
Meals	Lunch from £7.95.
	Dinner, 3 courses, about £35.
Closed	Never.
Directions	A9 north from Dunblane, then A823 south at Gleneagles. On left in village.

Roger & Bea McKie
Glendevon,
Perthshire FK14 7JY

Tel	0845 371 1414
Email	info@anlochan.co.uk
Web	www.anlochan.co.uk

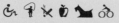

Windlestraw Lodge

There are few better distractions in Scotland than following the river Tweed; fishing lines glisten in the sun, lambs bleat high on the hill, ospreys glide through the afternoon sky. This is the river which brought prosperity to Scotland, its mills a source of huge wealth in Victorian days. Windlestraw, a supremely comfortable country house, stands in evidence; it was built as a wedding gift for a mill owner and sits on the side of a hill with timeless views down the valley. Outside, a fine copper beech shades the lawn. Inside, a dazzling refurbishment has softened the grandness giving the feel of home. You get stripped floors, painted ceilings, roaring fires, a panelled dining room. Light pours in through windows at the front, gilt mirrors hang on walls, fat sofas encourage idleness. There are binoculars with which to scan the valley, a terrace for afternoon tea, a sitting room for a quiet snooze. Country-house bedrooms are fine or finer; two are sublime, all come with crisp linen, those at the front have super views. Don't miss Alan's fabulous food or a round of golf at Peebles. Brilliant.

Price	£130-£180. Singles from £80. Half-board from £105 p.p.
Rooms	6: 5 doubles, 1 twin.
Meals	Lunch by arrangement. Dinner, 4 courses, £40.
Closed	February.
Directions	East from Peebles on A72. Into Walkerburn; house signed left on western flank of town.

Julie & Alan Reid
Tweed Valley, Walkerburn,
Scottish Borders EH43 6AA
Tel   01896 870 636
Fax   01896 870404
Email reception@windlestraw.co.uk
Web   www.windlestraw.co.uk

Ballochneck

Up the long rutted drive, past the curling pond (you can in winter) to Donnie and Fiona's 'big hoose' and a rocking good time. The house looks imposing, big and Scottish, but Donnie (also big and Scottish) is down the high steps with a smile and some banter in record time. He wants to show you his fires (blazing away in every room) and the enormous, beautiful bedrooms in sumptuous colours with bâteau beds and acres of crisp linen. There's the copper bathroom to marvel at (with another working fire) and several stunning views. He'll also want to tell you little stories about a picture, perhaps, or some evening or other he had with so-and-so — and take you to the games room at the top of the house with the full-sized billiard table and the purple walls. His charming wife Fiona (who has a gift for interior design using quirky colour combinations) is the perfect foil, calmly efficient and an accomplished cook. Only food and wine are taken seriously; the rest is laid back. Shooting, fishing, walking and the divine Donnie: what an antidote to work and the city! *Children over 12 welcome.*

Price	£145–£160.
Rooms	3: 1 double, en suite; 1 double, 1 twin sharing bathroom (let to same party only).
Meals	Lunch, 4 courses, £20, by arrangement. Dinner, 4 courses, £32.50. Packed lunch £10.
Closed	Christmas & New Year
Directions	At Buchlyvie, right onto B835 towards Aberfoyle. Entrance 200 yds on left after bridge. 1 mile along drive to house.

Donnie & Fiona Allan
Buchlyvie,
Stirling FK8 3PA

Tel	01360 850216
Fax	01360 850376
Email	info@ballochneck.com
Web	www.ballochneck.com

Mackay's Rooms

White beaches, turquoise sea, waves, cliffs, waterfalls, huge tumbling skies and mountains. Robbie and Fiona (local, young and brimming with energy) have brought it all inside with natural wood, stone, slate, seagrass and colours that reflect the landscape – heathers, blues and neutrals. Downstairs is comfortable and intimate – vanilla candles flickering in glass, a merry fire burning away, an interesting mix of modern and old furniture. Bedrooms are individual in style and vary much in size but all have excellent new beds, contemporary lighting, flat-screen TVs, DVD players, iPods and the same gorgeous natural colour schemes; purple saxifrage, moss campion and primrose yellow. Bathrooms are new, some with power showers, all with thick white towels and slate soap dispensers. Eat sublime food: cullen skink (fish soup), local venison, Highland beef, homemade puddings at chunky tables with high-backed leather chairs. The smell of peat fires drifts in the wind, gulls cry and the sea soothes – a place to free the heart and restore one's soul.

Price	£80–£110.
Rooms	7: 4 doubles, 2 twins, 1 single.
Meals	Dinner by arrangement.
Closed	November-Easter.
Directions	A838 north from Rhiconich. After 19 miles enter Durness village. Mackay's is on the right hand side opposite memorial.

Fiona Mackay
Durness,
Sutherland IV27 4PN

Tel	01971 511202
Fax	01971 511321
Email	fiona@visitmackays.com
Web	www.visitmackays.com

The Albannach

It may take a while to get here, but you won't regret it for a moment. The coast is magical, its glimmering seas, rugged mountains and empty roads a tonic for the soul. Add to this a night or two at the Albannach and you find paradise in the Highlands. Ostensibly this is a restaurant with rooms – Colin and Lesley's faultless food is worth the trip alone – but the house is no less alluring, so climb up to find fat white sofas in the conservatory, an open fire in the panelled snug, and cherry red walls in the baronial dining room. The house is one room deep with views from the front of water, village, mountain. Bedrooms are divine, big or bigger, all dressed in Sunday-best fabrics with Farrow & Ball colours, silky curtains, carafes of water and Bose sound systems. The suites are majestic with unbeatable bathrooms, and the simpler rooms are not simple at all; everything here is fantastic. As for the food, expect the best, perhaps duck with fois gras, red pepper soufflé, Lochinver halibut with a champagne sauce, sublime apple tart with calvados gelato. Walk, fish, some people swim. Heaven.

Price	Half-board £125-£165 p.p. Singles £190. Winter weekend breaks available.
Rooms	5: 1 double, 1 twin/double, 1 four-poster, 2 suites.
Meals	Half-board only. Lunch, by arrangement, from £12. Dinner, 5 courses, £50 for non-residents.
Closed	January & February.
Directions	North from Ullapool on A835, then A837 for Lochinver. In village, left, over bridge, for Baddidarrach. House signed left after half a mile.

Colin Craig & Lesley Crosfield
Baddidaroch, Lochinver,
Sutherland IV27 4LP

Tel	01571 844407
Email	info@thealbannach.co.uk
Web	www.thealbannach.co.uk

2 Quail Restaurant & Rooms

This is a small jewel in the Scottish crown, too modest to sing its own praises and all the better for it. It's a restaurant with rooms run in the Mediterranean tradition, with Michael and Karensa doing everything themselves with quiet flair. The exterior of this 1896 terrace cottage gives little hint of the pleasures within, but inside you find a double-fronted house that shines in homely splendour. There are fresh flowers, Buchanan tartan, Zoffany wallpaper and antique pine. It's hugely intimate, with a sitting room on one side of the hall and a snug dining room for 12 on the other (make sure you book). Here you eat Michael's exceptional food, four courses of heaven, perhaps fresh asparagus with truffles, lobster and langoustine with a saffron sauce, fillet of beef with roasted artichokes, then hot mint soufflé with dark chocolate cream. You sleep as well as you've eaten. Rooms are spotless and warmly furnished with comfy beds, decent linen, wool carpets and good bathrooms. Royal Dornoch is close for golf as are Brora and Bonnar Bridge. A treat.

Price	£110.
Rooms	3: 1 twin/double, 1 twin, 1 double.
Meals	Dinner, 3 courses, £38. Not Sunday or Monday; only Friday & Saturday in winter.
Closed	Occasionally.
Directions	From Inverness, A9 north for 44 miles, then right on A949 for Dornoch. Restaurant on left before cathedral.

Michael & Kerensa Carr
Castle Street, Dornoch,
Sutherland IV25 3SN

Tel	01862 811811
Email	stay@2quail.com
Web	www.2quail.com

Glenmorangie, The Highland Home at Cadboll

Glenmorangie – glen of tranquillity. And so it is; this is heaven. Owned by the eponymous distillery, this 1700s farmhouse of thick walls and immaculate interiors stands in glorious country, with a tree-lined path down to the beach; see your supper landed by fishermen, or search for driftwood instead. A perfect place and a real find, with levels of service to surpass most others, where staff are attentive yet unobtrusive, and where the comforts seem unending. Bedrooms are exceptional: decanters of whisky, *fleur de lys* wallpaper, tartan blankets and country views. Rooms flood with light, there are bathrobes and piles of towels, the best linen and blankets, and the cottage suites are perfect for families. Downstairs, the portrait of the Sheriff of Cromarty hangs on the wall, a fire crackles between plump sofas in the drawing room, and views of the garden draw you out. The walled half-acre garden is both beautiful and productive, with much for your plate: superb dinners, five courses, are served in intimate dinner party style. All this, and golf at Royal Dornoch, Tain and Brora.

Price	Half-board £165–£195 p.p.
Rooms	9: 6 twins/doubles, 3 cottage suites.
Meals	Half-board only. Light lunch from £7. Dinner for non-residents, £45.
Closed	3-23 January.
Directions	A9 north from Inverness for 33 miles to Nigg r'bout. Right on B9175, for Nigg, over r'way crossing for 1.5 miles, then left, following signs to house.

Martin Baxter
Fearn, By Tain,
Ross-shire IV20 1XP

Tel	01862 871671
Fax	01862 871625
Email	relax@glenmorangieplc.co.uk
Web	www.theglenmorangiehouse.com

The Torridon

An 1887 shooting lodge built for the Earl of Lovelace with 58 acres of lawn and field racing down to the shores of Upper Loch Torridon. You're in the middle of nowhere, but you wouldn't be anywhere else. Mighty mountains rise around you, red deer, sea eagles and otters pass through. Inside, sparkling interiors thrill: a huge fire in the panelled hall, a zodiac ceiling in the plush drawing room, 300 malts in the pitch pine bar. Huge windows pull in the view, walkers pour off the hills to recover in luxury, there's a telescope with which to scan water and mountain. Bedrooms are a real treat, some big, others bigger, all packed with spoiling extras. Newly refurbished rooms have a smart contemporary style (padded headboards, cool colours, silky throws, super bathrooms), others are deliciously traditional (country-house colours, warm florals, old armoires, a shower in a turret). Don't miss the two-acre vegetable garden, a work of art in itself. It provides much for the table, so feast on fresh food sublimely cooked. Cattle graze in the fields, magnificent Liathach waits to be climbed. Brilliant.

Price	Half-board £130–£162.50 p.p. Suites £232.50 p.p.
Rooms	19: 10 doubles, 1 twin/double, 1 single, 2 four-posters, 5 suites.
Meals	Half-board only. Lunch from £5. Dinner, 5 courses, £40 for non-residents. 7-course tasting menu £60.
Closed	January.
Directions	A9 to Inverness, A835 to Garve, A832 to Kinlochewe, A896 to Annat (not Torridon). In village, right by sea.

Daniel & Rohaise Rose-Bristow
Torridon, By Achnasheen,
Wester Ross IV22 2EY

Tel	01445 791242
Fax	01445 712253
Email	info@thetorridon.com
Web	www.thetorridon.com

Tigh an Eilean

Tigh an Eilean is the Holy Grail of the west coast – when you arrive you realise it's what you've been looking for all these years. A perfect place in every respect, from its position by the sea in this very pretty village, to the magnificence of the Torridon mountains that rise all around... this area is one of the wonderlands of the world. And Shieldaig itself has a strong sense of community, the hub of which is the pub – like the shop, owned by the hotel – where locals come to sing their songs, play their fiddles, drink their whisky, and talk. Most surprising of all is the hotel. Christopher and Cathryn, ex-London lawyers loving their new career, run an airy and stylish inn – all tartan cushions on window seats, sensational views, homemade shortbread, bedrooms that are comfy and bathrooms that sparkle. No TVs, no telephones, but kind, gentle staff who chat and advise. Friendly sitting rooms have plump sofas, Farrow & Ball colours and the odd tweed chair, an honesty bar and an open fire. Dine on Hebridean scallops in the restaurant, or try the pub: fewer frills but lots of fun.

Price	£150. Singles from £70.
	Half-board from £115 p.p.
Rooms	11: 5 doubles, 3 twins, 3 singles.
Meals	Bar meals from £5.
	Restaurant dinner £42.50.
Closed	November–March.
Directions	On loch front in centre of Shieldaig.

Christopher & Cathryn Field
Shieldaig, Loch Torridon,
Ross-shire IV54 8XN

Tel   01520 755251
Fax   01520 755321
Email   tighaneilean@keme.co.uk

Tomdoun Hotel

A quirky little place wrapped up in the middle of nowhere: in good weather Reception moves onto the veranda and the dogs sunbathe on lilos. Below, the blissful river Garry jumps from one loch to another; beyond, Glas Bheinn rises from the forest. Interiors are stylishly unpretentious (posh, but old!) with piles of logs and vintage luggage in the hall, a country-house dining room for breakfasts, and a smouldering coal fire in the lively bar. Come to fish – the hotel has rights on the loch and river – and if you're lucky, they'll cook your catch for supper. If not, settle for langoustine and cockles from Skye, or halibut fresh from Lochinver. A Swiss filmmaker liked the place so much he returned to shoot a movie; Sheila is now a star. Exquisite walking in the wild and peaceful glen, with Loch Hourn 20 miles upstream (where the road runs out). Bedrooms are simple, homely, nicely priced, full of colour; those at the front have huge Glengarry views. There's loads to do: 35 munros to climb, clay-pigeon shooting, white-water rafting, water-skiing, abseiling, mountain biking.

Price	£80–£110. Singles from £35.
Rooms	10: 3 doubles, 2 family, all en suite; 3 doubles, 1 twin, 1 single all sharing 2 baths.
Meals	Packed lunch £7.95. Bar meals from £9.95. Dinner, 3 courses, from £18.95.
Closed	24 & 25 December.
Directions	A82 north from Fort William, then A87 west from Invergarry. After 5 miles, left for Glengarry. Hotel 6 miles up on right.

Michael & Sheila Pearson
Glengarry, Invergarry,
Inverness-shire PH35 4HS

Tel	01809 511218
Email	enquiries@tomdoun.com
Web	www.tomdoun-sporting-lodge.com

Kilcamb Lodge

A stupendous setting, with Loch Sunart at the end of the garden and Glas Bheinn rising beyond. As for Kilcamb, it has all the ingredients of the perfect country house: a smart yellow drawing room with a roaring fire, a dining room that's won just about every award going and super-comfy bedrooms that don't stint on colour. The feel here is shipwreck-chic. There's a 12-acre garden with half a mile of shore, so follow paths to the water's edge and look for dolphins, otters and seals or watch duck and geese; if you're lucky, you may see eagles. Back inside you'll find stained-glass windows on the landing, a ship's bell in the bar, fresh flowers in the bedrooms. Come down at eight for a four-course dinner and feast on goat's cheese and chive mousse, cream of celery and stilton soup, roast venison with a juniper jus, then lemon curd crème brûlée. Warmly decorated bedrooms have all the trimmings: super king-size beds, padded headboards, big white towels, shiny bathrooms. Ardnamurchan Point is up the road and worth a visit: it's the most westerly point in mainland Britain. *Minumum stay two nights at weekends in May.*

Price	£150–£175. Suites £225. Singles from £95.
Rooms	10: 7 doubles, 3 suites.
Meals	Lunch from £4.50. Dinner, 4 courses, £45.
Closed	January. Limited opening November & February.
Directions	From Fort William, A82 south for 10 miles to Corran ferry, then A861 to Strontian. Hotel west of village on left, signed. A830 & A861 from Fort William takes an hour longer.

David & Sally Ruthven-Fox
Strontian, Argyll PH36 4HY

Tel	01967 402257
Fax	01967 402041
Email	enquiries@kilcamblodge.co.uk
Web	www.kilcamblodge.co.uk

Doune

Drive for miles and arrive at the water's edge where the mighty mountains of Knoydart rise to the east and Loch Nevis fuses with the sea. Be met by boat at Mallaig and taken to one of the most inaccessible parts of the Scottish mainland. Ever imagined landing in paradise? Here is a village of three families with no roads and a glorious view – Skye across the Sound of Sleat. Hear the water lapping, the call of a bird... and the whoops of joy of other guests as the combination of solitude, beauty, comfort and hospitality triggers an overpowering happiness. Hike (with a guide if you wish) and see no one all day, dive and find your own supper. Food is exceptional – maybe something from the sea, then a perfect venison pie. Along the veranda are three little pine-lined bed and shower rooms, with bunk galleries for children, hooks for clothes, easy chairs for watching the weather. There's a lodge for groups with simple bedrooms and an open-plan lay-out. The sunsets are breathtaking, the wind whistles, and townies will never know darkness like this. *Boat pick-up Tues & Sat only, so minimum stay three nights.*

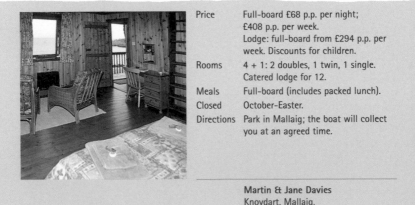

Price	Full-board £68 p.p. per night; £408 p.p. per week. Lodge: full-board from £294 p.p. per week. Discounts for children.
Rooms	4 + 1: 2 doubles, 1 twin, 1 single. Catered lodge for 12.
Meals	Full-board (includes packed lunch).
Closed	October-Easter.
Directions	Park in Mallaig; the boat will collect you at an agreed time.

Martin & Jane Davies
Knoydart, Mallaig,
Inverness-shire PH41 4PL

Tel	01687 462667
Fax	08700 940428
Email	martin@doune-knoydart.co.uk
Web	www.doune-knoydart.co.uk

Hotel Eilean Iarmain

One of the prettiest spots on Skye – a whitewashed hamlet at the end of the road. The Sound of Sleat wraps itself around the place and fishermen still land their catch 30 paces from the front door. Across the water Robert Louis Stevenson's lighthouse paddles in the shallow and the mountains of the mainland rise. Inside, the Hebrides of old survives, part shooting lodge, part gentlemen's club: tartan carpets, hessian on the walls, the papers by the fire in the morning room and a new Smuggler's Den where Gaelic whiskies can be savoured. Bedrooms in smart country style are split between the main house, the garden house and the stables, the latter for sparkling two-storey suites that sport crisp fabrics and new pine. Next door in the bar, the occasional ceilidh breaks loose and fiddles fly, but there's also a touch of refined culture in the art gallery round the corner. Sir Iain – born in Berlin, christened in Rome, schooled in Shanghai – is Skye through and through, and deeply involved in regenerating the woodland terrain to the south of the island. He'll teach you the odd word of Gaelic, too. Bring your kilt.

Price	£100–£200. Singles from £75. Suites £220–£250.
Rooms	15: 7 doubles, 4 twins, 4 suites.
Meals	Bar meals from £7.50. Lunch £12.50. Dinner, 4 courses, £33.
Closed	Rarely.
Directions	A87 over Skye Bridge, then left after 7 miles onto A851, signed Armdale. Hotel on left after 8 miles, signed.

	Sir Iain & Lady Noble Eilean Iarmain, Sleat, Isle of Skye IV43 8QR
Tel	01471 833332
Fax	01471 833275
Email	hotel@eileaniarmain.co.uk
Web	www.eileaniarmain.co.uk

Viewfield House

Scottish aristocracy meets high colonialism on a quiet hill above Portree. From its grand hall to its tiny turret bedroom the Victorian factor's house is stuffed with hunting trophies, eastern ornaments and a flurry of antiques, blending grandeur with touches of humour brilliantly. It's a fine ancestral seat, dates to 1790, and has huge windows in the sitting room, roaring fires, dark panelling, oriental rugs and unique 100-year-old wallpapers. Upstairs is a warren of bedrooms. Most are big, some are vast, all come in country-house style with traditional fabrics, well-laundered sheets and sea views from those at the front. Outside, you can climb through woods to Fingal's Seat for 360° views, or swim in a loch. Head further afield and sink into Skye — wildlife, mountains, sea lochs and castles all wait. Light suppers are on tap in the grand dining room where old ancestors peer down from the walls, so try Russian vegetable soup, honey roast ham salad, then rhubarb crumble with ice cream; alternatively, eat out and dine on Skye's natural larder. There's highland porridge for breakfast, too.

Price	£80–£120. Singles £40–£60.
Rooms	12: 4 doubles, 3 twins/doubles, 2 twins, 2 singles all en suite; 1 double with private bath & shower.
Meals	Light supper £3–£14. Packed lunch £5.20.
Closed	Mid-October–mid-April.
Directions	On A87, coming from south, driveway entrance on left just before the Portree National filling station.

Hugh Macdonald
Portree,
Isle of Skye IV51 9EU

Tel	01478 612217
Fax	01478 613517
Email	info@viewfieldhouse.com
Web	www.viewfieldhouse.com

Greshornish House Hotel

A wise man once said, "Skye is not a place, but an intoxication." This low-slung, white-painted manor house sits right beside the loch and the views stretch as far as the Trotternish peninsula. Neil and Rosemary have only been here a few years but already they've stamped their personality on the place; the rooms they have done so far are warm, peaceful, calming and relaxing. Bedrooms are mostly large, some still waiting for the magic wand, but all have excellent views over the water or the gardens, expensive bed linen and deep peace. In the restaurant, fish is as fresh as it can be, with scallops straight from the loch, and langoustine and lobster plucked from Dunvegan Bay. Dig into Talisker crab cakes, pan-fried halibut, basil panna cotta and a strawberry consommé. The hearty appetite of the walker is well understood here and conservatory breakfasts will set you up for anything; a game of tennis or croquet, a stroll around the garden or an energetic walk. Take your binoculars for otter, eider, heron and maybe a sea eagle – and watch out for sheep on the road to get here.

Price	£100–£170.
Rooms	9: 4 doubles, 2 twins/doubles, 1 twin, 2 family.
Meals	Lunch, 2 courses, from £14.95, by arrangement. Dinner from £34. Packed lunch about £6.
Closed	Christmas. Occasionally in winter.
Directions	A87 through Portree towards Dunvegan. 4 miles after Portree left on A850 for Dunvegan; signed to the right, 2 miles down single track road.

Neil & Rosemary Colquhoun
By Portree,
Isle of Skye IV51 9PN

Tel	01470 582266
Fax	01470 582345
Email	info@greshornishhouse.com
Web	www.greshornishhouse.com

Entry 275 Map 10, 11

Stein Inn

A small inn down by the water where Angus cooks super food and refuses to put up his prices. The position is perfect, Skye at its loveliest. You're bang on the loch on a road that goes nowhere. Razorbills and guillemots fly low over the water, islands sparkle in the distance, fishermen land their catch on the jetty, sunsets streak the sky red. Inside, stone walls, smouldering fires, pine cladding and a bustling bar that's crammed with locals at weekends. There are maps on the walls, nautical curios, a pool table at the back. Bedrooms above fit the bill perfectly. They're spotless, colourful, nice and comfy, with a warm country style and an honest price. Some are big, some are small, compact bathrooms are more than sufficient. Back downstairs you can dig into impossibly fresh food from a menu that changes daily, perhaps carrot and sweet potato soup, whole Dover sole fresh from the loch, then homemade profiteroles and chocolate sauce. Corncrakes and sea eagles pass through, the northern lights sparkle in winter, Dunvegan Castle is worth a peek.

Price	£52–£74. Singles £26–£37.
Rooms	5: 2 doubles, 2 family, 1 single.
Meals	Lunch & dinner £3–£20.
Closed	Christmas Day & New Year's Day.
Directions	From Isle of Skye bridge, A850 to Portree. Follow sign to Uig for 4 miles, left on A850 for Dunvegan for 14 miles. Hard right turn to Waternish on B886. Stein 4.5 miles along loch side.

Angus & Teresa McGhie
Stein, Waternish,
Isle of Skye IV55 8GA

Tel	01470 592362
Fax	01470 592362
Email	angus.teresa@steininn.co.uk
Web	www.steininn.co.uk

Scarista House

All you need to know is this: Harris is one of the most beautiful places anywhere in the world. Beaches of white sand that stretch for a mile or two are not uncommon. If you bump into another soul, it will be a delightful coincidence, but you should not count on it. The water is turquoise, and coconuts sometimes wash up on the beach. The view from Scarista is simple and magnificent: field, ridge, beach, water, sky. Patricia and Tim are the kindest people, quietly inspiring. Their home is island heaven: coal fires, rugs on painted wooden floors, books everywhere, old oak furniture, a first-floor drawing room, fresh flowers and fabulous Harris light. The golf club has left a set of clubs by the front door in case you wish to play (the view from the first tee is one of the best in the game). A corncrake occasionally visits the garden. There are walking sticks and Wellington boots to help you up the odd hill. Kind local staff may speak Gaelic. And the food is exceptional, maybe twice-baked crab soufflé, seared loin of Harris lamb, marmalade tart with plum compote. A perfect place.

Price	£175–£199. Singles from £120.
Rooms	5: 3 doubles, 2 twins.
Meals	Dinner, 3 courses, £43.50. Packed lunch £5.50.
Closed	Christmas & February.
Directions	From Tarbert, A859, signed Rodel. Scarista 15 miles on left, after golf course.

Patricia & Tim Martin
Isle of Harris,
Western Isles HS3 3HX

Tel   01859 550238
Fax   01859 550277
Email   timandpatricia@scaristahouse.com
Web   www.scaristahouse.com

Tigh Dearg

This far-flung island chain is worth every second it takes to get here. Come for huge skies, sweeping beaches, carpets of wild flowers in the machair in summer, stone circles, ancient burial chambers, white-tailed eagles and fabulous Hebridean light. It's hard to overstate the sheer wonder of these bleakly beautiful islands, five of which are connected by a causeway, so drop south to Benbecula (*Whisky Galore* was filmed here) or Eriskay (for the Prince's Strand, where Bonnie Prince Charlie landed). Up on North Uist, you'll find 1,000 lochs, so climb North Lees for wonderful watery views, then tumble back down to the island sanctuary of Tigh Dearg. The house is a delight, immensely welcoming, full of colour, warmly contemporary, with windows that flood the place with light. Swanky bedrooms come with suede headboards, power showers, bathrobes and beach towels, bowls of fruit and crisp white linen. In the restaurant, lobster, crab, squid, sole all come straight from the water. Walk, ride, fish, canoe, then return and try the sauna. Come in November for the northern lights. Fabulous.

Price	£80–£139.
Rooms	8 twins/doubles.
Meals	Bar meals from £7.50. Dinner, 3 courses, £25.
Closed	Never.
Directions	North into Lochmaddy. Left, signed Police Station. Hotel on left after 200 yds.

Iain MacLeod
Lochmaddy, Isle of North Uist,
Western Isles HS6 5AE

Tel	01876 500700
Fax	01876 500701
Email	info@tighdearghotel.co.uk
Web	www.tighdearghotel.co.uk

Wales

Photo: Quentin Craven

Neuadd Lwyd

Tudor kings came from this village, their forefathers buried in the tiny church that stands beyond the garden gate. Six sublime acres wrap around you, sheep graze in the fields, views shoot off to a distant Snowdon. The house, an 1871 rectory cloaked in wisteria, has been refurbished in lavish style and smart Victorian interiors shine. The drawing room floods with morning light, has deep sofas, polished wood floors, loads of books and a crackling fire; French windows open onto the south-facing terrace for sunny afternoons. High-ceilinged bedrooms are immaculate and full of beautiful things: cut-glass Venetian mirrors, ornate marble fireplaces, beautifully upholstered armchairs, Provençal eiderdowns; the two bigger rooms have slipper baths. Best of all is the cooking. Susannah and co-chef Delyth trained at Ballymaloe and whatever can be is homemade; delicious breads, fabulous oat cakes, jams, compotes, sorbets, ice creams. You may get Gorau Glas cheese soufflé, rack of Anglesey lamb with minted pea purée, warm pear and frangipani tarte, a plate of Welsh cheeses. Coastal paths will help you atone.

Fabulous food makes Neuadd Lwyd tick. Susannah and Delyth met at Ballymaloe and are passionate about using the freshest ingredients. A kitchen garden offers up organic vegetables and soft fruit, happy hens provide the eggs. Neighbours on the island do the rest. Wild berries and elderflower are 'sourced' from the next-door churchyard, meat and poultry come from a local farm, game is from an island estate, and sea bass and lobster are hauled from Anglesey's waters. Gorau Glas stars on the cheese board, while beers are whisked over the Menai Strait from a micro-brewery in Glan Conwy.

Price	£125–£145. Singles £80–£110. Half-board from £82.50 p.p.
Rooms	4: 3 doubles, 1 twin.
Meals	Dinner, 4 courses, £35.
Closed	Sundays & Mondays.
Directions	A55 north over Britannia Bridge. 2nd exit (A5025) for Amlwch, then left for Llangefni (B5420). After 2 miles, right signed St Gredifael's Church. 1 mile up lane; on right.

Susannah & Peter Woods
Penmynydd,
Anglesey LL61 5BX

Tel	01248 715005
Fax	01248 715005
Email	post@neuaddlwyd.co.uk
Web	www.neuaddlwyd.co.uk

SPECIAL
GREEN ENTRY
see page 17

Entry 279 Map 5

Jolyon's Boutique Hotel

Down in Butetown, the captain's house stands on Cardiff Bay's oldest residential street. Bang opposite, the regenerated docks are home to the Welsh Assembly, the Norwegian Church and the Millennium Centre. At Jolyon's boutique B&B hotel run in the Mediterranean style, you get quietly groovy interiors. Bedrooms start on the ground floor and work their way skywards to the one at the top with a private roof terrace. The higher you go, the better the view. In the basement is a bar made from reclaimed 1840 timbers encased in stainless steel; stop for an espresso, a trappist beer or a glass of pear and strawberry cider. An old harmonium rests against an exposed stone wall; sink into red leather sofas and gaze at contemporary art. Spotless bedrooms aren't huge, but nor are they small, and light floods in so none feel cramped. You find Moroccan lanterns, French armoires, Dutch marble, Canadian oak, Indian teak, Philippe Starck loos in airy bathrooms (you can watch TV while you soak in a couple). Jolyon will tell you where to eat: Capsule, for cocktails and *calzone*, is a must.

Price	£89–£150.
Rooms	6 doubles.
Meals	Pizzas from £8.
Closed	Never.
Directions	M4 junc. 29, then A48(M) for Cardiff. Take exit marked 'Docks and Bay'. Straight ahead, past Millenium Centre & 1st left.

Jolyon Joseph
5 Bute Crescent,
Cardiff CF10 5AN

Tel	02920 488775
Fax	02920 488775
Email	info@jolyons.co.uk
Web	www.jolyons.co.uk

Harbourmaster Hotel

The harbour at Aberaeron was created by an Act of Parliament in 1807. Shipbuilding flourished and the harbourmaster got his house on the quay with big views over Cardigan Bay. Step in to find that winning combination of seductive good looks, informal but attentive service and a menu overflowing with fresh local produce. The airy open-plan dining room/bar has stripped floors and a horseshoe bar for good beers and wines; plans to extend are in the offing, walls will soon open up and the bar will move next door and find a terrace. Wind up the staircase to super little bedrooms that come with shuttered windows, loads of colour and quietly funky bathrooms. You get Frette linen, Welsh wool blankets and a hot water bottle on every bed in winter. There are flat-screen TVs and DVD players, watery views and tide books. Come down for supper and try fishcakes with lime mayonnaise, rack of lamb with sweet potato chips, and poached pear with honey ice cream. There are bikes to borrow; cycle tracks spin off into the hills, coastal paths lead north and south. *Minimum stay two nights at weekends.*

Price	£110–£140. Suite £140–£150. Singles £65. Half-board from £80 p.p.
Rooms	9: 4 doubles, 2 singles, 1 suite. Cottage: 2 doubles.
Meals	Lunch from £10.50. Dinner, 3 courses, around £30.
Closed	Christmas & New Year.
Directions	A487 south from Aberystwyth. In Aberaeron, right, for the harbour. Hotel on waterfront.

Glyn & Menna Heulyn
Pen Cei, Aberaeron,
Ceredigion SA46 0BA

Tel	01545 570755
Email	info@harbour-master.com
Web	www.harbour-master.com

Escape Boutique B&B

Bill Bryson raved about Llandudno – the unspoilt front with its bright white hotels and pier, the bustling shops and restaurants behind. Just a short walk from the sea, the house on the hill with its Victorian features intact – stained-glass windows, ornate carved fireplaces – has been stunningly transformed into a world of wood floors, cool neutral colours, Italian cream leather and glass chandeliers. Sam and Gaenor have cut not one corner so everything is the best: huge pocket-sprung mattresses, Farrow & Ball colours, acres of crisp linen, gorgeous goose down, beautifully designed bathrooms with a roll top bath or a drench-me shower. Bedrooms are spotless, some have sea views and breakfast is a feast of Conwy Gold Award sausages and serious coffee. Best of all are the easy-going owners who organise pretty much anything you want – or leave you to your own devices. The comfortable sitting room with honesty bar would make this a great place for a weekend house party; there's even a pretty garden in which to sip something cool before a stroll into town. *Minimum stay two nights at weekends.*

Price	£80–£120.
Rooms	9 doubles.
Meals	Restaurants & pubs within walking distance.
Closed	Rarely.
Directions	A55 from Chester into North Wales; junc. 18 Llandudno (A470). Follow signs to promenade; left into Church Walks & past Great Orme Tramway. House on right.

Sam Nayar
48 Church Walks, Llandudno,
Conwy LL30 2HL

Tel	01492 877776
Fax	01492 878777
Email	info@escapebandb.co.uk
Web	www.escapebandb.co.uk

The Kinmel Arms

St George – just a handful of cottages – so the locals must be pleased that one of their own (the lovely Lynn, who grew up near here) has returned, with husband Tim, to turn the old place into a sparkling restaurant with rooms. Walk in to a light, open-plan space of cool, neutral colours, hard wood floors and a central bar with new stained-glass detail above; then through to a conservatory-style restaurant painted a cheery yellow, with marble-topped tables and Tim's photographs and paintings on all the walls, inspired by the North Wales landscape and his climbing travels. Behind are four gorgeous suites, each with wide French windows to a decked seating area facing east for glorious sunrises – you breakfast here on goodies from your own fridge. Expect huge beds with crisp linen, high ceilings and fresh yellow walls, flat-screen TVs, luxurious porcelain bathrooms with vast towels and designer radiators. Everything is geared towards relaxation – the rooms, the food, the wine, the independence. You're a hop from that stunning coast – and Snowdonia – while great walks start from the door. Fabulous.

Price	£135-£175.
Rooms	4 suites.
Meals	Continental breakfast only.
	Light lunch £3.25-£8.95.
	Dinner, 2 courses, from £15.
Closed	Sunday evenings & Mondays.
Directions	A55, junc. 24 from Chester; left;
	0.25 miles to top of Primrose Hill.

Tim Watson & Lynn Cunnah-Watson
The Village, St George,
Abergele, Conwy LL22 9BP

Tel	01745 832207
Fax	01745 822044
Email	info@thekinmelarms.co.uk
Web	www.thekinmelarms.co.uk

Entry 283 Map 5

The Lion Inn

A simple inn lost in the hills of North Wales. You are more likely to hear birdsong, bleating sheep or a rumbling tractor than a car. The village was the setting for the first Cadfael novel, which is partly based on fact; St Winifred was buried at the priory here. In summer you can sit at colourful tables on the pavement and watch buzzards circle high in the sky, in winter you can sip your pint by a fire that burns on both sides in the bar. Downstairs, there are blue carpets and sprigs of hawthorn decorate stone walls. Upstairs, bedrooms are an unexpected tonic, warm and cosy, nicely stylish, super value for money. There are Farrow & Ball paints on old stone walls and Canadian pitch pine furniture, rustic wooden beds with crisp white linen and Welsh wool blankets, spotless bathrooms, flat-screen TVs and DVD players too. Big breakfasts set you up for the day — porridge, croissants, free-range eggs — so burn off the excess on Snowden or ride your bike through local forests. The mobile library passes once a month. Portmerion and Anglesey are both close. *Minimum stay two nights at weekends.*

Price	£69. Singles from £39. Family £79-£89.
Rooms	5: 2 doubles, 1 twin, 1 family, 1 single.
Meals	Lunch from £7 (Saturday & Sunday only). Dinner, 3 courses, about £20. Not Sunday & Monday.
Closed	Mondays.
Directions	A55 to Abergale, A544 south to Llansannan, B5384 west to Gwytherin. In village.

Dai Richardson & Rose James
Gwytherin, Nr Betws-y-Coed,
Conwy LL22 8UU

Tel	01745 860123
Fax	01745 860556
Email	info@thelioninn.net
Web	www.thelioninn.net

Manorhaus

It's a little like rural France here – an old country town that climbs a hill with a sea of lush country all around. Wash up at Manorhaus and you discover a perfect little townhouse retreat. It's Georgian on the outside, distinctly groovy within, the hotel doubling as a gallery with fine contemporary art on every wall; it's all for sale and each bedroom shows the work of a different artist. Downstairs: a sitting room in white and blue, a restaurant with stripped wood floors and a small cinema in the Tudor basement. Upstairs you find a library for books, maps, CDs, DVDs, then a sauna and steam room to help you recover after a day in the hills. Keep going and you come to a sweep of funky bedrooms. Some are bigger than others but all have super bathrooms, oodles of character and style and king-size beds with crisp white linen and goose down bedding. One has a freestanding bath, another has huge views off to a distant ridge. Delicious food is fresh and local: Menai mussels, Welsh beef, warm treacle tart. Mountain biking can be arranged, Offa's Dyke is close for walkers. *Minimum stay two nights at weekends.*

Price	£95-£125. Suite £150.
	Half-board £72.50-£95 p.p.
Rooms	8: 7 doubles, 1 suite.
Meals	Lunch (Friday-Sunday) £16.
	Dinner, 3 courses, about £25.
Closed	24-30 December.
Directions	M56; A55; A494 to Ruthin. Follow signs to town centre, up hill; Well Street on left when entering square.

Christopher Frost & Gavin Harris
Well Street, Ruthin,
Denbighshire LL15 1AH

Tel	01824 704830
Fax	01824 707333
Email	cjf@manorhaus.com
Web	www.manorhaus.com

Tyddyn Llan

Everything is orchestrated superbly here. Your entry is into a smart country home – there's no reception desk – where owners Bryan and Susan Webb greet you with the promise of deep comfort and some exquisite modern cooking. There are three sitting rooms, a log fire, carefully chosen antiques and a dining room with a gentle, French country feel: blue-grey panelling and soft floral drapes. Eat at white-clothed tables on fresh, locally sourced produce lovingly cooked: grilled scallops, Welsh black fillet of beef au poivre, calves' sweetbreads with pancetta, whimberry crème brûlée. Bedrooms vary in size but all are cosy and well-designed in a traditional style with warm colours, lush towels and every indulging extra. Treat yourself to tea on the veranda after a game of croquet on the lawn… or walk the Berwin Ridge which rises to 2,000 feet. Or come with rod and wellies to fish trout and grayling on the river Dee. Great comfort and fine food in an astonishingly beautiful Welsh valley.

Price	£110–£260. Singles from £95. Half-board £95–£160 p.p.
Rooms	13: 8 doubles, 4 twins, 1 garden suite.
Meals	Lunch £21–£28. Dinner £35–£40; tasting menu £60. Sunday lunch £23.50.
Closed	Two weeks in January.
Directions	From A5 west of Corwen, left on B4401 to Llandrillo. Go through village, entrance on right after tight bend.

Bryan & Susan Webb
Llandrillo, Corwen,
Denbighshire LL21 0ST

Tel	01490 440264
Fax	01490 440414
Email	tyddynllan@compuserve.com
Web	www.tyddynllan.co.uk

The Hand at Llanarmon

Single-track lanes plunge you into the middle of nowhere. Lush valleys rise and fall, so pull on your boots and scale a mountain or find a river and jump into a canoe. Back at the Hand, a 16th-century drovers' inn, the pleasures of a country local are hard to miss. A coal fire burns on the range in reception, a wood fire crackles under brass in the front bar and a wood-burner warms the lofty dining room. Expect exposed stone walls, low beamed ceilings, old pine settles and candles on the mantelpiece. There's a games room for darts and pool, a quiet sitting room for maps and books. Delicious food is popular with locals, so grab a table and enjoy seasonal menus – perhaps game broth, lamb casserole, and orange and coriander sponge served warm with a cointreau syrup. Bedrooms are just as they should be: not too fancy, cosy and warm, spotlessly clean and with crisp white linen. A very friendly place. Martin and Gaynor are full of quiet enthusiasm and have made their home warmly welcoming. John Ceiriog Hughes, the Welsh Shakespeare, came from these hills. Special indeed.

Price	£70-£110.
Rooms	13: 8 doubles, 4 twins, 1 suite.
Meals	Lunch from £4.50. Sunday lunch £17. Dinner £8-£25.
Closed	24-26 December.
Directions	Leave A5 south of Chirk for B4500. Village 11 miles ahead and signed.

Gaynor & Martin De Luchi
Llanarmon Dyffryn Ceiriog, Llangollen,
Denbighshire LL20 7LD

Tel	01691 600666
Fax	01691 600262
Email	reception@thehandhotel.co.uk
Web	www.thehandhotel.co.uk

Entry 287 Map 5

Egerton Grey Country House Hotel

A Victorian rectory set in seven acres of lawn, orchard and terraced gardens, with views to the front of a viaduct striding across the valley; the path that runs beneath it leads to the sea. Inside, an unreformed country house, a looking-glass onto the Twenties. Step in to rugs on parquet floors, busts and oils, marble fireplaces and Cuban panelling. French windows in the breakfast room open onto a small terrace that looks the right way; keep going and you find a grand piano and a wood-burner in the splendid double-aspect drawing room, and a sunroom with views down the valley. Wind up the baronial oak staircase, past a portrait of Elizabeth I, to a landing packed with eccentric curios. Country-house bedrooms, some big, some smaller, have armoires, fresh flowers, ornamental fireplaces, colourful wallpaper. One in the eaves opens onto a tiny balcony, several have claw-foot baths, all have robes. Spin back down for a good dinner, perhaps ham hock and duck terrine, roasted monkfish, light chocolate mousse. Cardiff airport is within a mile; its traffic is infrequent and passes briefly.

Price	£140–£160. Singles from £90. Half-board from £90 p.p.
Rooms	9: 7 twins/doubles, 2 four-posters.
Meals	Lunch from £10. Dinner, à la carte, about £30. Sunday lunch £18.50.
Closed	Never.
Directions	M4 junc. 33. Follow signs to Cardiff airport. Hotel signed left at small r'bout by airport. On left after 500 yds, signed.

Richard Morgan-Price & Huw Thomas
Porthkerry, Barry,
Glamorgan CF62 3BZ

Tel	01446 711666
Fax	01446 711690
Email	info@egertongrey.co.uk
Web	www.egertongrey.co.uk

Holm House

A glittering hotel down by the sea: stylish, intimate and hugely spoiling. A two-year renovation has covered every square inch with something lovely, so step into this grand Edwardian house and find half-panelled walls, vintage wallpaper and a mirrored bar that doubles as a sitting room. Interiors mix Art Deco touches with contemporary flair. Downstairs, doors everywhere open onto a balustraded terrace with formal gardens below and a sparkling sea beyond; on a good day you're on the Côte d'Azur. You gather before dinner for canapés and a glass of champagne on the house, then slip into the airy restaurant for delicious comfort food, perhaps chicken liver pâté, fillet of lamb, chocolate tart with orange confit. Beautiful bedrooms come with Frette linen, super beds, designer fabrics and Italian ceramics in smart bathrooms. Rooms at the back look out to sea, one has a TV embedded in the bathroom wall, another comes in creamy leather; two have balconies. There are loungers on a first-floor sun terrace, a spa for treatments and a hydrotherapy pool. Cardiff is close. Heaven. *Minimum stay two nights at weekends.*

Price	Half-board £87.50–£175 p.p.
Rooms	12: 4 suites, 6 doubles, 2 twins.
Meals	Half-board only. Lunch from £12.50.
Closed	Never.
Directions	M4 junc. 33, then A4232 south. Follow signs to Penarth town centre (not marina). Along seafront, up hill, 1st right; 4th house on right.

	Susan Sessions
	Marine Parade, Penarth,
	Glamorgan CF64 3BG
Tel	02920 701572
Fax	02920 709875
Email	info@holmhouse.co.uk
Web	www.holmhouse.co.uk

Ty'n Rhos

This small country house packs quite some punch. It stands in 50 acres of sound-proofed grounds, with sheep in the fields, shrubs flanking the lawn and a path running down to a small lake. Step inside and you're drawn into a splendid conservatory that opens onto a stone terrace for long views off to Anglesey. Recently refurbished bedrooms come in plush country-house style with well-dressed beds, thick fabrics and nicely upholstered armchairs. Two rooms downstairs open onto the terrace, those that look north have fine views, and binoculars with which to scan the horizon. All are good and restful. Back downstairs you find chess and backgammon in a sofaed sitting room and an airy dining room where you are treated to Martin's delicious food, perhaps mussel, tomato and saffron soup, roast loin of lamb with an apricot stuffing, apple tart with bay leaf ice cream. He was once head chef at Bodysgallen Hall and cooks with huge passion, growing much for the table in a productive kitchen garden. The wild beauty of North Wales waits on your doorstep. Brilliant. *Minimum stay two nights at weekends.*

Price	£100–£140. Singles from £75.
Rooms	9: 2 doubles, 6 twins/doubles, 1 single.
Meals	Light lunch in summer from £15. Dinner, 3 courses, from £35.
Closed	Never.
Directions	A55 junc 11, then A4244 west. Straight over 1st roundabout and signed right after a mile. On left.

Jan & Martin James
Seion, Llanddeiniolen, Caernarfon,
Gwynedd LL55 3AE

Tel	01248 670489
Fax	01248 671772
Email	enquiries@tynrhos.co.uk
Web	www.tynrhos.co.uk

Rhiwafallen Restaurant with Rooms

North Wales may be a touch far flung, but its star shines brightly these days and ever-growing numbers are flocking in to explore its magical landscapes. Luckily, a smattering of stylish hotels has mushroomed to look after the lucky souls who venture forth; this intimate restaurant with rooms is one of the best. Roll up the drive to find old stone walls, ducks on the pond and a pebbled terrace overlooking the fields. Inside, cool interiors are warm and restful with candles in the fireplace and the odd bust of an eastern deity, but it's the bedrooms that take the biscuit, each one brimming with understated grace. The style is crisply contemporary: Egyptian cotton and goose down duvets, modern art and flat-screen TVs, fancy bathrooms and fluffy cotton bathrobes. One has a claw-foot bath in the room itself, another has its own balcony. Pull yourself away for Rob's glorious food, perhaps local crab, Welsh lamb, raspberry and lemon grass trifle. You eat in a canvas-shaded conservatory with doors that open onto the terrace in summer. Snowdon is close, as are wild beaches for seaside walks.

Price	£100–£150. Singles from £80.
Rooms	5 doubles.
Meals	Sunday lunch £17.50. Dinner, 3 courses, £27.50. Not Sunday or Monday.
Closed	Rarely.
Directions	South from Caernarfon on A487. Right onto A499 for Llandwrog. Through village and on left after 0.5 miles.

Rob & Kate John
Llandwrog,
Caernarfon,
Gwynedd LL54 5SW
Tel   01286 830172
Web   www.rhiwafallen.co.uk

Plas Bodegroes

Close to the end of the world and worth every second it takes to get here. Chris and Gunna are inspirational, their home a temple of cool elegance, the food possibly the best in Wales. Fronted by an avenue of 200-year-old beech trees, this Georgian manor house is wrapped in climbing roses, wildly roaming wisteria and ferns. The veranda circles the house, as do long French windows that lighten every room; open one up, grab a book and pull up a chair. Not a formal place – come to relax and be yourself. Bedrooms are wonderful, the courtyard rooms especially good; exposed wooden ceilings and a crisp clean style give the feel of a smart Scandinavian forest hideaway. Best of all is the dining room, almost a work of art in itself, cool and crisp with exceptional art and Venetian carnival masks on the walls – a great place to eat Chris's Michelin-starred food. How about French onion soup, roast mountain lamb with rosemary jus, and apricot and ginger parfait with pistachio praline? Tear yourself away and explore the Lleyn peninsula: sandy beaches, towering cliffs and country walks all wait. Snowdon is close, too.

Price	£110–£170. Singles £50–£80. Half-board from £95 p.p.
Rooms	11: 7 doubles, 2 twins, 1 four-poster, 1 single.
Meals	Sunday lunch £18.50. Dinner £40. Not Sunday evenings.
Closed	December-February; Sunday & Monday.
Directions	From Pwllheli, A497 towards Nefyn. House on left after 1 mile, signed.

Chris & Gunna Chown
Pwllheli,
Gwynedd LL53 5TH

Tel	01758 612363
Fax	01758 701247
Email	gunna@bodegroes.co.uk
Web	www.bodegroes.co.uk

Plas Tan-yr-allt

A sublime country house on the side of a hill with majestic views from the terrace stretching for miles across land and sea. There's history, too. The poet Shelley lived here in 1812, fleeing to Ireland after a ghost shot at him in the middle of the night; the event inspired Mary Shelley to dream up Frankenstein. These days you find nothing but relaxed country life; an honesty bar and a fire in the drawing room, the daily papers and fine art in the library, and lively communal dinner parties in the dining room each night. Nick and Michael receive with warmth and humour – this is a country-house B&B, not a hotel – and parties are welcome to take the whole place over. Airy bedrooms are predictably divine. Expect padded window seats, thick fabrics, Farrow & Ball colours, perhaps a sofa at the end of your bed. Also: crisp linen, fancy bathrooms and fresh flowers. You're in 47 acres of garden and hillside, you can climb to the top of the rock that soars behind and gaze down the Welsh coast. Snowdon, Anglesey and Portmerion are close. This one is hard to leave. *Minimum stay two nights at weekends.*

Price	£110-£150. Singles £90-£125. Half-board from £82.50 p.p.
Rooms	6: 3 doubles, 1 twin, 2 four-posters.
Meals	Dinner, 3 courses, £35.
Closed	2 weeks in January.
Directions	Leave Tremadog on A498 for Beddgelert. Signed on left after 0.5 miles. House at top of hill.

Michael Bewick & Nick Golding
Tremadog, Porthmadog,
Gwynedd LL49 9RG
Tel   01766 514545
Email   info@tanryallt.co.uk
Web   www.tanryallt.co.uk

Penmaenuchaf Hall

A long, windy road leads to the Hall and it's worth taking just for the views. Stand at the front of the house, on the Victorian stone balustrade, and gaze down on the tidal ebb and flow, or amble round the back to banks of rhododendrons, azaleas and camellias and a rising forest behind. Inside, all is immaculate bordering on sumptuous: rugs, wooden floors and oak panelling, flowers erupting from jugs and bowls, leather sofas and armchairs, open fires and lavish drapes. And, everywhere, those views. Impressive detail in the bedrooms too, with their vanity mirrors, underfloor heated bathrooms and every spoiling extra. They come in all shapes and sizes, the big being *huge*, the small being warm and cosy; one room up in the eaves has a fine bergère bed. In the dining room, stiff white napery, a dress code and the best of modern British, with fresh local produce and herbs from the garden. Fish in their 13 miles of salmon river, return to snooker, backgammon and a grand piano. You'll warm to Mark's sense of humour, too. *Children over six welcome. Pets by arrangement.*

Price	£135-£205. Singles £90-£135.
Rooms	14: 7 doubles, 5 twins/doubles, 1 four-poster, 1 family.
Meals	Lunch £5-£18. Afternoon tea from £6. Dinner, 4 courses, £35. Also à la carte.
Closed	Rarely.
Directions	From Dolgellau, A493 west for about 1.5 miles. Entrance on left.

Mark Watson & Lorraine Fielding
Penmaenpool, Dolgellau,
Gwynedd LL40 1YB

Tel	01341 422129
Fax	01341 422787
Email	relax@penhall.co.uk
Web	www.penhall.co.uk

Penhelig Arms

It's small, friendly and rather smart, and the way things are done here is second to none. Village life pours through: old boys drop by for a pint, passing friends stop for a chat, families book in for a birthday lunch. Robert and Sally do things from the heart and generous prices draw a loyal crowd. Across the road the Dyfi estuary bursts into Cardigan Bay; sands appear at low tide. Inside, homely inn rooms are small but sweet and all come with sea views. But if you want something fancier you can have it: Bodhelig House has big, airy rooms with sofas, some with French windows that open onto tables and chairs outside; super-cool Penhelig House is a waterside suite over two floors with a private terrace; a self-catering designer cottage, 50 paces along the waterfront, has views that shoot down the estuary, and its own terrace. The food truly is fabulous, the fish straight from the sea, and there are rump-steak burgers for committed carnivores. Super art adorns the walls in the restaurant and a fire burns in the local's bar. Coast and hills beckon, so bring the boots. *Minimum stay two nights at weekends.*

Price	£79-£130. Singles from £45. Half-board £69-£96 p.p.
Rooms	16 + 1: 4 twins/doubles, 5 doubles, 1 single. Bodhelig House: 5 suites. Penhelig House: 1 suite. Cottage for 2.
Meals	Bar meals from £7. Dinner, 3 courses, about £30.
Closed	Christmas Day & Boxing Day.
Directions	North from Aberystwyth on A487. Through Machynlleth, then A493 to Aberdyfi. Inn on right entering village. Parking opposite.

Robert & Sally Hughes
Aberdyfi,
Gwynedd LL35 0LT

Tel	01654 767215
Fax	01654 767690
Email	penheligarms@saqnet.co.uk
Web	www.penheligarms.com

The Bell at Skenfrith

The Bell stands by an ancient stone bridge in a much-ignored valley with hugely beautiful hills rising behind and a Norman castle paddling in the river a hundred yards from the front door. A sublime spot – and the inn is as good. It dates to the 17th century, but its crisply designed interiors ooze a cool country chic. In the locals' bar you find slate floors, open fires, plump-cushioned armchairs and polished oak. In summer, doors fly open and life decants onto the terrace at the back; views of wood and hill are interrupted only by the odd chef pottering past on his way to a rather productive kitchen garden. Stripped boards in the restaurant give an airy feel, so stop for delicious food served by young, attentive staff, perhaps roasted red pepper soup, breast of local duck and fig tarte tatin with lemon and thyme ice cream. Bedrooms above are as you'd expect: dressed in fine fabrics, uncluttered and elegant, brimming with light, some beamed, others overlooking the river. Idyllic circular walks start from the front door and sweep you into blissful country. A perfect place. *Minimum stay two nights at weekends.*

Price	£105–£185. Singles from £80 (Monday-Friday).
Rooms	8: 3 doubles, 1 twin/double, 2 four-posters, 2 attic suites.
Meals	Bar lunch from £14. Sunday lunch £21.50. Dinner, à la carte, about £30.
Closed	Mondays November to Easter; 2 weeks January/February.
Directions	From Monmouth, B4233 to Rockfield; B4347 for 5 miles; right on B4521, Skenfrith 1 mile.

William & Janet Hutchings
Skenfrith,
Monmouthshire NP7 8UH

Tel	01600 750235
Fax	01600 750525
Email	enquiries@skenfrith.co.uk
Web	www.skenfrith.co.uk

Beaufort Arms

A 16th-century village inn with a terrace at the front for a pint in summer, a snug beamed bar for the rugby, and a music festival in the second week of June (hop from pub to church for rock, jazz, folk and classical). At the inn flagged floors, exposed stone walls and low beamed ceilings have been spruced up to give a fresh traditional feel; not contemporary, just warmly inviting. A pretty entrance hall of half-panelled walls and rippling glass takes you back to the 1920s. A very friendly place with lots to drink: local ales, Belgian beers, French coffee, New World wines. Choose from boarded menus in the big bar (Slovakian meatballs, beer-battered hake) or skip over to the dining room for something more fancy (pan-fried monkfish with a peach and rocket salad). Bedrooms in the main house are stylish. Some have pleasant views, a couple have sleigh beds, all come with crisp white linen and pretty throws; those in the old stables are simpler, smaller, less expensive. The A40 passes quietly nearby, making access easy. Raglan's exquisite medieval castle is close, as are the mighty Brecon Beacons.

Price	£70–£100. Singles from £60.
Rooms	15: 8 doubles, 6 twins, 1 single.
Meals	Lunch & dinner £5–£25. Sunday lunch £12.95–£14.95.
Closed	25 & 26 December.
Directions	M4 junc. 24, A449 north, then A40 west and immediately left into village. On right opposite church.

Eliot & Jana Lewis
High Street, Raglan, Usk,
Monmouthshire NP15 2DY

Tel	01291 690412
Fax	01291 690935
Email	enquiries@beaufortraglan.co.uk
Web	www.beaufortraglan.co.uk

The Crown at Whitebrook

An unbeatable combination of attentive service, sublime food and impeccable style make this a real find for those in search of affordable luxury. The Crown is a small restaurant with rooms in a tiny village that's wrapped up in the Wye Valley. Forest rises all around, goats graze in fields, deer amble by in summer. Walks start from the front door, so climb to the ridge for imperious views or head south to Tintern Abbey. Don't stray too far. Bedrooms are a real treat, seriously comfortable, with crisp linen, pretty colours, decanters of sherry and fluffy white bathrobes. The smaller rooms are exceptional value, but splash out on bigger ones for sofas, armchairs and a little more space, huge walk-in showers, sparkling deep baths, perhaps a four-poster bed; all come with an astonishing array of hi-tech gadgetry including a movie library and internet access through the TV. As for the food, it's Michelin-starred and utterly delicious, perhaps seared langoustine and crab risotto, chargrilled loin of wild venison, then confit of rhubarb with apple sorbet. Whatever can be is homemade and flavour floods from every bite. Brilliant.

Price	£100–£120. Singles from £75.
Rooms	8: 6 doubles, 2 twins/doubles.
Meals	Lunch (Wed-Sun) from £19.50. Dinner (Wed-Sat), 3 courses, £37.50.
Closed	Late December to early January.
Directions	M4 junc. 24, A449/A40 north to Monmouth, then B4293 south. Up hill. After 2.7 miles left for Whitebook. On right after two miles.

Michael Obray
Whitebrook, Monmouth,
Monmouthshire NP25 4TX

Tel	01600 860254
Fax	01600 860607
Email	info@crownatwhitebrook.co.uk
Web	www.crownatwhitebrook.co.uk

Lake Vyrnwy Hotel

A blissful pocket of rural Wales, with high hills of forest and grazing land cradling the lake; it was excavated by hand in 1891, took two years to fill and now provides Liverpool's water. The hotel was built shortly afterwards so civic dignitaries could come for the weekend and fish the 400,000 trout that were released into the water. The view is *stupendous*, the lake stretching five miles into the distance, home to rolling mists and sunburst. Walk or cycle round it, canoe, sail or fish on it, all can be arranged. Birdwatchers will be in heaven, the walking is fabulous, but if you want to hole up in country-house comfort, you can; a plush drawing room, an armchaired library, a new conservatory, a terraced bar and an award-winning restaurant for fresh local produce all look the right way. Some rooms in the house are seriously grand (in one you can soak in a claw-foot bath while gazing down the lake), others are snug in the eaves and come in warm country colours. There's a spa, too, and 14 new bedrooms have balconies. A place to return to again and again. *Minimum stay two nights at weekends.*

Price	£100–£210. Singles from £90. Half-board £67.50–£120 p.p.
Rooms	52: 49 twins/doubles, 2 four-posters, 1 suite.
Meals	Lunch from £8.50. Bar meals from £8. Dinner, 3 courses, £34.
Closed	Rarely.
Directions	A490 from Welshpool; B4393 to Lake Vyrnwy. Brown signs from A5 at Shrewsbury as well.

The Bisiker Family
Llanwddyn,
Montgomeryshire SY10 0LY

Tel	01691 870692
Fax	01691 870259
Email	res@lakevyrnwy.com
Web	www.lakevyrnwy.com

Cnapan

Cnapan is a way of life – a family affair with three generations at work in harmony. Eluned makes the preserves, Judith excels in the kitchen, Michael looks after the bar and Oliver, the newest recruit, serves a mean breakfast. It is a very friendly place with locals popping in to book tables and guests chatting in the bar before dinner. As for the house, it's warm and cosy, charmingly home-spun, with whitewashed stone walls and old pine settles in the dining room, comfy sofas and a wood-burner in the sitting room, and a tiny telly in the bar for the odd game of rugby (the game of cnapan, rugby's precursor, originated in the town). There are maps for walkers, bird books, flower books, the daily papers, too. Spill into the garden in summer for pre-dinner drinks under the weeping willow, then slip back in for Judith's delicious food, perhaps parsnip soup, breast of Gressingham duck, honey ice cream. Comfy bedrooms, warmly simple, are super value for money. You're in the Pembrokeshire National Park here; beaches and clifftop coastal walks beckon. *Minimum stay two nights at weekends.*

Price	£80. Singles £47.
Rooms	5: 1 double, 3 twins, 1 family. Extra bath available.
Meals	Lunch from £7.50. Dinner from £27. Not Tuesday evenings from Easter to October.
Closed	Christmas, January & February.
Directions	From Cardigan, A487 to Newport. 1st pink house on right.

Eluned Lloyd & Michael & Judith Cooper
East Street, Newport, Fishguard,
Pembrokeshire SA42 0SY

Tel	01239 820575
Fax	01239 820878
Email	enquiry@cnapan.co.uk
Web	www.cnapan.co.uk

Llys Meddyg

This quirky restaurant with rooms has a bit of everything: rooms that pack a designer punch, super food in a sparkling restaurant, a cellar bar for drinks before dinner, a fabulous garden for summer treats. The house – the town's old doctor's surgery – is built of pretty stone upon which a trim Virginia creeper now roams. Inside, Victorian interiors have a warm contemporary finish. In the restaurant, where candles burn serenely under a teardrop chandelier, there's Welsh cheese soufflé, pan-fried sea bass, Grand Marnier frangipane tart. Excellent bedrooms are split between the main house (high ceilings) and the one behind (quieter). All have the same fresh style: Farrow & Ball colours, good art, oak beds with crisp linen, fancy bathrooms with fluffy robes. Three have computers stuffed with music and film, others have flat-screen TVs and DVD players, one has a super-cool bathroom in Jerusalem stone. Best of all is a lush garden with a mountain-fed stream pouring past. By day it becomes an open-air café. There's even a small sofa-clad marquee for cocktails before dinner.

Price	£90–£110. Suites £120–£130. Singles from £70.	
Rooms	6: 2 doubles, 1 twin/double, 3 suites.	
Meals	Lunch from £7 (June to mid–Sept). Dinner, 3 courses, about £30. Not Sunday/Monday in winter.	
Closed	Never.	
Directions	East from Fishguard on A487. On left in Newport towards eastern edge of town.	

Louise & Edward Sykes
East Street, Newport,
Pembrokeshire SA42 0SY

Tel	01239 820008
Email	contact@llysmeddyg.com
Web	www.llysmeddyg.com

Penally Abbey

A fabulous position up on the hill with a ridge of sycamore and ash towering above and huge views to the front of Carmarthen Bay. Caldy island lies to the east, the road ends at the village green, a quick stride across the golf course leads to the beach. Up at the house, a fine arched window by the grand piano frames the view perfectly, so sink into a chesterfield in front of the fire and gaze out to sea. The house dates to 1790 and was once an abbey; you'll also find St Deiniol's, a ruined 13th-century church that's lit up at night. Sprawling lawns are yours to roam, bluebells carpet the wood in May. Bedrooms are all different: grand four-posters and wild flock wallpaper in the main house; a simpler cottage feel in the coach house; warm contemporary luxury in St Deiniol's Lodge. Steve's gentle, unflappable manner is infectious and hugely relaxing; don't expect to feel rushed. Elleen cooks in the French style, much of it picked up in the kitchen of a château many years ago; her Tenby sea bass is exquisite. The Pembrokeshire coastal path passes by outside; don't miss it. *Minimum stay two nights at weekends.*

Price	£140–£220. Half-board from £105 p.p.
Rooms	17: 6 doubles, 1 twin all en suite; 1 double with separate bath. Coach house: 4 doubles. Lodge: 5 twins/doubles.
Meals	Lunch by arrangement. Dinner, 3 courses, £35.
Closed	Never.
Directions	From Tenby, A4139 for Pembroke. Right into Penally after 1.5 miles. Hotel signed at village green. Train station 5 mins walk.

Steve & Elleen Warren
Penally, Tenby,
Pembrokeshire SA70 7PY

Tel 01834 843033
Fax 01834 844714
Email info@penally-abbey.com
Web www.penally-abbey.com

Milebrook House Hotel

Your arrival at the old family home of writer and explorer Wilfred Thesiger (he lived here from 1922 to 1939) is expectedly comforting. The parquet floor in the hall smells of lavender floor wax, the clock ticks quietly, the flowers are fresh and Beryl is likely to come out of the kitchen in her apron to greet you. Much space and comfort in the bedrooms where fabrics are blended, beds excellent, lighting adjustable, the furniture modern and the service attentive and unobtrusive. In the walled kitchen garden flowers and vegetables are grown for the table – a table to reckon with, by all accounts; the new chef is winning recognition for his skilful British cooking. Outside, wild terrain, too, devoted to a mature arboretum and wildlife pond, and terracing, a gazebo, a pergola with roses growing over obelisks and a croquet lawn. At the end of these gorgeous gardens are pheasants, moorhens, red kites, kingfishers, herons and the Welsh border; you may fish on their stretch of the river Teme. Deeply tranquil country, a wonderful place to unwind. *Minimum stay two nights at weekends.*

Price	£99.50-£105. Singles £64-£68.50. Half-board (min. 2 nights) £62-£74 p.p.
Rooms	10: 5 doubles, 4 twins, 1 family.
Meals	Lunch from £11.95. Not Monday lunchtimes. Dinner £30.95.
Closed	Rarely.
Directions	From Ludlow, A49 north, then left at Bromfield on A4113 towards Knighton for 7 miles. Hotel on right.

Rodney & Beryl Marsden
Milebrook, Knighton,
Powys LD7 1LT
Tel 01547 528632
Fax 01547 520509
Email hotel@milebrook.kc3ltd.co.uk
Web www.milebrookhouse.co.uk

The Lake Country House & Spa

Deep in the silence of Wales, a country house intent on pampering you rotten. Fifty acres of lawns, lake and ancient woodland sweep you clean of city cobwebs, and if that's not enough a spa has been added, with an indoor pool, treatment rooms and a tennis court by the lake. Sit in a hot tub and watch guests fish for their supper, try your luck on the nine-hole golf course, or saddle up near by and take to the hills. Come home to afternoon tea in the drawing room, where beautiful rugs warm a brightly polished wooden floor and chandeliers hang from the ceiling. The hotel opened over 100 years ago and the leather-bound fishing logs go back to 1894. A feel of the 1920s lingers. Fires come to life in front of your eyes, grand pianos and grandfather clocks sing their songs, snooker balls crash about in the distance. Dress for a delicious dinner – the food and wines deserve it – then retire to cosseting bedrooms. Most are suites: those in the house are warmly traditional, those in the lodge are softly contemporary. The London train takes four hours and stops in the village. Resident geese waddle. Marvellous.

Price	£170–£220. Singles from £115–£155. Suites £250–£300. Half-board £105–£150 p.p.
Rooms	30: 6 twins/doubles, 12 suites. Lodge: 12 suites.
Meals	Lunch, 3 courses, £21.50. Dinner, 3 courses, £42.50.
Closed	Rarely.
Directions	From Builth Wells, A483 west for 7 miles to Garth. Signed from village.

Jean-Pierre Mifsud
Llangammarch Wells,
Powys LD4 4BS
Tel   01591 620202
Fax   01591 620457
Email   info@lakecountryhouse.co.uk
Web   www.lakecountryhouse.co.uk

The Felin Fach Griffin

Delicious food, a friendly bar and honest prices make the Griffin a must for those in search of a welcoming billet close to the mountains. It's quirky, homespun, utterly intoxicating and thrives on a mix of relaxed informality and colourful style. The timber-framed bar resembles the sitting room of a small hip country house, with sofas in front of a fire that burns on both sides and backgammon waiting to be played. Painted stone walls throughout come in blocks of colour. An open-plan feel sweeps you through to the restaurant, where stock pots simmer on an Aga; try roasted scallops, Welsh lamb, vanilla crème brûlée with Piña Colada. Bedrooms above are warmly simple with comfy beds wrapped in crisp linen, framed photography on the walls, good books and the odd piece of mahogany furniture (but no TVs unless you ask); tongue and groove bathrooms have White Company lotions. A road passes outside, quietly at night, lanes lead into the hills, and a small organic kitchen garden provides much for the table. The Beacons are close, so walk, ride, bike, canoe – or head to Hay for books galore.

Price	£97.50. Four-poster £125. Singles from £67.50.
Rooms	7: 2 doubles, 2 twins/doubles, 3 four-posters.
Meals	Lunch from £12. Dinner, 3 courses, about £30. Not Monday lunchtimes.
Closed	25 & 26 December.
Directions	From Brecon, A470 north to Felin Fach (4.5 miles). On left.

Charles & Edmund Inkin
Felin Fach, Brecon,
Powys LD3 0UB

Tel	01874 620111
Email	enquiries@felinfachgriffin.co.uk
Web	www.felinfachgriffin.co.uk

Gliffaes Hotel

Gliffaes is matchless: grandly comfortable but as casual and warm as home. It's a house for all seasons – not even driving rain could mask its beauty. Wander the 33 acres of stunning gardens and woodland or bask in the sun on the buttressed terrace as the river Usk cuts through the valley 150 feet below. Tea is a feast of scones and cakes laid out on a long table in a sitting room of polished floors and panelled walls, served by a winter fire; dinner is an Italian-influenced feast. Membership of the Slow Food movement means local, seasonal food is used as much as possible – the fish and meat in this area are outstanding. With the Suter clan at the helm – they've been welcoming guests for nearly 60 years – improvements are always underway. The free-standing roll top bath with a view is gathering a fan club, a mix of fresh, bold and elegant fabrics have spruced up the rooms, furniture is chosen to suit and original Welsh paintings are becoming a feature. Fisherfolk can cast to their hearts' content on a prime 2.5-mile stretch overlooked, perhaps, by red kite and buzzards. *Minimum stay two nights at weekends.*

Price	£88–£210. Singles from £78.50.
Rooms	23: 3 doubles, 14 twins/doubles, 6 singles.
Meals	Light lunch from £3.50. Dinner £32.
Closed	First 4 weeks in January.
Directions	From Crickhowell, A40 west for 2.5 miles. Entrance on left, signed. Hotel 1 mile up windy hill.

James & Susie Suter
Crickhowell,
Powys NP8 1RH

Tel	01874 730371
Fax	01874 730463
Email	calls@gliffaeshotel.com
Web	www.gliffaeshotel.com

Fairyhill

The Gower peninsular has legions of fans who come for its glorious heathland, its rugged coastline and some of the best beaches in the country. Fairyhill is bang in the middle of it all, but just to ensure absolute silence, it is wrapped in 24 acres of its own. Follow your nose and discover a stream-fed lake, an ancient orchard, a walled garden with asparagus beds and, somewhere, a family of Muscovy ducks. Inside, an informal house-party feel comes courtesy of Andrew and Paul, who've been here since 1992. Most bedrooms are big and fancy, a couple are smaller and simpler. The plush ones have painted beams, striking stripes, bold colours, immaculate bathrooms. Mattresses are Vi-sprung, but if that's not enough you'll find a treatment room, so book a massage. There's croquet on the lawn in summer and seriously good food all year round. Lamb, poultry, beef and cheese come from Gower, so tuck into duck eggs with white asparagus mousse, grilled lemon sole with beurre noisette, twice-glazed lemon tart with sour-apple ice cream. Fabulous walking, too. *Minimum stay two nights at weekends.*

Price	£165–£275. Singles from £145. Half-board from £110 p.p.
Rooms	11: 6 doubles, 5 twins/doubles.
Meals	Lunch from £15.95. Dinner £30–£40.
Closed	1st three weeks in January.
Directions	M4 junc. 47; A483 south; A484 west to Gowerton; B4295 to Llanrhidian; through Oldwalls & 1 mile up on left.

Andrew Hetherington & Paul Davies
Reynoldston, Gower,
Swansea SA3 1BS

Tel	01792 390139
Fax	01792 391358
Email	andrew@fairyhill.net
Web	www.fairyhill.net

Quick reference indices

On a budget?
These places have a double room for £70 or under.

Events
The whole building can be hired for an event.

Weddings
Want to tie the knot? You
can here.

Quick reference indices

Quick reference indices

Singles

These places either have a single room or charge no single supplement.

Quick reference indices

If you have any comments on entries in this guide, please tell us. If you have a favourite hotel or a new discovery, please let us know about it. You can return this form or visit www.sawdays.co.uk.

Existing entry

Property name: _____

Entry number: _____ Date of visit: _____

New recommendation

Property name: _____

Address: _____

_____

Tel: _____

Your comments

What did you like (or dislike) about this place? Were the people friendly? What was the location like? What sort of food did they serve?

_____

_____

_____

_____

_____

Your details

Name: _____

Address: _____

_____

_____ Postcode: _____

Tel: _____ Email: _____

Please send completed form to:
BH, Sawday's, The Old Farmyard, Yanley Lane, Long Ashton, Bristol BS41 9LR, UK

Have you enjoyed this book? Why not try one of the others in the Special Places to Stay series and get 35% discount on the RRP *

British Bed & Breakfast (Ed 12)	RRP £14.99	Offer price £9.75
British Bed & Breakfast for Garden Lovers (Ed 4)	RRP £14.99	Offer price £9.75
British Hotels & Inns (Ed 9)	RRP £14.99	Offer price £9.75
Pubs & Inns of England & Wales (Ed 4)	RRP £14.99	Offer price £9.75
French Bed & Breakfast (Ed 10)	RRP £15.99	Offer price £10.40
French Holiday Homes (Ed 4)	RRP £14.99	Offer price £9.75
French Hotels (Ed 4)	RRP £14.99	Offer price £9.75
Paris Hotels (Ed 6)	RRP £10.99	Offer price £7.15
Spain (Ed 7)	RRP £14.99	Offer price £9.75
Italy (Ed 4)	RRP £14.99	Offer price £9.75
Portugal (Ed 4)	RRP £11.99	Offer price £7.80
Croatia (Ed 1)	RRP £11.99	Offer price £7.80
Greece (Ed 1)	RRP £11.99	Offer price £7.80
Turkey (Ed 1)	RRP £11.99	Offer price £7.80
Ireland (Ed 6)	RRP £12.99	Offer price £8.45
Morocco (Ed 2)	RRP £11.99	Offer price £7.80
India (Ed 2)	RRP £11.99	Offer price £7.80
Green Places to Stay (Ed 1)	RRP £13.99	Offer price £9.10

*postage and packing is added to each order

To order at the Reader's Discount price simply phone 01275 395431 and quote 'Reader Discount BH'.

② Hotel   ① **Suffolk**

③ Wentworth Hotel

④ Come for a little time travel; this stretch of the Suffolk coast will sweep you back to sleepy England at its loveliest: fishing boats on shingle beaches, an estuary for super walks and a music festival in summer. The Wentworth matches the mood perfectly; it's warmly old-fashioned, quietly grand, full of its own traditions. Michael's family have been here since 1920, when scores of fishermen worked the shore; the few that remain haul their boats up onto the beach across from the hotel terrace. Inside you find a warm seaside elegance, nothing too racy; instead, sunshine colours, fresh flowers, flickering coal fires, oils on the walls and shelves of books. Also: delightful sitting rooms, a bar for all seasons, and part of the hotel resembles a grand ocean liner. The restaurant looks out to sea, comes in Georgian red and spills onto the sunken lawn in summer for views of passing boats. Bedrooms (many with sea views) are plush: Zoffany wallpaper, reds and golds, French armoires, comfortable beds. Joyce Grenfell used to stay for the Aldeburgh Festival and has a room named after her. *Minimum stay two nights at weekends.*

⑤ Price	£108–£220. Singles from £63. Half-board £57–£120 p.p.
⑥ Rooms	35: 24 twins/doubles, 4 singles. Darfield House: 7 doubles.
⑦ Meals	Lunch from £7.50. Dinner from £15.
⑧ Closed	Never.
⑨ Directions	A12 north from Ipswich, then A1094 for Aldeburgh. Past church, down hill, left at x-roads; on right.

Michael Pritt
Wentworth Road, Aldeburgh,
Suffolk IP15 5BD

Tel   01728 452312
Fax   01728 454343
Email   stay@wentworth-aldeburgh.co.uk
Web   www.wentworth-aldeburgh.com

⑩   ⑪   Entry 183 Map 4